PROFITS WITHOUT PANIC

Investment Psychology for Personal Wealth

Jonathan Myers

NICHOLAS BREALEY
PUBLISHING

LONDON

First published by
Nicholas Brealey Publishing Limited in 1999

36 John Street
London
WC1N 2AT, UK
Tel: +44 (0)171 430 0224
Fax: +44 (0)171 404 8311

1163 E. Ogden Avenue, Suite 705-229
Naperville
IL 60563-8535, USA
Tel: (888) BREALEY
Fax: (630) 428 3442

http://www.nbrealey-books.com

ISBN 1-85788-217-2

Library of Congress Cataloging-in-Publication Data

Myers, Jonathan
　　　Profits without panic : investment psychology for personal wealth
/ Jonathan Myers
　　　　　p. cm.
　　　Includes bibliographical references and index.
　　　ISBN 1-85788-217-2 hb
　　　1. Investments--Psychological aspects. I. Title II. Title:
Investment psychology for personal wealth.
HG4515.15.M93 1999
332.6′01′9--dc21

99-11373
CIP

British Library Cataloguing in Publication Data
A catalogue record for this book is available from the
British Library.

Printed in Finland by WSOY.

The information contained in this book is for guidance only and neither the publisher nor the author shall be held liable for readers' choice of investments. Readers are reminded of the need always to seek professional and independent financial advice, so that investment decisions are made within the context of full, personal financial circumstances.

Contents

1

Overcoming Fear, Greed and the Madness of Markets

A major shift towards liquidity protection is really not a market phenomenon. It's ... a fear-induced psychological response.
Alan Greenspan, Federal Reserve Chairman

PROFITS WITHOUT PANIC IS ABOUT AVOIDING THE MANIA OF investment markets and not getting swept along by the crowd or your own misperceptions. In the following pages, you will find practical tools to help you develop the financial self-awareness that leads to investment success. Whether you're a professional or a private investor, this involves understanding your personal reactions in relation to your chosen market, applying effective financial strategies and realistically analyzing the mistakes you make without applying ill-conceived reasons or getting caught up in biased thinking.

You will learn how research in investment psychology and behavioral finance points the way to making good investment decisions and avoiding bad ones – not just by choosing which investment is best, but also by watching over it, making it work for you, and taking appropriate action in the market at the best possible times. But more than this, you will see how some of the latest ideas that I and others have developed come together to form a different approach, one that goes beyond the purely financial and provides a method of valuing investments more efficiently.

Making the same old mistakes

The ability to make profitable investment choices is exceptionally important in today's world, because stock ownership now represents a greater slice of personal wealth than at any other time, greater even than bricks and mortar. At the end of 1990, the US Federal Reserve reported that approximately 33 percent of US households owned stock valued at $3.1 trillion. By the end of 1997, this had grown with unprecedented speed to a staggering $11.4 trillion, with 44 percent of US households placing their money in a broader range of investments, either directly in the market or indirectly through mutual funds. In comparison, home ownership rose from $6.0 trillion to $8.7 trillion over the same period. Yet despite this massive rise in investment, investors are still making a range of avoidable mistakes.

Money is increasingly used for volatile, short-term speculations in fashionable sectors at the expense of quality investments and long-term real wealth. While some speculations may turn out to be good-quality purchases several years down the line, more usually they represent unstable paper assets with an uncertain future. The trouble is that when stock markets climb, vigorous overoptimism seems to be the driving force behind the buying rather than any sound evaluation of investment potential. Any downside is dismissed with the belief that profits will continue on the same upward trajectory. Then, when markets fall, an overdose of pessimism leads many people to sell their investment inappropriately, suffering a heavy loss in the process.

Nor does technology necessarily help. With high-powered computers in more homes than ever before, investors believe that they are making better-informed decisions as their eyes and ears are more readily attuned to up-to-the-second market changes. All they need is the right type of information, on the right type of system, and they'll be well on the way to spotting the trend and achieving their financial goal. The reality is somewhat different, and that golden opportunity they're searching for stays just out of their grasp. As John Markese, the president of the American Association of Individual Investors, recently put it:

Investors are still making the same mistakes today as they were twelve years ago. But now they're using a $3000 computer and making seven-dollar trades on the Internet. Their mistakes are a great deal more expensive than they used to be, far more frequent, and considerably faster.

Investors may end up with some very beautiful graphs and charts, but when *under- or overreaction* in the market increases, the crowd mentality interferes with a true assessment of prices, making timing and choice of investment far more difficult.

Furthermore, investors reinforce each other's actions in an upward or downward spiral of activity in a way previously inconceivable. At the dawn of the twenty-first century this is more important than ever. With electronic trading, markets are highly interconnected. In the words of Richard Grasso, CEO of the New York Stock Exchange: 'There's a global trend towards free-market principles and equity-fused capital markets.' Investment and market volatility now interact at an ever-escalating international level – when one market sneezes, another catches a cold on the other side of the world.

Psychonomics – a new approach to unlocking value

As the realization develops that a more comprehensive awareness is vital to achieving financial success, the predominance of analytical finance is being rivaled by investment psychology. This gives rise to a broad-spectrum approach called *psychonomics*, which emphasizes the relationship between investors' unique, internal characteristics – the internal market inside their heads – and the pressures and reinforcing effects of the external financial markets. Harmonizing both sides of this relationship is the way to secure consistent profits, and depends on factors such as how susceptible to influence and media hype you are; your personal biases, desires, expectations, life situation and goals; as well as your ability to make sound financial evaluations. To a far greater extent than most investment books and theories will lead you to believe, these human traits dictate the choices that investors make and are the energizing force behind price changes and market activity.

The term psychonomics isn't simply a contraction of psychology and economics, but refers to a mass of disparate factors that need to be considered together or integrated for a solution. Psychonomics, therefore, has wide application because some of the most important components of particular investments and economies, in terms of real value, cannot be measured directly, nor can they be considered in dollars and cents. These include *weightless* factors that have an indirect impact on true worth, such as the value of brand loyalty, corporate relationships, human capital or creativity. In addition, weightless factors also have a delayed effect. For example, management or political decisions may cause changes in business practice several months or years in the future. These elements may not be accounted for in conventional financial analyses due to their varied and subjective nature, but they are essential in determining the potential of an investment.

Two ways to attribute value

Psychonomics shows that, in reality, there are only two ways in which value can be attributed to a financial opportunity. The first is to increase your ability to determine the *intrinsic value* of an investment – its fundamental or tangible value, together with its weightless component. Successful investors are particularly good at this type of analysis. They tend to have developed a feel for the relevance of non-financial factors that affect company performance and future growth. They apply a mixture of objective and subjective evaluation. That's not to say that they don't ever make mistakes – for example, no one can ever guess exactly what the next major technology is going to be and what it will be worth – but they get their decisions right more often than they get them wrong.

The second way of attributing the correct value to an investment is to reduce the chance of making *systematic errors* – these are errors of the same type that are made on a repeated basis and occur either because you are influenced by your internal biases to make irrational decisions, or because you are influenced by the investment crowd through news or other sources of information. A great deal of behavioral finance research has centered on these psychological tendencies which we all have. For example, we tend to see patterns in investment price histories because we have a vested interest in believing that we have identified an exploitable trend. We also tend to believe that trends will continue regardless. So in a raging bull market, we expect to keep making crazy, above-average returns and dismiss the more reasonable, long-term opportunities. Even more telling about human nature perhaps, the pain of *losing* a dollar is much more intense than the pleasure of gaining one.

Avoiding systematic errors

The fact is that, unlike the random walk theory that economists have argued extensively in favor of in the past, stock prices don't always follow random patterns. According to Richard Thaler, professor of behavioral finance at Chicago University Business School, human irrationality often causes market changes due to patterns of activity produced by investors' perception of risk. In the real world, investors make decisions on the basis of hunches, tips, fashions, rumors or simple fears about losing. Add in the intriguing finding that investors often see other people's decisions as less rational than their own 'superior' ones, and you can easily see how prices have a tendency to drift up and down in concert – or produce market momentum – due to very specific investor behaviors. One example is *anchoring*, where investors presume that a stock price must be correct at the level at which they buy. If ABC stock initially stands at $5 and its market keeps rising further, each new price high is anchored to its previous high in the minds of later investors, say to $6 and then to $7. While investors may accept that ABC can fall back to $6, far fewer will accept that it could fall back to $5 or below. This effect leads even more investors to buy ABC, moving it further away from a realistic price and increasing its likelihood of eventual collapse.

Another psychological phenomenon is *framing*, identified by Daniel Kahneman and Amos Twerski, which shows that decision making about investment alternatives is sensitive to the way in which the choice is initially framed. Generally, investors go for the choice that 'appears' less risky – simply because the choice made is the one that's more psychologically comfortable and appealing rather than because it's the best choice. It's all about your personal assessment and, again, comes down to perception and bias. But when many investors all make trading decisions in this manner, there is heightened volatility, with the market shooting up to peaks and down to troughs as uncertainty about price direction increases exponentially.

Now suppose that, instead of being uncertain, you are supremely confident that the stock market is going to soar. And sitting on huge gains, it's easy to believe that things can only keep getting better. But *overconfidence* leads many investors to make inaccurate estimates about future market performance, as well as minimizing the possibility and impact of downturns. In 1996, as the worldwide market bull continued to charge ahead, Robert Shiller, a professor of economics at Yale, questioned 400 investors over whether they agreed with the following statement: 'If there's another crash like October 1987, the market will surely be back to its former levels within a couple of years or so.' Eighty-two percent of respondents agreed.

When this type of overconfidence dominates, investors find it incredibly hard to entertain the notion that their emotions are ruling their actions. Nevertheless, test after test shows that stock market swings exceed investor expectations far more than anticipated. This is all extra fuel for market volatility, as investors react out of surprise and anxiety, believing that conditions are either far better or far worse than they actually are.

Of course, we could say that investors follow the latest fashionable strategy or act rashly out of fear, greed or even madness, and leave it at that. But the reasons are more complex and it's important to understand what's going on so that the twofold purpose of investment is satisfied: to make a high financial return and to provide a pool of capital for industry or business development.

Basically, there's an interactive process taking place between all the varied internal pressures underlying your mindset and the external pressures of the market. These all act on your decision-making abilities. Get the psychological balance in your approach wrong and you're more likely to misperceive real worth and, consequently, take unrealistic action. At these times, market prices have more to do with psychological variables than financial ones. As a result, once you begin to separate out these internal and external elements, it becomes easier to see the opportunities. Furthermore, because investors have been shown to make similar types of mistakes, when you know what to look for these mistakes can be exploited for substantial gains.

Understanding why you act as you do, and the type of investor you are, will allow you to use strategies more effectively and make better-suited financial decisions that you can live with comfortably. It is about knowing how aggressive or cautious you are – or need to become – and the way you handle risk. As a result, not only will you avoid speculative trading but sudden market movements can be placed in context; for example the October 1997 drop precipitated by the Asian economies and the August 1998 drop said to have resulted from Russian economic woes, continued concern over Asia, and expensive valuations on leading domestic stocks. And, if something similar happens again, you won't buy and sell out of panic because you will understand your responses better, know the signs to look out for in the trading environment and be prepared.

It is these types of effects resulting from a range of biases and misperceptions that produce market inefficiencies and signal trading opportunities for the shrewd investor, as the gap between basic value and market value alters. Indeed, these effects lead to powerful strategies and, with an estimated $72 billion presently invested with funds applying psychological principles, behavioral finance experts are no longer confined to the universities. One such example is LSV Asset Management in Chicago, run by finance professors Josef Lakonishok, Andrei Shleifer and Robert Vishny. LSV's investment approach, based on the trio's research findings, is to identify stocks that are just beginning their recovery phase. Besides searching for value anomalies, they also seek out lingering effects due to momentum as a result of people's slowness to respond to earnings announcements, dividends and stock splits. You'll learn more about how this works in Chapter 2.

Clearly, successful investment is brought about not by impetuous trading, but by realistically assessing intrinsic worth or reducing the chances of making systematic errors, or a combination of the two. Keep this thought firmly fixed in your mind as you progress through the book.

Is market value correct?

While some of the strongest findings from psychology show how individuals behave differently with others to the way they would behave on their own – there's apparent safety in numbers – one of the ironies of financial economics in previous years is that investors were led to believe that markets were rational places. Stocks or other investments were, according to the economists, valued at a price that reflected not only their true worth but all possible known information that could affect them in the future. This idea was embodied in the *efficient market hypothesis*.

For the economist, rationality and value were inherently linked and the assumption was that investors behaved rationally at all times and the future was already discounted by the present valuation. However, there were anomalies in investor behavior that the theory couldn't account for, such as when companies announced unexpected earnings surprises. Furthermore, there was no explanation of how a change in investor perception suddenly caused an upsurge of interest for no obvious reason when the company's fundamentals hadn't altered, or why prices often leaped when research discoveries were made.

There is an old joke about two professors of finance discussing the merits of the efficient market hypothesis while walking along Wall Street. Coming across a $100 bill, they debated whether to pick it up or not. One argued in favor of picking it up on the assumption that someone else's loss was his gain, while his friend argued that it wasn't worth picking up because if it was real someone else would already have picked it up, therefore it couldn't be real. Take this view to its ultimate conclusion, and in a wholly efficient market there is no foresight about possible future breakthroughs if there is no indication of them in the present. There cannot be a scientific or technological advance because somebody would already have done it. The information would be known and would have been reacted to. Under this premise, the world's first mammalian clone, a sheep called Dolly, cannot exist at this point in time, because if her existence were possible someone would already have created her. This, of course, is absurd. The last time I heard, Dolly was alive and doing very well. Try telling her that she doesn't exist!

Exploitable investment opportunities

One of the repercussions of a psychonomic approach is that it forces a reassessment of what rationality is all about and how it relates to stock valuation. In fact, psychonomics represents a considerable divergence from current approaches, where professionals often talk about the excess price as being the difference between fundamental value and market value. According to their view, this difference is accounted for by rational investor behavior, which causes changes in supply and demand as investors reassess future earnings growth, potential corporate expansion, and hoped-for dividend increases.

The psychonomic model is more wide ranging and shows how market value can also be determined by irrational investor perceptions, with error, bias, emotion and panic accounting for the excess price. And it is the degree of excess price, embodied in market value, that produces exploitable investment opportunities. As Warren Buffet, one of the world's greatest investors, has suggested: only look at the market to see if anyone's done something foolish that day on which you can capitalize. Figure 1 helps to explain the significance of the psychological aspects of a stock price.

The most significant attribute of the psychonomic model is that it is dynamic. The psychological price component, resulting from the mass sentiment of investors at any particular moment, can account for a little of the overall price or it can account for a great deal of it. There will always be some psychological component to the price because of the way the market values potential profit; that is, because it hasn't materialized yet, investors buy and sell according to their perceptions of what might happen, which may be correct or it may be a complete overreaction.

Theoretically, there is a point at which the psychological price accounts for all the stock price, encompassing both weightless and fundamental value, and this would be a stock at fever pitch at the height of a speculative bubble, with everybody buying for no more solid reason than that everyone else is buying. Alternatively, it would be a stock priced way below its basic value when there is no intelligent justification. As you will see in the coming chapters, you may not be able to

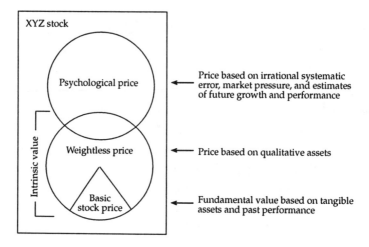

Figure 1 *Psychonomic components of a stock price*

measure all the subjective components fully, but you can learn how to handle them – and this will give you a highly profitable edge.

Rational some of the time

All of this adds up to the fact that there cannot be total rationality in a market in the economic sense. Valid as well as invalid expectations, attitudes and personal psychology fuel investors' actions with the result that prices change. All we can ever say is that the market is rational some of the time. And the main reason that the market behaves in this manner is that it is made up of individual investors who are sometimes financially rational and sometimes not.

In fact, all financial markets are affected by mass emotion and madness at some time or other. In this context, hedge funds attempt to smooth out market irrationality and to profit in both rising and falling markets by using a variety of investment tools – derivatives, futures, stocks, bonds and so forth. The recent international calamities of these intensely speculative funds – Long Term Capital Management's $3.5 billion loss, for example – highlights the fact that market irrationality cannot be easily controlled, nor risk abolished, simply by using sophisticated mathematical techniques alone or by optimizing different types of investment instruments. Like the boy who put his finger in the crack in the dam to stop the water flowing, it only works until the crack gets too big. Once irrational crowd behavior overwhelms stringent financial models, or 'realistic' evaluations, the effects cascade over the strategy. Then, as hedge funds react and move very large quantities of money quickly, their activities rapidly affect the very markets in which they're trading, causing further dramatic changes in prices.

A financial market therefore varies in its rationality according to whim, fashion and the pressures of the crowd. To be successful at investment means accepting this interplay between investors' actions in the market and then facing the situation head on. You can't change the market, but you can develop your own perspective. Just because other investors are overreacting to the latest piece of 'hot' news, like fish all changing direction at the same time, doesn't mean that you have to. As an individual investor, to be *rational* means to develop the ability to control your emotional characteristics so that you make the best possible decisions and are not swayed by other market players. If you achieve this, you will, in a sense, be harmonizing the internal market inside your head with the external market in the wider world – and then you won't be panicked into dealing.

P.R.O.F.I.T.S.

This book uses the P.R.O.F.I.T.S. framework of psychonomic rationality to provide an easy way of linking these psychological and financial themes (Figure 2). P.R.O.F.I.T.S stands for Profits, Relationships, Outlierism, Flexibility, Information, Traps and Strategies, and each chapter focuses on a different combination of these elements. A simple definition of psychonomic rationality is: *the maximization of your ability to evaluate fundamental and weightless factors of an investment while minimizing any tendency to make systematic errors.* The underlying idea is that gaining mastery of all the elements of P.R.O.F.I.T.S. is necessary to achieve greater control over your financial actions when dealing in uncertain or volatile markets.

Profits Without Panic is divided into two parts. Part One deals with your investment actions in relation to financial markets, demonstrating

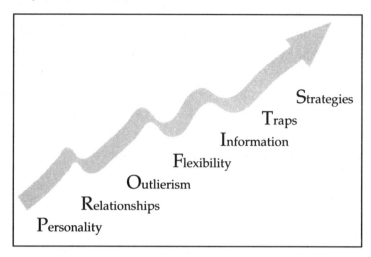

Figure 2 *The P.R.O.F.I.T.S. framework*

how psychology drives markets through bull and bear phases. You'll see how neither panic nor listening to the doom and gloom of media experts is an acceptable option if you want to be a successful investor. The crowd may move in unison, but you don't have to move with it.

Psychonomic rationality points the way to avoiding systematic errors and profitably exploiting the opportunities that arise. By this approach, you will see how to identify changes in other investors' responses – when they are making systematic errors – and how you can develop effective strategies as a result. You will also see how to assess intrinsic value more accurately, and be trained to spot many of the crowd pressures creating the crazy market values that cause investors to get burnt by entering the market too late in a cycle.

By gathering financial, weightless and psychological value together and considering them as psychonomic components, *Profits Without Panic* goes much further than many current books on investment. Its approach has two unique repercussions. The first is that it allows more accurate assessments of how a company's assets are priced than is possible using only financial measures. It becomes much easier to assess quality companies in sectors such as information technology or medical research that have nominal tangible assets – for example plant, property and machinery – but show massive market gains. Conversely, companies that are poor quality – at home or in emerging markets – but have high market value are more easily identifiable as likely to hit the rocks. In this way, you will be able to evaluate precisely why companies are performing as they are, without trying to forecast performance on the basis of a balance sheet alone or an analyst's recommendation.

The second repercussion is that industries' perception of themselves and their place in the overall economy is more easily observable when you start examining non-financial factors. Corporate leadership and the decisions taken may be very good and feed into sustained expansion and hikes in profits. But corporate leadership can also delude itself, just as individual investors can. This explains why, even when a balance sheet or an announcement can be glowing, the rot is beginning to set in. As these organizations constitute the stock market, the overall effect can be dramatic in terms of boom and bust cycles or economic crashes. You will discover how to spot the signals before it's too late and you're swept along on a wave of market hysteria.

Self-awareness for better decisions

Part Two deals with personal investment at a deeper level by looking at how developing self-awareness leads to improved financial decisions. It will become easier to see where you may have gone wrong with your investments in the past, or why you sometimes did well with one particular strategy and at other times lost money. Successful investors make high returns because – either by experience or by instinct or both – they have systematized their approach. The book considers in detail how they achieve this and highlights common characteristics of successful investors. These characteristics can easily be incorporated into your own approach to improve your performance.

Assessing your previous investment achievements is often a good way to renew your investment situation. Practical techniques for doing this are examined, along with explanations for why you may have become caught up in a cycle of behavior. For example, you may have held on to a falling investment though you clearly knew that, like a bottle of soured wine, you might as well have taken the money and poured it down the drain! You'll also see how to profile the type of investor you are and how this leads to making more appropriate investment choices, taking into account the level of risk that's right for you.

Also described in detail are the investment traps that exist for the unwary, such as schemes and scams, as well as the reasons for so many investors being repeatedly gullible. Why, for example, do investors senselessly gamble their money, follow the latest speculative fad, or even believe the latest astrological market prediction? For a psychonomic approach to be effective, you need to know what a trap looks like so that you won't get sucked in.

By the end of the book you will have a better idea of how your personal characteristics, far from being a drawback, can in fact be utilized for greater financial success.

Part One

Investment Psychology and Market Awareness

2

Psychonomics: Investment Strategies That Work

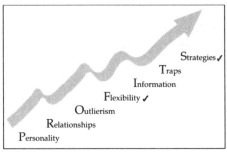

Strategies ✓
Traps
Information
Flexibility ✓
Outlierism
Relationships
Personality

A NY METHOD THAT ALLOWS YOU TO CHOOSE ONE INVESTMENT over another is a strategy. This could be by some rule of thumb or by analysis.

The irony is that good strategies are easy to find – it is their implementation that is hard, because it involves going against popular wisdom and your own intuition. But it is precisely the capacity to go against the crowd – and what is accepted as human nature – that makes for successful investment.

Psychonomic rationality combines objective and subjective evaluation in order to determine investment value more accurately. At the same time, you need to keep your emotions in check, while focusing outwards from your inner self to the real world of financial markets. By applying the P.R.O.F.I.T.S. framework, this balanced outlook is achievable. In other words, psychonomic rationality provides a method of implementing investment strategy to greatest effect.

Let's look briefly at each of the components of the framework.

Personality

Every investor is an individual with their own life goals, personal biases, beliefs and attitudes. They also differ in the amount of risk they feel comfortable with and whether they tend to be greedy for success or fearful of failure. These predominant characteristics lead to specific financial choices.

Many of these characteristics depend on the *type* of investor you are, which in turn dictates your overall approach. You could be cautious, emotional, technical, busy, casual or informed, and you'll get the opportunity to discover which you are when you read Chapter 8.

People often fail to take account of all the important aspects of their personality and how it is modified by their circumstances. They may also try to suppress their natural investor type, believing that if they change their performance will improve. Successful investment is not about changing but about developing.

Relationships

When you deal in the market, you form a relationship with another investor. In fact, you often form a relationship with many investors. Buyers and sellers are matched up and prices fluctuate as a result of the number of investors who want to be part of the trade. If more investors want to be buyers, prices will rise. If more want to be sellers, prices will fall.

Other relationships also have an effect on investment dealing. Your family and any other group you're attached to influence your decisions. Sometimes they promote a certain course of action or modify it, while at other times their involvement may actually conflict with your investment choices and goals.

Relationships between individuals within companies are a particularly important factor, as they have a crucial bearing on stock prices. If relationships are poor – for example one department doesn't know what another is doing, no one seems to care about customers, or trust has broken down between individual employees – this will ultimately affect corporate performance.

Outlierism

Outlierism, which can also be called *contrarianism*, refers to investors who move outside of the investment herd. Being an outlier means being your own person and making your own decisions. Successful outliers are often mavericks, but characteristically they stick to their chosen course of action or view when they believe it to be right.

Picture several gazelle quietly munching grass by a waterhole. They seem calm and supremely intent on their meal, but a part of their brain remains on guard duty. When, without warning, a lion charges at them from some hidden vantage point, they all take off with lightning speed – only the straggler gets caught. This is the outlier who, in an attempt to feast a little bit longer, pays the ultimate price. It is the perceived danger of straying too far from the investment crowd that keeps most investors – private and professional – together. They think there's safety in numbers, so staying within the accepted behavioral framework of the herd mentality prevents financial loneliness and risk.

The true outlier is not contrary for the sake of it, but bases their decisions on available information, experience and considered judgment. Sometimes this means going in the same direction as the crowd if that is appropriate, while at other times high gains can be made by having the confidence not to follow the crowd. The trick is to know when to act with the crowd and when to go your own way.

Flexibility

Profits remain elusive when investors keep making errors of the same type. For example, investors often overreact to information by pushing prices too high or too low. They believe that bad news will give rise to more bad news, and that good news will lead to more good news. Even when the evidence suggests that investment performance cannot be sustained, they are not sufficiently flexible in their thinking to realize that news can change or that they may have overreacted.

Many investors are resistant to altering their approach and tend to be emotionally locked in to their thinking patterns. As Josef Lakonishok at the University of Illinois has shown, the human mind often fights against change because the familiarity of a previous psychological style is comfortable. As a result, investors are likely to repeat the same types of behavior, making poor decisions in a never-ending loop.

Those investors who are sufficiently flexible in their approach will know the best times to change tack and find bargains. As you will see later, specific investment strategies are based on this idea.

Information

The use of information is vital in making good investment choices – whether it's the TV news, brokers' circulars or your own analysis. But what type and how much information do you need? You have to know your sources and how to use them effectively. It's also one thing to be informed, it's quite another to be an information junkie. Unfortunately, many investors imagine that more information equates with being better informed.

Successful investors sift their information and use it wisely. After all, you want to have enough time to enjoy your success.

Traps

Following the experts because they appear plausible and carry the weight of authority behind their words is a trap for many investors. So is the tendency to be gullible and fall into schemes and scams.

Traps also cover a range of subconscious fallacies that cause investors to delude themselves in some way. For example, according to Werner De Bondt, professor of finance at the University of Wisconsin-Madison, when people only remember their victories, they tend dramatically to underestimate the prospect of defeat.

Confirmation bias explains the tendency to collect and interpret financial information in a way that supports your previous beliefs about a stock's likely performance and where, once a stock's been traded, any negative facts that should cause you to reconsider are ignored. This dovetails with another trap into which private and professional investors repeatedly fall: *sunk cost bias*. Here, on the basis of the effort initially involved, investors justify past financial decisions even when the reasons are no longer valid.

Greed and fear are arguably the most intoxicating of traps. Investors get on the bandwagon in the hope of easy profits and fuel a speculative bubble that will eventually burst, leaving a great many investors with nothing more than egg on their face and a sick feeling in their stomach. At these times, psychonomic rationality dictates that you stand back and ask yourself whether the action you're about to take makes sense.

Strategies

Whatever type of investor you are, and assuming that you're sufficiently rational that your emotions don't rule your decisions, success is a matter of applying the right strategy. Whether you want to be actively involved in your investments or you want to take a back seat and let someone else make the decisions, there's a strategy that will suit you.

Strategies represent a systematic method of sifting opportunities, simply and efficiently, while enabling you to select a level of risk that is comfortable for you. Without a successful strategy, and however well you know yourself and your reactions to investment choices, you are shooting in the dark – you may have a very good gun but you can't see the target.

Using the framework

The P.R.O.F.I.T.S. framework represents the main themes of *Profits Without Panic* – personality, relationships, outlierism, flexibility, information, traps and strategies – which together form a psychonomically rational approach to successful investment. The diagram at the beginning of each chapter indicates the individual themes that will be focused on.

Choosing a strategy

In reality, strategies are either passive or active. A passive approach is rather mechanical and could involve selecting a low-risk, indexed portfolio. An active approach is more flexible and can be applied to many different classes of investments, where you choose the level of risk that is most comfortable for you. It is down to personal preference whether you go for small capitalization stocks, growth stocks, blue chips or speculative funds in emerging markets. Whatever type of investor you are, there is plenty of scope to explore different opportunities – providing that you use a workable strategy and avoid systematic errors.

Passive strategies

Buying the index

Most money managers attempt to maximize returns on a portfolio by periodically altering its constituent stocks. But because this active strategy often fails to provide the high gains that clients want, it has become less popular among investors. As a result, many investors feel that rather than try to outperform the stock market, it is better to attempt not to do worse. This passive approach involves buying a good spread of index leaders, like the top 100 stocks in a leading index, and then just holding on to them.

Within the last 10 years a multitude of index funds have sprung up, from Vanguard Fund Managers and Prudential Insurance to Richard Branson's Virgin. They are most likely to perform well because they mirror the performance of major stock markets, where the long-term trend is upwards.

There are a number of other benefits too. Because the holding is managed by a fund, you're less likely to get anxious and sell. The fund is diversified and risk is therefore minimized. Long-term investment is more likely because you feel that your money is in expert hands. And commission charges are minimal or nonexistent because no management is involved.

Furthermore, whereas actively managed funds are volatile because they keep trading to maximize their returns, index funds are more stable. Index strategies work well because they factor out the human element of the fund manager. Over time, the strategy is consistent and is not influenced by personal motives or personality.

This type of strategy is useful if you are very cautious – it is a couple of small risk steps up from bank and building society term deposits. Many pension schemes use this approach as part of their overall strategy.

The easy way to become rich

Investors avoid the upswings and downswings of the market, with its associated risk, all the time, yet aren't fully aware of it. If, like many people, you pay money regularly into a pension scheme, you automatically assume that your money is looked after and will grow to provide a good sum at the end of the period. You don't worry about anything more than that. This approach works for two very good reasons: it is enforced saving and, over a period of years, there is a compounding effect. Taken together, it produces a strategy that factors out human error.

Most people never develop the discipline to make regular contributions into any other form of investment vehicle. On the contrary, if you know you can get at your money easily, a holiday or a new car or a loft extension for Grandma soon whittles away the nest egg. But if you could develop this discipline and your strategy was to make regular payments into a savings plan of your own construction, would you make more money?

If you look at some of the projections of pension and insurance schemes, it's quite amazing how little interest they pay. In fact, the fund managers don't have to be that good because you're paying the money in regardless of their performance and it keeps compounding. Simple building society deposits, compounded for the same length of time, can pay more. Moreover, if you had the discipline to make regular contributions over about 35 years, not only would it compound but you'd get to keep all the fund; with some pension schemes there are stiff penalties for early withdrawals and transfers, or your money is kept by the fund for the whole period and only used to pay an annuity when you retire. It may seem unfair, but that's what you're paying for.

I'm not suggesting that you take your money out of any investment scheme – many occupational pension schemes, such as those in the UK health services, are some of the best around – but you should be aware of how you're making your money and where other good opportunities lie. It takes very little money to use this strategy and the long-term reward can be worth the discipline involved.

Now comes the clever bit: combine a strategy of regular saving with indexing, making yearly contributions into an index fund rather than a savings plan. This could produce a high profit. Figure 3 compares the return on a savings plan with that of an index fund, based on 10 percent of salary invested over 35 years – returns assume yields of 8 percent and 11 percent respectively, and a starting investment of $1500.

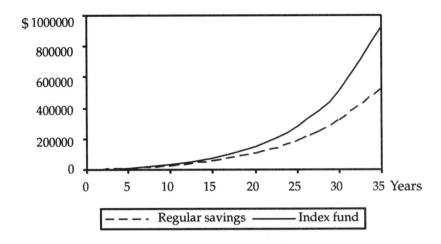

Figure 3 *There's high profit in long-term indexed investment*

Even if your portfolio includes high-risk vehicles, you should always incorporate low-risk vehicles to hedge against any unforeseeable losses. Regular saving – with a managed pension scheme and a self-constructed long-term savings plan – is a good way to achieve this. And it might turn out to be one of the best strategies you'll ever use.

Active strategies

To be contrarian just for the sake of it is like the guy who always wears a scarf whether the climate is cold or hot: it smacks of obstinacy. To go against accepted wisdom and implement an active strategy, there must be some good evidence that your decisions are valid.

One of the strongest findings of behavioral finance is that, in a three- to five-year period, there is a tendency – remember, this is not an absolute – for previous poor performers to begin to do well and for previous good performers to begin to perform less well.

In other words, value stocks turn into glamor stocks, and glamor stocks turn into value stocks. Value stocks have low ratings, for example low price to earnings (PE) ratios (the market price of a company's stock divided by its earnings), while glamor stocks, or growth stocks as they're also known, have high ratings because they're sought after by investors.

The idea of equating winners with glamor stocks and losers with value stocks was tested by Werner De Bondt of the University of Wisconsin-Madison and Richard Thaler of the University of Chicago Business School, who formed a portfolio of 'winner' and 'loser' stocks. They found that the 35 'loser' stocks in their portfolio subsequently outperformed the 'winner' stocks, during the next three-year period, by 25 percent.

What happens is that investors believe the stories and the market hype surrounding glamor stocks. They buy and keep buying. Eventually, the price rises to a level above what is financially realistic and investors finally see that the stock has become too expensive. Prices then reverse.

The fact that investors are slow to come round to a true assessment of stocks is what drives prices up or down. This is a result of the difficulty that many people have in giving up a firmly held belief. Often, too, they have a vested interest in maintaining their holding. Their thinking is dictated by a failure to admit that a changed situation necessitates a change of action. As a result, they wait too long to trade. Many people also hate to sell a stock if it falls below the level at which they bought it. This is sometimes referred to as the *disposition effect*. So investors don't cut their losses until later when the price has dropped even further. The strategy of these investors is unformed and they are buffeted around the market by the actions of the herd, never truly making their own systematic investment decisions.

Although initially there may have been a good reason for the downward price rerating, as time passes and the company puts its affairs in order, the real outlook changes. But this fact is overlooked. Once investors have perceived the stock as a bad bet, the price falls. With minimal news hitting the market – it's no darling of the analysts and rarely focused on – investors become discouraged and keep trading out, pushing the price ever lower. Investors have again overreacted by being slow to respond to changed conditions. This provides the opportunity.

Using a value strategy, clued-up investors buy stocks that are weak in the hope that they'll eventually become strong. Essentially, these are good-quality stocks but their price is dependent on misperception. This is a long-term view but, when the price begins to rise, the approach is proven correct.

Nevertheless, this swing between value and glamor stocks is a cycle and you don't know what stage in the cycle you're at, so buying what you believe to be a value or 'loser' stock with great potential may mean that you have to sit on it for a long time – and that's hard, especially when you see opportunities that you're missing. If you mistime it, could you really wait five years on just a hope?

Momentum stocks

If you've ever pulled up sharply in a car and felt the seatbelt cut into your shoulder, you've experienced momentum. In a physical sense, it is the tendency for objects to keep moving when the force that was propeling them has stopped.

If XYZ Industries has recently been a poor performer, investors believe that it will remain a poor performer until there is a weight of evidence to convince them otherwise. Similarly, if it has performed exceedingly well in recent months, investors often believe that it will continue to do so. This is momentum thinking, which may well fly in the face of sound evidence to the contrary. For example, the PE ratio may be way above the sector average and the projected earnings may not justify the high price that investors are paying. Momentum strategies that take advantage of this systematic error have become more popular in the last 10 years.

Investors can be overly cautious when confronted with situations that call for clear thinking. They wait too long to act and miss the best opportunities for profit. And in the same way, once the investment is on the move, they plough in. It's the *barn door closing effect*, where investors are saying to themselves: 'Hey, wait a minute, this is a good opportunity. I've got to be quick though, otherwise everybody else will get in and I'll miss the chance to make any money.'

An example of this is in mutual funds, when performance improves above around 10 percent and is publicized. Suddenly, new money entering the fund increases. Once in the fund, investors are slow to react to information suggesting that poor performance is just around the corner. At the extreme, they fudge the information, misinterpreting the facts and failing to act because they don't want to admit to themselves that they could have chosen a bad fund.

Within this behavior lies opportunity. Josef Lakonishok, professor of finance at the University of Illinois and partner in LSV Asset Management, has shown that high-momentum stocks – based on their previous six months' gains or on dazzling earnings surprises – out-perform low-momentum stocks by 8–9 percent in the following year. In other words, the momentum behavior of investors, coupled with a swift appraisal of new information, is used to signal which stocks are starting the upward phase of their cycle.

The longer you wait, however, the more other people will have spotted the opportunity and the more expensive the stock will become. Very soon it isn't a momentum stock any more but a growth stock (see Table 1). As investors catch on, the higher premiums paid for momentum stocks are justified because they don't have to wait so long for improvements compared to highly underrated value stocks.

Nevertheless, for many of these stocks it still isn't easy to identify which ones are on the move but undervalued by the market. Besides using financial yardsticks like performance ratios or relative strength, which are discussed in Chapter 5, spotting these types of undervalued stocks can be done using published forecasts, such as the consensus earnings forecasts of the S&P 500 index. You then need to figure in where you believe this stock is going to go. If, however, the forecast is more than 30 percent above what it was a year ago, then it may already have peaked – but then again, you don't know for sure. This is where an informed guess based on instinct, experience and psychonomic rationality comes in.

Strategies that look for value stocks on the basis of momentum rely on the fact that out-of-favor stocks have begun to turn around, as other investors have spotted their potential. Investors are buying stocks when they are already moving in the hope that they will move even more. In the medium term this can be a highly profitable approach if you trade at the right times. But it's important to remember that this strategy is not dependent on the stock itself but on investors' perception of its future value. To paraphrase finance professor Robert Vishny, you don't necessarily make money by buying the best stocks in the market this way, but by buying the stocks that everyone thinks are going to be the best.

Table 1 *You have to be alert to catch the best momentum stocks*

Market activity	**Investor response**
Stock undervalued with a static price *forgotten by the market*	Investors wait
Stock on the move *past its lowest and cheapest price*	Investors slow to trade but increasingly active
Stock soaring *a rising glamor stock*	Investors waited too long, now buying at a heavy premium

A profitable momentum edge

Momentum effects also work on combinations of stocks. Research on portfolio returns by Andrew Lo and Craig Mackinlay showed that there was a correlation between one week's return and the next, where about 4 percent of the price change of next week's return could be predicted from this week's. When the constituents of the portfolio were altered to contain small-capitalization companies, rather than an equal amount invested in each stock of the New York Stock Exchange, the effect was enhanced to around 10 percent. Although the effect only works for portfolios, not for individual stocks, and only in the short term, that is, daily and weekly returns, there appears to be an observable lead/lag pattern – big stocks lead little stocks. For example, Microsoft goes up dramatically and a few days later there's a price jump in other computer software manufacturers.

The strategic investor

What should be apparent is that applying a strategy is more than just deciding when to buy and when to sell according to some predetermined notion. Most importantly, it's about having the right mental approach.

From a psychonomic perspective, two sides of the coin – financial criteria and approach – need to be integrated for you to be an effective investor. You may start out using a strategy with the best of intentions, but irrational motives, misperceptions and beliefs can lead to poor decisions.

Here, then, are some of the main systematic errors that you need to learn to avoid:

❒ Overestimating your skills, attributing success to ability you don't possess and seeing order in information or data where it doesn't exist.

❒ Expressing a preference for an investment, then distorting any other information in order to add weight to your decision.

❒ Inability to alter long-held beliefs, even when confronted with overwhelming evidence that you should.

❒ Remembering successes and minimizing or forgetting failures.

❒ Being impatient to sell a good stock.

❒ Thinking in extremes – the highly probable news is considered certain, while the improbable is considered impossible.

❒ Taking a short-term viewpoint. Recent market losses lead to suspicion and caution, while recent gains lead to action.

❒ Assuming that lack of market or price movement represents stability, while volatility represents instability – the *stability misperception.*

❒ Following the crowd and being heavily influenced by other investors or compelling news, failing to check out the real facts (see Chapter 6).

❒ Making predictions based on limited information as if you have special foreknowledge.

❒ Thinking of investments as pieces of paper rather than part ownership of a company.

❒ Becoming obsessed with prices and trend watching, rather than solid information.

Many of these errors will be discussed in the coming chapters. But overall, they really only have one effect – you take a financial decision that lacks accuracy.

Strategy is about taking the right decision, in the right way, at the right time. And, from a psychonomic perspective, these errors are strongest when uncertainty, inexperience, attitudes and market pressures come together to undermine your decision-making ability.

To expand on this, let's now turn to the way you focus on an investment, the way fashion influences you and getting your timing right.

If it wasn't for human nature, you'd be rich!

How do you avoid focusing on individual stocks when you're attracted to them or they have glowing recommendations from a variety of experts? First, you avoid falling in love with your investment or, indeed, being enticed or influenced by a great story. Instead, you need to view your stock dispassionately in the context of similar stocks and the forces acting on it. Second, you need to resist the inclination to view your investment from a narrow perspective, based on limited information or the urge to trade out of a volatile market. As already intimated, investors are more likely to follow the crowd than develop a rational strategy that can be applied to a portfolio of stocks or a sector over a chosen period of time.

Using this approach, if you need to sell, you won't get bogged down in an internal 'should I, shouldn't I?' debate. Nevertheless, starting out with a good strategy and a good intention is not enough. Human nature being what it is, it's still easy to be swayed.

Researchers in this field, such as Alex Bavelas, have shown that one of the main reasons that people find it so hard to stick to a strategy is that they tend to complicate things. They believe that highly successful investors are privy to specialist knowledge which is extremely difficult to learn. And when they start looking at investment charts and graphs, this seems to bear out their preconceptions. A successful strategy must be complex, they conclude, throwing to one side any straightforward approach that in time would have been profitable. But the simplest solutions are often the correct ones, as science and technology have proved thousands of times.

Suppose you and another person, Sue, have started a new job in an industrial X-ray department where samples of metal plates for passenger airplanes are being examined for defects. The manager says that

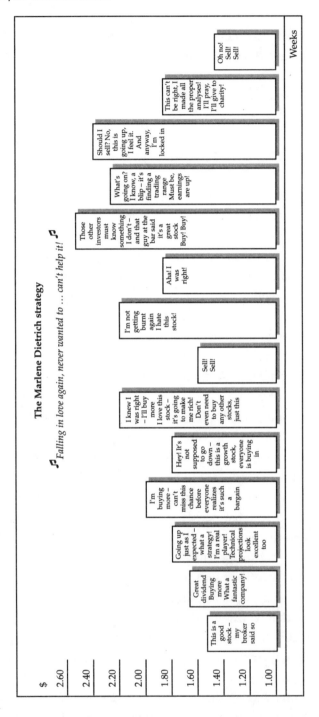

Figure 4 *Is this how you pick stocks for profit?*

you'll first need to learn how to distinguish between good and faulty samples and this takes some practice. To help, a computer simulation has been set up. In front of each of you are a screen and two large buttons labeled Good and Faulty. As the screen shows different samples, you and Sue have to guess whether the sample is good or faulty by pressing one of the buttons. The screen will then flash either Right or Wrong in response.

What you don't know is this: you get true feedback. When you're right, the screen flashes Right, and when you're wrong, it flashes Wrong. Very quickly, you learn to discriminate the good and faulty samples, getting around 80 percent correct.

However, Sue doesn't get true feedback. Instead, she gets feedback based on your guesses. Whether she's right or wrong, her computer only flashes Right if you've already guessed right, and Wrong if you've already guessed wrong. Sue looks deep in thought as she tries different tactics to improve her skill.

The manager comes back and explains that you've both been taking part in a experiment to help the company's training program. He asks what strategy you applied to make your guesses. You reply that simple rules, based on observable features, worked best. Sue replies with an intricate explanation, stressing the complexity of the problem and accounting for why a strategy that worked sometimes didn't work on other occasions.

When you hear Sue's explanation, how do you react? What happens with many people is that they're impressed by complicated theories. It must be a good explanation, goes the old joke, because I can't understand a word of it! So you think that your strategy is nowhere near as good as Sue's, and assume that Sue must have done better than you.

The manager then wants you to make a new plate analysis. 'Who will do better this time?' he asks. Sue believes that she can improve her performance and you agree with her. But, interestingly, you also believe that she will do better than you.

What happens? Sue doesn't improve at all, while you do worse because you've changed tactics, trying to use a strategy based on Sue's complex strategy! Sounds crazy? That's exactly the type of error that investors make all the time.

Following fashion

Investors may complicate their actions because they believe that they're using a valid strategy when in fact they're basing their decisions on an external, prevailing attitude. This is slightly different from the herd instinct, where investors are influenced to conform to a pattern of behavior even when they know it may be wrong.

Fashion exerts a powerful effect. Its overriding characteristic is that its build-up is slow, almost unnoticeable. It takes time for mass attitudes to be transformed. But once they are, investors are more likely to put their money in instruments that have suddenly become in vogue.

Two forces are especially important when fashion influences you: the way you *frame* the questions that need to be asked before an investment is made – you met this effect in Chapter 1 – and the way you're *conditioned* to the prevailing fashion. Here, we look at how to overcome these tendencies.

Framing the question

Suppose that you're holding stocks in two different companies. The combined worth of this portfolio is $10. ABC Industries was bought at $5, while DEF Associates was bought at $2.50 but is now priced at $2. Would you be happy to sell DEF Associates at a loss?

If you frame the question differently to yourself and consider the combined worth of the two stocks, would this change your view? Would you now be happy to sell the portfolio for an overall gain of $3 per unit?

Fashion has biased the way we frame our financial questions. Success is measured by our ability to profit and a loss of any sort is unacceptable. Strange as it seems, the pain of losing a dollar is much greater than the pleasure of gaining a dollar. People cannot accept a small overall loss even if it means a larger overall gain. In addition to this, investors tend to focus on a particular stock rather than taking a broader view.

You're assessing a company and you look at the data, company material and brokers' reports to answer the question: 'Is it a good company?' If all the information looks acceptable, you think it is a good company and buy as many shares as you can afford. But what is the question you *should* have asked yourself?

Consider the type of information you still need to obtain. For example:

1   What does the market think of this stock – is it expensive or cheap?
2   Is it a glamor stock or a value stock?
3   Is the company working in an area subject to fashion or rapid change, such as clothes or electronics?
4   How much profit do I estimate I can make?
5   For how long should I hold the stock for the maximum return?
6   Will I be looking for better returns elsewhere when my holding period has ended?
7   How many shares should I buy?
8   Is the stock going to be a constituent in my portfolio?
9   Am I buying the stock for a good financial reason or because someone gave me a 'hot tip'?
10 Am I buying the stock because a feeling or a story is compelling me?

The way in which you make decisions depends on the way you frame your questions. Asking whether it's a good company is not enough. Either you're framing the question in the wrong context by basing your assessment on how the company appears to you, or your frame is too narrow and you're not taking into account market and other influences, as well as your particular investment needs.

To insulate yourself against a gut response to variable conditions, where you might trade out of panic or rationalize a loss, what you should be asking from all possible angles is: 'Is it worthwhile to be an investor in this company?'

Conditioned to fashion

Fashion dictates that particular strategies and particular stocks are 'in'. This year's 'most likely' may be an upcoming gene-splicing company, while next year fund managers may be falling over themselves in a rush to place assets in the latest emerging market.

What matters here is that investors *feel* that they have acted correctly when they buy. And they believe this to be so because everyone is using the same style of thinking to reach their decisions. No one is willing to step out of line too far. They've followed the fashion and if their investments do badly, the loss is more easily digested if they can convince themselves that they've done all they can.

As simple as it seems – and yet so hard – the way to overcome being conditioned to fashion is to ask yourself with absolute honesty whether your investment decision is in fact your own. Successful investment is about making your own mind up, not letting someone else make it up for you. Consequently, high gains are made not just by deciding which stocks to deal in, but also by making your own decisions about when to deal.

Getting your timing right

With all the internal and external pressures acting on your decision-making abilities, finding the best moment to trade is a difficult task. Moreover, it's incredibly hard to be a true outlier. You may believe you're making the best possible contrarian decisions, but panic and fear lurk beneath your investment choices, causing you to buy and sell at the wrong times.

When the market is dropping like a stone, even the most intelligent and experienced investor can be swayed to make a decision out of a gut response. Did investors buy after world markets fell on Black Monday in October 1987, with a carefully considered strategy and in the sure knowledge of which quality stocks were trading at significant discounts? On the contrary, investors sold and kept on selling and timing went out the window! The most prudent time to buy was a few days later, once it could be clearly seen that markets had bottomed out and that investors had overreacted.

If you get your timing right, however, large market anomalies can serve as a dealing opportunity, the optimal moment to buy or sell being dependent on assessing market conditions in general and a company's financial fundamentals in particular. These two elements together create the backdrop to informed choice. You'll see in more detail how to make these analyses in Chapter 5. For now, the question is why so many investors appear to lose their heads and trade irrationally, or even procrastinate, when market and fundamental information suggests they should act in a different way? One thing is certain, these investors are not all acting in a contrarian manner and simply getting their timing wrong through bad luck.

A tendency to follow the investment herd is part of the answer. The other part lies with fashion again, along with several internal emotional effects that produce a misperception of reality, which moves you away from a profitable strategy – for example, the desire to keep things as they are because it's too uncomfortable to face the decisions that need to be taken at the precise time they should be addressed. So you keep your money tied up in poor investments and miss the best market opportunities, or you put off sorting out a portfolio that you inherited. Hence, while market and personal biases may cause you to panic, leading you to buy at the wrong times or sell when you should hang on, they can just as easily lead you to hang on when you should sell.

Why you might not sell when you should

Assuming that you've got a good stock, ideally you wouldn't ever sell – you'd just keep it tucked away and let it increase in value over the years. When you retire, you'd cash it in for a fat profit and go and live on a yacht in the Caribbean, drinking champagne and watching beautiful sunsets.

What is a good stock today may not be a good stock tomorrow. The reality is that there are times when you must minimize further losses, sell, and take whatever profit there is by offloading poor-quality stocks.

Behavioral finance highlights three common reasons for investors not taking action when they should.

Being unbudgeable

You've made your mind up and nothing is going to alter your course. It may be down to ego and a reluctance to admit to yourself that your decision may not have been perfect, but often investors simply over-identify with a particular stock. You fall in love with the stock and love is very difficult to break free of, because it involves a relationship and personal justifications for staying put. For example, you may have a fantasy that is looking to become a reality, or ownership answers a specific need within you, such as a heightened sense of self-importance.

For some investors, when a stock drops there is also a type of happiness. It may be financial narcissism, but because these investors expect to do badly, they take pleasure from being right when their expectations are borne out. Perverse as this pleasure is, they feel happy in the knowledge that they predicted the outcome correctly and stay put for further pain without gain!

Forming mental accounts

Imagine that you've decided to buy a computer and have been saving up for several months the $3000 you need. Your bank issues three cashier's checks for $1000 each. When you get to the store, to your horror you find that one of the checks is missing. You search around, but it's lost. The only way to raise the $1000 to buy the computer, which you desperately need, is to sell an old, poor-quality investment called XYZ Electronics. Would you do it?

Now imagine that you've spent $3000 on ABC Industries stock, a blue-chip, high-quality company. Over the next few weeks the fundamentals remain just as good, but for no obvious reason ABC drops then begins to stabilize, ending at a reduction in price of 33 percent. Every piece of information you examine suggests that ABC will climb back to where it was. Would you see this as an opportunity and sell XYZ Electronics so that you can buy more ABC stock?

In both cases there is a loss of $1000. But whereas most people would put the physical loss of the check down to bad luck and buy the computer if they really wanted it by selling a poorly performing investment, far fewer people would sell the investment to top up ABC with another $1000. These investors would rather hoard their money in savings accounts paying low interest or in other investments when the fundamentals suggest that they should sell out.

The reason, according to researchers such as Amos Twerski of Stanford University, is that we separate our money into mental accounts. In the first instance, the loss of the check is treated as a debit from one mental account, the cost of the computer is in another mental account, and the money in XYZ Electronics is in a third mental account. Because of this, it's easier to act and buy the computer after the loss of the check. In your mind the accounts remain separate and you still perceive the computer as costing $3000.

When it comes to ABC Industries stock, the original $3000 is considered as a debit to the 'ABC investment account'. Extra money for more stock is also perceived as a further debit to this account, bringing the total to $4000. Whether it is a feeling of uncertainty about ABC's future or another reason, not releasing money or selling bad investments so that your assets are put to the best possible use actually costs you more in the end.

Many investors justify staying with poor performers such as XYZ Electronics on the basis of sunk cost bias – having already invested time, money, loyalty or effort, there is a psychological tendency to maintain the investment even if it is losing money. Furthermore, it seems that as losses increase the entrapment increases too, because investors believe that if they sell not only will their losses be high, but they will also miss the chance of making up the losses if things change for the better. They imagine that things will improve because they consider their investment to be worth more than it is.

In addition, there is a natural tendency to believe that what you own or have accomplished yourself is of high value. This was nicely demonstrated by researchers who gave a coffee mug to a group of people and asked them to write down what their lowest selling price would be. A second group of people were asked to write down the highest price they would pay for the mug. You would expect the prices to be near to each other so that trading could develop. But in fact sellers valued the mug at around $5.75, while buyers felt that a fair price was around $2.25.

Sellers, it appeared, endowed the mug with greater value than did potential buyers, because they owned it. This *endowment effect* can easily lead you to rate your own investments higher than the market does.

Failing to take responsibility

For many investors, failing to take responsibility is the result of a false sense of loyalty. You may feel that your company is somehow involved with the public good or provides a needy service, such as a medical supply company selling to developing countries. Here, though the company could be losing money heavily, it's easy to convince yourself that your investment is being used in an honorable and productive manner. Managers will often attempt to encourage this type of loyalty – and even believe their own justifications wholeheartedly. But lofty ideals – either developed through your own biases and perceptions about the world or engendered by managers – are not a good rationale for remaining in an investment.

There may be a far simpler reason for being overly loyal to an investment. If dear old Uncle George recommended DEF Associates 20 years ago, you hang on to the investment because you always liked Uncle George and trusted his judgment. The trouble is, Uncle George died nine years ago, and you feel that if you take financial responsibility and sell, you're somehow slighting his memory. As a result, you tuck DEF Associates away for another 20 years, even though its performance has declined.

Seasonal variation

Timing, of course, doesn't just apply to selling but to buying, and investors are always looking for an easy way to pinpoint the best time to buy. The January effect, where smaller-capitalization companies and value stocks appear to outperform larger-capitalization companies, is well documented. Every year between around mid-December and mid-January there is a flurry of activity in this sector. I'll talk later in the book about capitalization as a factor, but for now remember that one of the most likely reasons for this sudden upsurge is the pressure on fund managers to do their housekeeping. At the year end, these funds need to demonstrate that they've performed well over the previous 12 months. It's much nicer to run ads when Mr. Manager can show Mr. Public that all the stocks in the fund's portfolio have made excellent gains – and no losers either! So fund managers are looking to keep their winners and get rid of their losers.

A contrarian approach may dictate that a particular loser should do well at some future point. Fund managers know this; they are not doing you any favors by dumping their old stock. But they cannot hold on to the stock because it is the short-term perception that's important. They have to be seen to be riding the winners – not only by you, the public, but also by their senior managers and fund directors.

Yet high-risk funds do exist precisely to mop up these undervalued stocks, which is one reason for their end-year price rise. Often called something like Small Companies Portfolio or International High Risk Fund, some of these do very well from this approach, providing that investors take a longer-term view. However, your approach to these types of investment instruments should include a range of criteria, rather than just capitalization or the fact that they're out of favor, to get a more rounded picture of profit potential.

Another seasonal price fluctuation has given rise to the old stock market saying 'Sell in May and go away'. This is based on the fact that many investors and brokers go away on vacation during this period. As a result, the market is less active.

If there is a spring dip in the market, it seems to be getting earlier each year. Presumably these investors are taking earlier vacations – either they're very successful and are spending their profits, or they're stressed out and have been advised to take a rest! Furthermore, the dip is becoming less pronounced, which suggests that even on vacation, many investors are still in touch with the market. Certainly, with the advent of electronic trading and the global investment market, investors from all over the world are continually dealing in the major investment centers. So even if one country has a larger proportion of investors and brokers taking time off during the vacation season to soak up the sun somewhere, it's really a drop in the ocean compared to the overall numbers of investors still making trades. As such, the impact of seasonal variations is becoming much less significant than it used to be.

Implementing your strategy

Whatever strategy you choose, there are certain common elements to their successful implementation. The following list of tips should be considered before you make an irrevocable investment decision. Remember, the idea is to make profitable investments through a considered evaluation of possible opportunities, not to have an ego trip or to be panicked into buying or selling at the wrong times.

1 Understand that markets are supposed to move up and down.
2 Don't just look at individual stocks and their attractive stories.
3 You need to be swift, but a good stock today will be a good stock tomorrow.
4 Don't let a feel override hard facts.
5 Use a strategy that works across a range of stocks.
6 Don't try to outguess price movements.
7 Stick with your strategy – even if your stock hits a bad patch.
8 Don't be influenced by others to change your strategy if you believe that it will work.
9 Realize that markets work in your favor over the long term.
10 Short-term strategies are less likely to make you money and are more volatile than long-term strategies.
11 Choose a level of risk that you're comfortable with.
12 Think about the investment decision from various angles.
13 Use statistics and financial information as well as real information.
14 Never be panicked.
15 Don't follow fashion regardless of good sense.
16 Apply your strategy consistently, whether it's investments or regular savings.
17 Remember that good strategies don't always work well every moment of every day.

If you keep these simple tips in mind, you'll be making investments on the basis of financial realism rather than being swept along with the investment crowd or your own emotions. *You* will be the one in control over what happens to your money.

3

What Type of Market Are You Facing?

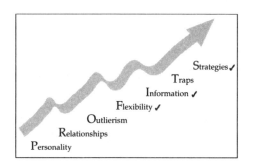

THE MARKET IS IN CONSTANT MOTION. AT SOME POINTS INVESTORS' actions may coincide, while at others they may not. Investors don't all act at the same moment with the same thought for the same reason. Uncertainty can cause investors to revert to instinctive behavior, but not every investor is going to be affected to the same degree. Furthermore, small changes in individual prices don't always add up to big overall changes. There may be times when the market misses out a stage, dropping or rising at different rates. As a result, the market can move differently at different times even when the same circumstances reappear.

Many market watchers have searched for a mechanism to explain this behavior. One of the latest methods for trying to achieve this is chaos theory. Applied to stock markets, analysis can show when there is more likelihood of large falls or rises in an index.

So how does this work? Imagine you have a tray on to which you slowly pour sand in a thin stream from a jug. The sand slowly forms a mound. At some point, however, as you keep pouring, parts of the mound collapse. And as you add more sand, there comes a point when a large part of the mound collapses. Even if the mound peaks for a moment, it will quickly lose shape or collapse under the force of more sand.

The connection to stock markets is obvious. The small collapses of the mound represent small corrections to the market index, while the large collapse represents a market with a heavy drop. Just as the sand mound is in constant motion – little changes, medium-sized changes, big changes – so too is the market. Even in the midst of a raging bull or bear market, there are still movements within movements – slight upswings against the overall downswings; slight downswings against the overall upswings – where investors are testing the waters or taking profits.

Trading and market stability

To trade successfully in this apparent chaos requires psychonomic rationality. You need to be sure that your investment actions are going to have specific effects, following the idea that under condition *A*, action *B* will cause *C*. Remember, the *market* doesn't have to be rational to capitalize out of it – *you* do. You can make better decisions if you know the type of market you're dealing with. Psychological factors such as sentiment then feed into this process, as well as interacting with external factors such as economic and political uncertainty.

The sand in the example never stops being poured, even if it's one grain at a time. The collapse and build-up of the mound are inevitable. Hence, a trend always reverses – you may not know how long you'll have to wait, but you can be sure that at some point the market will reverse. This is why it is always so difficult to think of the market in a logical way: the time component is continually changing. Looking at a graph or a table of figures doesn't give you any predictive knowledge. Considering the past performance of the market or a stock price and projecting it forwards only allows you to make an assumption about its future behavior. It isn't like a pendulum with a constant backwards and forwards motion; on the contrary, cycles are irregular, which makes things appear all the more confusing.

Once you appreciate this underlying principle of how the market operates, it becomes easier to accept the frequent and characteristic short-term fluctuations and volatile swings. Under these conditions, money can be made with a disciplined approach, while controlling any tendency to feel overconfident about the direction of prices and buy too high or sell too low.

In fact, there has to be fluctuation. The constant dips and rises, large and small, confer stability on the market. That may seem strange when most people's thinking suggests that the opposite should be true and a relatively quiet period of market movement is the stable period. This *stability misperception* highlights the fact that if most investors' thinking were true there would be no market movement and as a result no market in which to trade!

This dynamic financial market that allows for continual adjustment, with all the opportunities for a variety of trades, came about in a specific way. Historically, stock markets began for the purpose of allowing investors to trade stock easily when they wanted to and at a fair price. As an added facility to save time, without the need to have to meet the other party personally, someone else handled the administration and took a small commission. It was, and still is, a system that allows for fast, efficient and safe transition from commercial or government stock to money and vice versa. As the years passed, investors and speculators realized that money could not only be made by straightforward trading of stocks but also by the use of other instruments that allowed for debt or forward financial management of assets that didn't yet exist. As a result, government bonds, futures and options, as just a few examples, came into existence.

The stock market works because it is liquid. Investors buy and sell when they want at the best price they can get – not necessarily the fairest – in the quantities they want. Whether you're a buyer or a seller, you are brought together with someone else who will accept your deal; and it doesn't matter whether you are a private or an institutional investor or the amount that's to be traded. The price at which you trade conforms only to the pressures of supply and demand.

Underlying supply and demand, however, is a range of psychological and external forces, either personal or from the mass reactions of many investors. These display themselves in the up and down cycles and waves that reflect alterations in stock prices and market indexes. Supply or demand fixes the price at any given moment, but different investors perceive the market in different ways and react according to their particular analysis of information or their belief in whether a market or a stock is at a fair level. This results in a change in the liquidity of the market – and the market moves yet again.

Correction or crash?

So how do you tell the difference between different phases of market movement? Other than the fact that crashes tend to be sudden and violent whereas corrections leading to bull or bear markets tend to happen several times – much like an earthquake is preceded by several small tremors – the difference between a correction and a crash is a matter of degree. Hence, uncertainty may give rise to a correction, but when other factors are in existence it could lead to a crash.

Factors characteristic of market drops include the following:

- ❐ strong concern about the economic backdrop (such as global market changes, interest rates, trade deficiencies, corporate earnings, loan defaults)
- ❐ changes to the dominant investment market (for example, a major shift away from biotechnology stocks)
- ❐ increased short-termism
- ❐ increased short-term speculation
- ❐ reduced long-term investment
- ❐ changes in market procedures or the introduction of new technology for data handling or analysis.

Although there may be other reasons, what is important is that there is:

- ❐ increasing uncertainty – financial, economic or political
- ❐ increasing confusion about the course of future events or how best to manage the current situation
- ❐ increasing conformity to the opinions of the investment crowd
- ❐ increasing likelihood of personal misreaction to information.

In other words, investors haven't got the faintest idea what's going to happen, so they are unwilling to commit themselves, other than to make a quick dip into market waters and then swiftly retreat.

As conformity increases due to uncertainty and the pressures of the crowd, investors' actions become more uniform. Although this is counter intuitive – and you would think it would be possible to make a

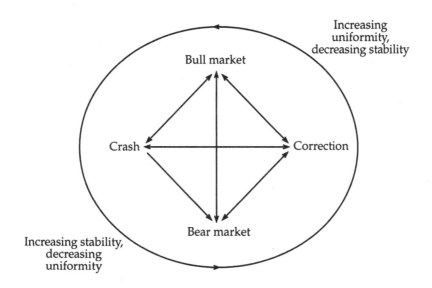

Figure 5 *The boom–bust relationship*

rational assessment and trade in the way that is best for you – the reality is that because there seems to be safety in numbers, you will follow the herd and invest as other do.

Against this backdrop of changes to the uniformity and liquidity of the market, Figure 5 shows how a bull market can change into a bear market via a series of corrections. A correction may also turn into a crash. And from a crash, the market can turn bearish or it can bounce back towards a bull market.

Real crashes are rare, but when a crash does occur it's highly unlikely to move into a bull phase straight away. The dust has to settle and investors need to become more certain of what the market is telling them about current events before they return in any large numbers. This is why a recession or high inflation may be presaged by a crash.

Short-term risk is at its highest at the top of a bull phase. Stocks are moving fastest in tandem with the market and show profits faster. This is why experts often promote fashionable glamor stocks at these times. It is also why, when the market suddenly falls, these same experts may recommend a contrarian approach. The logic is that there is greater potential for a rebound at the bottom of a bear market or a crash. But unless these experts are looking at all the relevant factors and whether the companies and economies they're promoting are fundamentally sound, they are simply creating more speculative investment.

Similarly, as a bull market continues on its upward path, the index may reach a certain point, then slow and waver around a large whole number, such as 5000 or 6000. Investors become increasingly nervous and talk about resistance levels, believing that a drop is more likely to occur and that they'll lose their recent gains. The market is perceived as a riskier place. In reality, the resistance is psychological: a market is just as likely to pass through 5000 as it is to pass through 5050. But if there are enough short-term investors who think this way, it becomes a self-fulfilling prophecy and the market falls.

What is hard for many investors to grasp is that all this is normal. The market moves into different phases to create checks and balances in the system. It is a self-correcting mechanism. The only time it can be said to be abnormal is when the market is in the grip of a speculative madness, which will be considered further in Chapter 10. But here again, the self-correcting mechanism comes into operation. As the mood suddenly reverses and sanity returns – even with a severe case of over-reaction – the market crashes.

When you are in this dramatic cycle, it is easy to get caught out and miss the best investment opportunities. Table 2 outlines a few of the common mistakes you should learn to avoid and why you might behave in this way.

Table 2 *When you miss the best time to trade*

How you behave	**Why you do it**
You become wedded to either a bull or a bear market	There is psychological comfort in moving with the market
You break discipline and sell, then get angry when the market continues on its original track	You alter your position in the market in the light of new 'expert' information

You buy more stock as it falls along with the market – averaging down	You believe that this is how to get rich and forget that an investment is only worth what people are willing to pay for it
The market moves against your expectations and you shy away from future trades	You forget that winning in the market is about getting it right *most* of the time
You won't accept that the market has moved into a bull phase and keep selling stock you don't own – selling short (or buying risky put options, which give you the right to sell stock at a predetermined price within a specified period)	You're taking your revenge on the market for previous losses and believe, for no sound reason, that you'll profit when the market falls
You're constantly trading on reported market swings. Losses and commission charges swallow the few small gains you make	Your strategy lacks discipline and consistency. You need to develop greater analytical objectivity

When the market is heading for a change

You should now have a better idea of how to tell the difference between a normal bull or bear market and a rapid, freefalling crash. But how do you find the best moment to trade? With increased uncertainty and uniformity in investors' actions, the market takes time to reach its peak – or to bottom out – and the knack is to know when other investors are about to have a violent mood shift. There has never been a sudden change in market performance where the information that caused the change was not known at some level – it just wasn't believed or thought to be important. Hence, there is always a little time to make a considered judgment.

This is time you can use to your benefit. Be aware of what you read, hear and see – magazines and TV reports among other sources will furnish the information. Chapter 6 gives you techniques for sifting and sorting information effectively. The most important thing you can learn from these sources is when to wait and watch. The best time to trade in undervalued, good-quality investments is going to be when the cycle has turned down, not near the top when everyone's telling you how wonderful the investment is. As the saying goes: Buy low, sell high!

The next section explains how to assess the market and gauge when to take action or when to wait and watch. The first is a behavioral method of analyzing information that leads to a major dip. The more you hear comments from the *five stages of a market cycle* reflected in media coverage, the more the cycle is moving. The second method is a technical one that examines the trend by a moving average. Use both together and you will have a powerful analytical approach.

The five stages of a market cycle

Stage one – Everyone's happy

- ❏ The market has been rising steadily for several months, or more, with hardly a pause.
- ❏ There is a heightened feeling of optimism about the market's performance. The sentiment is contagious and you wonder whether now is a good time to buy in.
- ❏ There is an explosion of investment and speculative opportunities, but it's hard to choose – investors are spoilt for choice.
- ❏ From colleagues at work to the taxi driver, everyone has a great tip for you!
- ❏ Bad political or economic news is minimized or dismissed outright.
- ❏ Small corrections that suggest a market change is imminent are dismissed as simple cases of profit taking or shaking out the nervous investors.

Stage two – The market becomes uniform

☐ The advice of experts and advisers, from financial journalists to brokers, begins to coincide. And the advice is very often of the form: 'A correction is coming – it may even be overdue – but there's still some mileage in the market before it's really at its peak.'

☐ Stock prices are at all-time record highs.

☐ The bars around the financial centers are doing a roaring trade.

☐ There is a feeling of wonder and enthusiasm as the market keeps on rising to new levels. You constantly hear comments like: 'The market is reestablishing itself' or 'The market is in uncharted territory' or 'The market's testing a new trading range.'

☐ No one wants to miss out – the barn door is thought to be closing and investors want to get on the bandwagon before it's too late (looking closely, you find there's greater activity but it is concentrated in a decreasing range of stocks).

☐ Mergers, takeovers and acquisitions increase (the defining point here is the association with more redundancies).

☐ Due to uncertainty about correct price levels, investors overreact to news, creating greater volatility in prices.

☐ In a self-reinforcing or *reflexive* process, the market begins feeding off its own false perceptions – the stronger the upward trend becomes, the stronger the prevailing opinion that the trend will continue, which fuels the trend still further.

☐ Yields on equities begin to fall in comparison to previous levels.

☐ Sudden small market dips and rises increase in frequency.

Stage three – Getting greedy

☐ It's hard to find good investment opportunities – everything is fully priced or overpriced.

☐ There is an increase in tipsheets with penny stock recommendations.

☐ Media ads for brokerage services are prevalent.

☐ Investors are buying with little regard for fundamental factors such as earnings and price valuations.

☐ Personal equity investment is at an all-time high – everyone and their granny are investing!

☐ There is a dramatic increase in speculative short-term trading in fashionable stocks and sectors.

☐ Consumer spending grows – either investors are spending some of their gains or they're spending capital they believe they've made (in which case, they're borrowing from another source in lieu of unrealized cash, as their profits are still on paper).

☐ Financial magazines feature articles illustrated by bulls – flying ones, dressed-up ones, or jumping over index values!

☐ Some financial people become lax, spending more time in the bar than looking after their clients. They think: 'There are always more clients.'

☐ Money increasingly flows into outlandish investment schemes, fueled by 'sharks' or media attention.

☐ What was previously controlled optimism about the investment outlook has now become euphoria.

Stage four – What went up comes down

☐ The mood changes suddenly and dramatically across the whole market.

☐ Headlines read: 'Billions Wiped off Stock Market; Fortunes Lost Instantly...'

☐ The bars around the financial centers are empty.

☐ The bad news is abruptly listened to – media pundits trot out previously underrated information to account for the market drop.

☐ Investors overreact to bad news, leading to heavy selling.

☐ Investors follow the crowd, burning their fingers as they rush to sell out.

☐ Experts say things like: 'This has been on the cards for some time.'

☐ Everyone's pessimistic about the future – they don't know when opportunities are going to materialize.

☐ Confusion reigns: market watchers can't make up their minds whether the drop is a one-off event or whether it's the beginning of a long-term or short-term trend – or even the dreaded recession.

☐ Experts who want to be seen to be different, or to gain an edge over their colleagues, begin pushing contrarian investment suggestions.

☐ TV and radio reporters start talking about great crashes and financial disasters – they are really enjoying themselves!

☐ Regulators, government agencies and financial institutions call for calm.

Stage five – Recovery

☐ Having been bitten, many investors are wary of entering the market.

☐ Overreaction in the form of procrastination begins to subside.

☐ Amidst the gloom, good advice suggests buying quality blue chips with strong balance sheets or reputable mutual funds or unit trusts.

☐ The number of mutual funds/unit trusts/investment funds begins to mushroom.

☐ The bars around the financial centers fill up again.

☐ Market confidence returns – with a vengeance!

☐ The cycle begins again.

This type of analysis will give you a fairly good idea of the type of market situation you're faced with, so that you won't be influenced to make bad trading decisions against your will, or be fed a line of hype from individuals whose own interests are paramount. Most importantly, remember that because human nature works as it does, the cycle is normal.

However, this is a loose method of analysis. Therefore, in addition to watching events, to choose the best time to trade you also need a more exact method.

Successful investment on the turn of the cycle

Markets, of course, never go straight up or down in a bull or bear cycle. Sentiment, and the particular concerns of investors, mean that there is profit taking or speculative buying as the cycle progresses. The overall bull or bear market can therefore last anything between a few months to several years. By the time investors realize that the market has actually turned the corner, the new direction may have already been in existence for some time and the absolute best moment to trade has passed.

Brokers know about market turns, don't they?

One step that has been taken to determine the market's direction is the *Sentiment Index*. Based on a poll of brokers and advisers, the proportions who are bullish, bearish or expecting a correction are estimated. Data is produced regularly by companies such as Investors Intelligence and Market Vane and published in *Barrons* and other leading journals.

A simple interpretation of the data would be: if opinion is bullish, the investor should be too; and if it is bearish, a similar logic would apply. However, in recent years this measure has become a popular contrary indicator, on the assumption that the market never does what you expect it to. So, a high proportion of bullish brokers (over 55 percent) is taken as a bearish indicator for the market; if most brokers are bears (bullish value below 15 percent) then the market is signaling a strong, bullish upturn.

The question is: does it work? Can the market be predicted in this way? Michael Solt and Meir Statman at Santa Clara University subjected the Sentiment Index to a study looking at how it performed over various time periods. The researchers concluded that it was useless as a forecasting tool, throwing up an almost equivalent number of false hits of market turns as it did true hits. The same type of results would be expected by chance alone.

Whether a contrarian view is taken or not, it appears that there is a big difference between what brokers may think or say is going to happen in the market and what actually does.

How do you know when the cycle's turned? One way is to watch index fluctuations. When the market falls and then rises, it has to rise to a point above where it previously was to continue being a bull market. If the market was at 4000, then drops to 3950, and then rises to 4100, the bull is still charging. And if after a spectacular run-up to a new peak, the market retreats to a lower level and then subsequently falls to an even lower level, there is a good likelihood that the market has turned and the bear has arrived.

Assuming that you've made an assessment based on the five stages of a market cycle and have a good idea of the current situation, the other method you can use to analyze market sentiment is the *moving average*. This makes things clearer by smoothing out volatile movements that would otherwise obscure the overall trend. Many software programs will be able to work this out automatically, using either market index figures that you input or data downloaded from the Internet. It is also straightforward to do it yourself the old-fashioned way.

To calculate the moving average, collect the data you need by keeping a record of the closing weekly prices of the stock market for the last 13 Fridays. It's called a moving average because after 13 weeks when you add a new week, you subtract the 13th week back, so the average moves through time. Record this movement on some squared paper and strike a line through the week you're subtracting; or you can use a spreadsheet program. You actually want two measures, 13 weeks and 5 weeks, and you'll end up with something like Table 3. When you add a new index value, the oldest value drops out – which is what you're crossing through in the 'Subtract last in' columns.

These averages themselves tell you a great deal about when the market has changed direction. You can also plot the market index, 5-week and 13-week averages on a graph. As an example, Figure 6 shows the graph for the Standard and Poors 500 Composite Index for 1997.

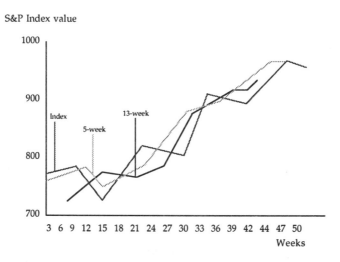

Figure 6 *S&P 500 with moving averages*

Table 3 *Calculating the moving average*

Date	S&P Index	5-Week Moving Average			13-Week Moving Average		
		Subtract last in	5-week total	Average	Subtract last in	13-week total	Average
Sept 05	929.05						
12	923.91						
19	950.51						
26	945.22						
Oct 03	965.03		4713.72	942.74			
10	966.98		4751.65	950.33			
17	944.16		4771.90	954.38			
24	941.64		4763.03	952.60			
31	914.62		4732.43	946.49			
Nov 07	927.51		4694.91	938.98			
14	928.35		4656.28	931.26			
21	963.09		4675.21	935.04			
28	955.40		4688.97	937.79		12255.47	942.73
Dec 05	983.79		4758.14	951.63		12310.21	946.94
12	953.39		4784.02	956.80		12339.69	949.21
19	946.78		4802.45	960.49		12335.96	948.92
26	936.46		4772.82	955.16		12327.20	948.25
	Add latest value here and subtract last in						

Although the index can be plotted on its starting point, in order to be more precise the averages have a time lag. For example, the 5-week average must start three weeks after the index start point, since three weeks is the mid-point of five weeks. It must also stop three weeks before the end of the plotted index period. A similar change is made with the 13-week plot using a time lag of seven weeks. This is the only way to match up the trend lines on the same graph.

At certain times the averages turn up or turn down, sometimes crossing one another. When the averages turn down it is time to get out of the market – when they turn up, that's the time to buy.

There are no absolutes about this procedure, as markets can do crazy or surprising things when you least expect. But it works as an indicator because prices and the markets *are* predictable to a degree. As behavioral finance makes clear, investors either misreact or take a while to digest information and act on it. So even though you'll be assessing the market with a slight delay, the table and graphical values, taken together, provide useful information about the future direction of the market.

How much risk is comfortable?

One of the results of using the moving average is that you can trade in the markets according to how cautious or aggressive you want to be. If you're cautious you'll use a 13-week timespan, while if you're more aggressive you'll use 5 weeks. Other timespans, such as 3-week, 9-week and 15-week, can also be chosen to suit your taste in risk.

However, though the cautious investor may have the benefit of more time in which to decide whether to enter the market or not, some profit is sacrificed because of the extra delay. A higher price will also be paid because the market and individual stocks will have risen during this period. Yet waiting a while longer than more aggressive investors does have its benefits. Short timespans are more volatile than longer timespans and so are more likely to give false indications of market turns. Aggressive investors who misread the market in this way are more likely to suffer losses.

Even so, an aggressive investor can still make money when there are false indications of a market turn, simply because, as mentioned above, it often takes a few weeks for information to be digested by other investors. Price changes in different stocks also move at different rates, again providing more time to act if you've carefully chosen some good stocks. Hence, if you take an aggressive stance – and are willing to subdue any tendency you have to stick around in the hope of squeezing more gain – you will be out of the market with some real profit ahead of the crowd before it turns down, when the 13-week average shows that a bull run is not going to materialize. Similarly, any losses will be minimized. And should the market surprise you and bounce upwards, you may not make as much as other investors on one deal, but you will be doing consistently better over time.

The signals are there if you look

Moving averages can be used together with the *advance–decline* line. This can be found in the financial press and is a measure, favored by analysts, of the number of stocks advancing to the number of stocks declining based on each day's trading for various indices. So, when advances exactly equal declines, this can be represented by a value of '0'. Ideally an index, with its associated moving average, should be going in the same direction as the *a–d* line. If it doesn't, this is a warning that market sentiment is likely to change direction.

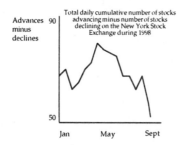

In April 1998, the *a–d* line peaked then began to fall, while at the same time the S&P 500 kept forging upwards, ahead of its moving average. This suggested that the aggressive focus of investors was becoming narrower and that the market was being energized by a decreasing number of stocks. In fact, the later bull market advances, ending with the downward corrections starting mid-July, were found to result from just a handful of large capitalization stocks like Microsoft, Wal-Mart and General Electric. In real terms, by discounting these stocks, the moving averages of the rest of the stocks in the index had either fallen in value already or were barely maintaining their positions.

The effects on the market of different types of trader

Different types of investors make different types of trades for a variety of different reasons. Most importantly, there are short-term and long-term traders. It is these two types of trader and their actions that, more than any other reason, cause the market to fluctuate in the way that it does.

Short-term traders are usually professional investors. They may be portfolio managers, but are more usually currency, bond or commodities traders. Their investment horizon can be anything from a few months down to seconds. They are much more likely to base their trading decisions on technical analysis, often taking split-second decisions to buy or sell as computer screens flash new information. They are less concerned with intrinsic or fundamental value than they are with instantaneous trends or exploitable technical anomalies.

Except where psychological influences cause all types of investors to react in certain ways, this book is concerned with long-term investors, whose investment horizon could be anything between a few months and several years. This is because the way to make money from investment is to understand the nature of the instruments being traded and for this you need time to analyze the opportunity, apply your strategy and make your decision. Fluctuations during a day mean little to a long-term trader's investment choices. The ups and downs of the market are factored in as the backdrop to informed decisions when there are good opportunities for buying or selling. Furthermore, the price itself does not need to be exact to be worthwhile, so a few points either way of the best price doesn't make a big difference to the decision to trade.

The vast majority of investors do not have access to professional traders' sophisticated computer trading programs or technical information. You should not try to compete with these short-term traders and the market volatility they cause should be ignored. If you still have a desire to emulate their approach, remember that it is usually young individuals in their early twenties who have the stomach to stay in that particular game. Their professional careers in this stressful area are often short, no more than a few years before they've had enough or burn out.

A range of investors is important to maintain a wide and sophisticated financial market. As long as there is a balance between all the different types of investor and trader, the market retains its liquidity and is stable. Hence a stable market is a dynamic market, one in which there is movement and volatility.

However, when the balance changes the market becomes unstable. This can happen for one of three reasons:

❐ Long-term investors stop trading in the market.
❐ Long-term investors become short-term traders.
❐ There are more short-term traders than long-term investors.

How does a sudden market swing happen?

Anything that causes the balance to change between long- and short-term traders will affect the market. But the normal volatility never gets too far out of hand because there is always some other investor who will see small rises and falls as a trading opportunity based on their personal analysis.

Major swings – which are historically rare – occur when the actions of the majority of investors and traders become uniform. Investors discount potentially useful information in favor of short-term technical indicators or trends. They follow the herd and the predominant opinion rather than fundamental market or company information. Rationality and good sense give way to instinct and financial survival.

The reason usually is that there is uncertainty about the future. When market sentiment reflects a gloomy outlook, there is a mad rush to trade; investors want to get out before the barn door closes. Everyone tries to squeeze some profit from the market before it all turns sour. But not everybody can and there are bound to be some who cannot act fast enough. They are the ones trading – and losing – in a falling market that rapidly picks up momentum. With most people's natural inclination to believe that there is safety in numbers, the market quickly goes into freefall as greed turns to fear and panic.

The crash that never was

Ten years after Black Monday, the Hong Kong stock market lost about one-third of its value in the space of a day. As the pace of the decline built up around political and economic fears, other stock markets around the world caught the mood. By 28 October 1997, the gloomy

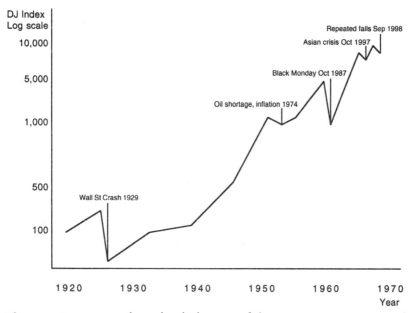

Figure 7 *Historical market behavior of the Dow Jones equity index*

outlook was at its peak. Everyone had been talking about a correction for some time and only a slight push was needed for markets to fall like a house of cards. The push came in the form of uncertainty about Hong Kong's future with respect to its new Chinese owners; a feeling that the US and Asian markets were overvalued; and uncertainty about European Monetary Union. In the way that investors always overreact, Wall Street and London fell heavily: 554 points off the Dow Jones and 457 off the Financial Times 100 at its worst point.

It wasn't hard to see that short-term investors were dominating. There was greater uniformity in investors' actions and oceans of red covered the trading screens as sell orders flashed through. At that moment it wasn't important whether such heavy selling was justified. The market had moved from being rational – where it based its valuations on fundamentals – to being psychologically driven and unstable.

Whether the market was actually crashing was a debatable point. For example, although the Dow Jones fell heavily, the fall only represented 7 percent of the market, while Black Monday saw a fall of 22 percent. Furthermore, many of the losses suffered by investors were on paper and never realized; those investors who hung on didn't take a mauling.

Successful investors who kept themselves informed as the market collapsed to a new level also knew that, since the beginning of the year, the Dow had still risen by 10 percent on balance. If you managed to keep your head and had some spare cash, this proved an excellent opportunity to buy good, market-leading, blue-chip stocks at bargain prices. And buy investors did. Within 24 hours the markets had reversed sharply.

Political or economic uncertainty

Some successful investors, Warren Buffet among them, dismiss the whims of political or economic change. To a large extent they are correct. Provided that a long enough investment viewpoint is taken, most changes and cycles can be ridden out. And if you have the courage to hang on in there in the face of what appears to be a very depressed market – where your investment appears to be worth far, far less than what you started with – you can profit substantially. But it is hard to do nothing for long periods when you believe you're losing money.

Political and economic cycles are connected to long-term trends – if they weren't, short-term technical trends would always dominate. Economics and the ability to exploit new markets are tied in to how companies perform; earnings and profit announcements affect market prices; the political environment creates the backdrop on which company performance depends – tax incentives, international trading links, ease of trading without government interference and so forth.

Furthermore, the markets are often a step ahead in that they embody the consensus opinion of how the future is going to proceed. So when there is a gloomy outlook, there is still uncertainty – with an associated under- or overreaction by investors according to their likes or dislikes – but at the points when the consensus is very strong, the market becomes more uniform as investors steer clear of long-term commitments. In effect, there is a general certainty that the future is uncertain. The result is that investors shift rapidly between markets in an effort to reduce perceived risk and find greater liquidity protection for their money. And where money has been borrowed to finance speculative investment, this market shifting and the price movements it produces are exacerbated as investors act to safeguard their positions.

According to Alan Greenspan, Chairman of the US Federal Reserve, this isn't a market phenomenon at all but a fear-induced psychological response. Consequently, just as they did in October 1998, investors may switch between international equities and bonds, driving these markets towards emotionally charged bull or bear phases in quick succession. On the other hand, large market drops can suggest large changes in a society. The Wall Street Crash of 1929 is one example where investor sentiment predicted long-term economic recession.

The key is to work out just how much of an impact the political and economic backdrop will have on your investments. The main problem, of course, is that this backdrop is hard to relate to the financial markets, due to conflicting reports and media coverage. Taking an extreme example, on the latest news the reporter announces that the market's crashing. A little later, someone else says it wasn't a crash but a correction. Then another expert takes the view that we're still in a bull run, while yet another commentator claims that the economy has turned. And everyone has an answer to why the market is reacting as it is.

Profiting from investment cycles

The investment crowd and the media exert a great deal of pressure on you to conform to the overall trend of the market. You move with the herd and the safety that you believe it provides. The trick to contrarianism is only to go in the same direction as the herd if you intend going that way in any case. If another direction has more potential, take that route instead. Where many investors go wrong is in assuming that contrarianism simply means doing the opposite to everyone else. All they are achieving by this irrationality is adding to the speculative fever of the crowd. It's all about developing a firm grip on reality – being aware of what's really happening in the market, not what everyone says is happening.

If you look for the reasons behind what is happening in the financial world and understand where you are in the market cycle, you are far more likely to succeed. Psychonomics isn't an exact science; there are simply too many unknown variables to account for. But everything has a reason, even if that reason is folly. Once you realize this and that the general trend of the market can be worked out by careful analysis of information, you will be more aware of inefficiencies in market valuations. Alternatively, you will have determined that the part of the cycle you're in is emotionally driven to heights of untenable psychological worth. As a result, although your assessment may not always be spot on, a comprehensive psychonomic approach that incorporates both behavioral and statistical analysis will, on balance, allow better identification of the best moments to trade – and that's a profitable edge.

This all appears to be highly rational. But if everyone is making rational assessments, won't this work against finding opportunities? In other words, are opportunities available because of the systematic errors of other investors, disappearing as soon as they're exploited?

I don't believe so. On the contrary, the better the market operates in response to your actions and the actions of other investors, the more chance there is of making sense out of what's happening and smoothing out volatility due to irrational investing. There will always be normal amounts of volatility because of the variety of traders who want to trade for different reasons. And this will continue to provide a range of opportunities that can be exploited for profit. Furthermore, the market is somewhat efficient, which means that as new information becomes known and acted on, it incorporates any change by altering valuations. What stays the same throughout is that there are buyers and there are sellers, all acting for their own reasons. More of one type or the other and the market swings towards boom or bust.

As you've probably realized by now, when it comes to analyzing the market for opportunities, even the most clued-up experts can easily get it wrong. Andy, a successful New York broker, put it like this: 'We spend our days looking at graphs, financial indicators, company reports and sector projections ... and then we guess!'

Ultimately, a calculated guess based on sound principles and experience will still put you way ahead of the crowd.

4

Investor Sentiment and Market Pressures

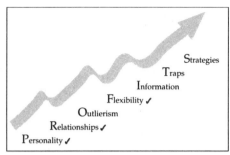

Strategies
Traps
Information
Flexibility ✓
Outlierism
Relationships ✓
Personality ✓

I F YOU WERE THE ONLY PLAYER IN THE MARKET, INVESTMENT WOULD BE a great deal simpler. You would be the only one affecting the market. Your profits – or losses – would be directly attributable to your actions. But the reality is other people are involved, and just like you they take action to gain from the best opportunities. The problem, therefore, is that as soon as more than one person is involved in a trade, you are each pitting your wits against the other. As this effect is magnified across the market, mass behavior takes over from financial realism, forcing investment prices up or down.

Investors' actions, individually and within groups, are interacting. Or in psychonomic terms, your internal market and the external market act on each other in a self-reinforcing manner.

As these interactive and group pressures fluctuate, there is a change in general investor sentiment. This in turn has a knock-on effect on personal financial behavior, such as individual biases and the way you react to information. When this happens, the speculative lure of the herd increases, with volatility and market ratings altering dramatically. Finding the most profitable opportunities amidst this confusion requires that you understand how these crowd pressures operate to change sentiment. You will then be able to avoid any tendency to value investments by adding unreasonable psychological value; or, indeed, to accept without question that an investment is priced rationally because that's the level at which the market has valued it.

Why can't we ignore market pressures?

Many investors deal in the market as if they were the main player because from their perspective their own likes take precedence. A failure to be aware of the viewpoint of others often lies at the heart of poor investment choices, because it doesn't take into account the variety of different people's tastes, perceptions and expectations. Moreover, when others take action, moving away from the view you perceive to be correct, you don't fully comprehend why they've done it.

As a result, investors only see the most observable market characteristic – the price. The more it changes due to trading pressure, the more this feature expands in their mental horizon, forcing out all other logical and sensible information. When prices are moving down, it becomes harder to comprehend why investors are behaving counter to the way you've already decided that prices should proceed. Or if they are going up, you feel euphoric that the price movement is exceeding your expectations. It simply doesn't penetrate your thinking that other investors are making decisions according to their own, different and personal outlook.

To beat the market you need a change in orientation so that you have a more global perspective, rather than seeing the market from only one point of view – your own.

It was the social scientist John Maynard Keynes who first compared good professional investment to a beauty contest. Many people try to guess who's going to win by considering what they like best about a particular contestant. You are mesmerized by those eyes, those lips, that figure. But invariably, the judges choose someone else. 'Are the judges crazy?' you say to yourself when they don't choose the contestant you believe should have won. You assume that other people see things the way you do. They don't: there are almost as many opinions and sentiments as there are investors. The trick is to work out, as rationally as possible, the general opinion and by so doing get a feel for where the market, and a particular price, is heading.

To work out the most likely winner of the beauty contest, you need to focus not on what you like best but on what you think the general view of the judges is going to be: what type of characteristics will they be attracted to? In other words, what will be their average opinion?

Second-guessing and the art of price forecasting

This approach has recently been developed by behavioral finance researchers, including Rosemarie Nagel and Richard Thaler, using number games with groups of people. The basic idea is this: write down a number between 1 and 100 that is two-thirds of the average guess of everyone else. So if five people choose the numbers 50, 40, 30, 20, and 10, then the average is 30 and two-thirds is 20. What number would you choose?

As Thaler shows, there are several possible alternatives:

- ☐ *Zero-level thinking*: 'This is too complicated for me so I'll just pick any number and hope for the best. Anyway, an average guess is probably around 50.'
- ☐ *First-level thinking*: 'Other people aren't really very clever with numbers and so I'm not up against very much. They'll pick numbers randomly or by some other simple method. This means that the average guess will be 50, so I'll choose 33.'
- ☐ *Second-level thinking*: 'People can be quite bright but I'm very good with numbers. They'll no doubt all choose 33, because they'll think they're not up against very much, so I'll choose 22.'

The numbers guessed most frequently in this version of the game were 0, 1, 22, and 33. 'Those who chose 0 and 1,' says Thaler, 'were thinking overly mathematically and not taking sufficient account of human behavior. While those who chose 22 and 33 were not giving others sufficient credit for their intelligence.' The average (rounded) guess was 13.

Thaler suggests that investors often think too much or too little. Furthermore, we try to foresee what average opinion expects average opinion to be and we can go on looking at deeper and deeper levels.

When rationality collides!

As far as your outlook is concerned, the development of financial and psychological rationality is a given: it may be the only thing stopping you from making unreasonable forecasts or following the herd. Yet when everyone is using an extreme level of rationality of the same type, and everybody is trying to outguess everyone else, there can be times when one investor's actions can interfere with other investors' actions and vice versa. This occurs because if everyone were to seek to beat the market by searching for opportunities with the same reasoning, logically no one would ever trade at all.

If that sounds strange, consider this: the comedian Groucho Marx is famous for the wonderful line that he wouldn't be a member of any club that would have him as a member. The logic goes: if they knew what he knew about himself, they wouldn't have offered – and if they did know, and they still wanted him, then their standards were too low in any case; but if their standards were that low, why should he want to become a member! Similarly, the 'Groucho Marx theorem' says: if you have stock that you want to sell to me, and I know that you are rational and you know that I am rational, and I know that you know that I am rational and so on, I will wonder what you know that I don't know. And if you think the stock is good, why do you want to sell it? And if it isn't worth the price you're asking, what makes you think I'm going to buy it? I won't want to be part of any deal that will have me as a buyer!

The implication is that after a significant drop in the market, investors are wary of stepping back in to deal. For a while, they are all biased by the same extreme rationality or mindset, believing that other investors have some hidden reason for not investing. This keeps the market unduly depressed until the cycle again picks up momentum and everyone attempts to find some edge that other investors have overlooked. Locating these opportunities is part of the fun, but it also means that it's only when other investors are operating and making trades for a variety of reasons that a true market exists.

☞ What should you do to profit?

Be aware of the general viewpoint of other investors when you deal in the market – look at the market from their perspective. Remember too that, although you want to find stocks that have been overlooked in order to get in early and eventually make a sizable profit, they mustn't be too difficult to find. If other investors can't locate the stock, the price will remain static. Most importantly, psychonomic rationality dictates that you don't tie yourself up in knots attempting to outguess the market.

Unreasonable expectations lead to greed and gravity

It's hard for many investors to accept that what goes up will eventually come down. When bull markets are rising everything seems great – it's a no-lose situation, isn't it? What's even harder to accept is that what has gone down will eventually begin to go up. In a bear market the mood is gloomy. Behavioral finance points out that investors have a tendency to see things in absolutes. Consequently, their expectations alter because a market event that is only probable is viewed as definite, while a market event that is improbable is viewed as impossible. These extreme viewpoints increase trading pressure as investors scramble for some edge.

Yet change is inevitable as long as the market exists and a sentiment will, in time, reverse. This forms the basis of a cycle: the constant ebbing and flowing of investor sentiment. Under normal conditions, momentum effects are produced. But as people over- or underreact according to their whim or fancy, the worst excesses of desire and anxiety fuel unreasonable expectations, with financial gravity taking over from the frenzied riot.

This effect was well demonstrated by Vernon Smith at the Arizona Economic Science Laboratory. Students were given mock accounts and asked to trade on behalf of fictitious clients. The first time, the students traded prices up and down in wild speculation, throwing money recklessly into the artificial market, their deals based on their expectations of where the trend was heading. But interestingly, with experience, subsequent trades became less impetuous. The students learned the folly of the system and how controlling their emotional response was the only way to gain a financial advantage.

When your expectation suddenly changes despite good intentions

In real life, unlike in an experiment, people don't always learn from their mistakes, even when they think they will. As sanity returns after making a bad deal, you may kick yourself and swear you'll start setting stop-losses on stock price changes – a price, decided in advance, at which you will sell – because you've learned that's the professional way to do it. But the chances are that you'll make the same error of judgment when another similar situation presents itself. It's human nature not to want to lose, and watching the price drop on your teletext screen causes too much pressure. You believe you're going to lose everything. So rather than double check investment fundamentals, the compulsion to get out of a seemingly bad situation – or to buy when everyone else is buying – overwhelms good sense, and even sensible stop-losses get forgotten.

Here are some other situations that people often face when personal expectations and general investor sentiment interact. How would you deal with them?

- ❒ A major stock in your portfolio, which you've had for two years and really like, announces poor earnings and a dividend cut accompanied by a profit warning – but the price rises. What do you do?
- ❒ You're holding several ounces of gold, bought at a market high. The price then dropped 20 percent and has been static for nine months. The market opinion is that the current pricing is right. Do you stay put or do you sell?
- ❒ A securities analyst says on television that the market has topped and a correction is imminent. How would this affect your investments?
- ❒ Your favorite stock, which previously yielded 7.5 percent, has just announced moderate earnings for the second quarter with a 0.5 percent increase in the dividend. The price drops by 10 percent over two days. Is it time to get out or should you ride the storm?

Investor sentiment can make you feel rich: a common factor running through these examples is that when the investment was bought, your expectations were that things could only get better. In a market regularly pushing new highs, this seemed inevitable as positive investor sentiment dominated. One result is that you feel richer, even though it's only on paper, and are more likely to spend and less likely to save. Economists call this the *wealth effect* and reckon that for every $1 rise in stock values, consumer spending rises by 4c. Conversely, when stock values drop by $1, spending slows by 4c.

This is a tenuous situation, because when things are looking good, investors spend money on anything from real estate and swimming pools to cars and vacations using money they haven't yet realized. They take high-cost loans to cover their expenditure or dip into their earnings and savings, in the belief that they will be able to pay it back later. But inevitably the stock market turns down. Shell-shocked investors suddenly feel anxious about their paper riches. Taking their cue from crowd sentiment, they sell their assets for no good financial reason and are left either having to swallow losses or facing debts. This wild overreaction not only results in the market sliding even lower as it feeds off its own false perceptions, but as consumer spending is reduced, retail sales and the companies meeting consumer demand are also adversely affected in terms of market position and future profits. This further interacts with stock valuations, exacerbating the downward spiral.

☞ What should you do to profit?

Always make up your own mind about the direction that future market events will take, so you are not pressured by the sentiments of others, so you will invest only if you can afford to stay in the market, and so you will not spend profits that you haven't actually received.

Don't wait for investor demand to rise

When investors believe that the stock market is likely to fall in the future, they will tend to hold more of their personal wealth in cash. In contrast, if the stock market is expected to rise, more money will be placed in equities.

On the face of it, such behavior seems logical. The trouble is, because expectation is a psychological phenomenon and not an economic one, the law of supply and demand is turned on its head. In the market for goods, if everybody wants to buy a TV set, then some enterprising businessperson will find a way to undercut their rivals and increase supply by selling more TVs. The intrinsic value of the TV eventually drops as it becomes cheaper to produce, so prices fall and demand can rise further with more shoppers buying.

In stock markets, however, when a price falls, rather than seeing it as a buying opportunity, investors imagine that someone else is acting on special information. This results in a mistaken belief that this is sufficient reason not to deal in the stock. Demand, now fueled by psychology rather than financial realism, may stay static or even decrease. Hence, precisely at the time when the intrinsic value of a good stock hasn't changed, the pressure of investor demand is at its lowest. It's as if there's a huge clearance sale on with numerous bargains to be had, but everyone stays away. In parallel, if general investor sentiment is that the market will rise and more people want to buy stocks, the response to this increased demand is to try to decrease the supply of stock by raising prices. Therefore, at the time when you want to deal, market pressures – resulting in added psychological value – are likely to be at their greatest.

☞ What should you do to profit?

Think hard about why other investors are taking the actions they are and whether external forces – or your own internal pressures resulting from unreasonable expectations and personal biases – are leading you to take rash or extreme decisions where you mindlessly follow the crowd. The market may be driven to unprecedented bull heights, or investors may be leaving in droves, but it is at these times that the real potential of a market situation or financial vehicle needs to be carefully assessed to reveal the best opportunities. Only then will decisive actions produce high returns.

Investors become prophets for profit!

Even the sanest person, who under normal circumstances would never try to second guess what the weather is going to be three days ahead, can take investment decisions as if they had a crystal ball providing them with magic predictive power. These investors make unreasonable forecasts – and continue to make unreasonable forecasts – as soon as they enter the markets. They've justified their decision, irrevocably, in their minds and 'know' where the trend is heading.

Why do investors believe that they can predict price movements solely on the basis of data? It's possible that by using a sample of price changes over a period of time, these people have what is almost a snapshot of their desired investment. Believing that this is representative of how things will develop, they act. This *fallacy of representativeness* can be illustrated by tossing a coin six times in a row. The general view is that the resulting pattern should show roughly equal numbers of heads and tails. In six coin tosses this may be so, but the greater the number of tosses, the more likelihood of a longer run of either heads or tails with the lengths of the runs being far more uncertain. This is indeed random, but transpose the effect to the stock market and investors believe that they've spotted a trend.

Consequently, with a tendency to be locked into past events based on limited information rather than looking forward, investors often fail to see randomness in patterns of data, such as statistics or graphs. This isn't to say that market prices cannot be predicted to some extent when a more comprehensive view is taken, but investors misguidedly assume that a stock price is more likely to keep rising after a rise than after a fall, and more likely to fall after a fall than after a rise.

Even with experience that should help them to discern their errors, they find it incredibly hard to give up their unshakable belief that they have identified an observable pattern. There is an emotional investment in maintaining the belief, and the fact that data patterns are only representations of the real world is easily forgotten. Under this *illusion of validity*, investors want to conclude that they see something important which confirms their judgment – therefore, they do. Hence, they erroneously believe that they can make informed predictions.

Nevertheless, this isn't a simple case of self-deception. The illusion of validity persists, according to Daniel Kahneman and Amos Twerski, even when its illusory character is recognized. And the phenomenon is widespread, occurring not only in investments but also in a range of human activities.

In basketball, for example, players are said to have a 'hot hand' when they have had a series of hits. This leads many experienced players, coaches and fans to believe that the player is more likely to score a hit after a hit than after a miss. The belief persists, even though Amos Twerski and his colleagues have demonstrated conclusively that the hot hand is an illusion and that a player is just as likely to have a run of hits after a miss as after a hit. And who are the strongest believers of this myth? Those very same experienced players, coaches and fans.

But supposing you're not prone to any biases or fallacies and understand the statistical rules in force, can a prediction be made solely on the pattern of data? Technical analysts will say that it can. The problem, however, is that with data alone you still don't know what stage or segment of the price movement is being looked at and you don't know – and have no way of measuring – what other influences there are or will be.

☞ What should you do to profit?

Be disciplined about forecasting, frequently asking yourself whether your range of predicted outcomes for your chosen stock is possible. Couple this with flexibility in your analysis to allow for revisions in your strategy due to changes in market conditions. And remember that the trend is only the general market view, which may be right or wrong. So don't follow the trend – however pretty the computerized graphs and bar charts are – without checking out the real investment situation.

Learn to avoid conforming to the crowd

Imagine that you have been asked to take part in an experiment on the effects of negative reinforcement on learning. Already in an adjoining room, separated by a glass screen, is a second volunteer who's wired to an electric shock generator. You're told to ask the second volunteer some questions. If he fails to provide the correct answer, you're to give him a shock.

Would you do it?

What about when you're told to increase the voltage to give bigger shocks? What would you do now?

When this experiment was conducted by the Yale psychologist Stanley Milgram, he found that volunteers would readily increase the voltage to 'fatal' levels when they'd previously been assured that the experimenter took full responsibility and that they were taking part in a valid experiment that would lead to important information being learned.

In fact, the volunteer who was being shocked was an actor working with the experimenter. But the real volunteers, not knowing this, conformed to the experimenter's demands – even to the point of giving lethal shocks while laughing hysterically as the actor screamed out in pain.

Carrying out variations on this set-up, Milgram found that when the experimenter left the room, the volunteer would sometimes reduce the voltage levels. So it appeared that it was the authority figure of the experimenter that promoted the behavior. Furthermore, if several volunteers were used together, the same effect occurred. But when one refused to administer the shocks, the others also refused to go along with the experiment.

What this study demonstrates is that the desire to conform to the pattern of the group is often stronger than the ability to act in your own way or to be contrarian. Moreover, when experts – who are viewed as authority figures – convey their ideas with the weight of their profession behind them, the tendency to conform is even stronger. Consequently, when you make an investment in the assumption that there is total consensus, there is a good likelihood that you'll converge to that position. The pattern of group behavior is so powerful that it overrides your decision-making ability – until one investor breaks out of the mold and the walls of the market come tumbling down.

One particularly strong personal bias that interacts with group behavior is people's innate need to impose order on their surroundings. Humans feel powerful when they are in control. As a result, it's human nature to respond to extreme conditions with an extreme response in an attempt to make sense out of your environment. The *principle of certainty*, developed by the psychologist R H Thouless, says that when there are influences in a group that cause either acceptance or rejection of a belief, the result is not to make the majority of people accept the belief with a low degree of conviction, but to make some hold the belief and others reject it with equally high degrees of conviction. This principle can be applied to political and religious beliefs as well as economic and financial systems. In other words, there will always be some people who take an extreme view in a group situation.

Investors are no exception – when there is a compulsion to impose order amidst limited information, information that is suggestive of future performance, or some subjective personal belief, extreme actions are taken. With total conviction, you act – or overreact. Seeing a graph with a gently up-curving trend line may utterly convince you that the future looks rosy for GHI Electronics and all your friends are buying. In fact, the information you have is insufficient and the opposite may be true – GHI may be heading for the doldrums, but only a full and rational analysis of a variety of factors can tell you this.

Add to this inclination to think in extremes the fact that you are unaware of the extent of any uncertainty or doubt that can be held by other members of the group, and another effect becomes apparent: it's easily assumed that everyone else is thinking to the same extreme as you are. Why? Because you confer your own attitude – or the attitudes you believe you hold, or would like to hold – on others.

The tendency to be influenced and to conform to the consensus, however, also depends on what the investment means to you and the amount of work that went into obtaining it in the first place. In essence, this involves not simply sunk cost but whether you view what you're buying as an investment or a speculation. The more speculative your treatment of the venture, the more you're likely to be influenced by media or hype and to trade at the wrong times.

Frank has just bought an apartment in central Manhattan for $300,000. It's a great apartment with a wonderful view overlooking Central Park. But every day as he goes out of his building, people come up to him with offers. The strange thing is, every day the offers get smaller, until, at the end of the month, Frank is offered $140,000. But

Frank's no fool and he reckons that the market in property changes. The going rate may be true at the moment, but next year, who can tell? There's no point in even attempting to predict what will happen. And anyway, he knows he likes the apartment, it's fully paid for, and he knows that there's something odd about the offers. So, Frank decides to ignore things.

Instead of an apartment, what would you do with 1000 shares of ABC Industries under the same conditions? Every day you see the published price drop further and further and you worry that it's going to drop even more. Your waking day becomes a nightmare and all you can see is a slowly dwindling stock price. There's no apparent reason – no company press releases or media reports of significant changes. The chances are that you'll say to yourself, 'All those people out there are selling, they must know something I don't.' You believe that the price will continue to sink. You try to second guess the market, but all you're left with is the negative forecast that it will never come right. What do you do? You conform, follow the herd and sell, overcome by the weight of investor pressure. And to add insult to injury, the price rockets the following day.

When a need for simple explanations forces you to conform

Most people like explanations that are uncomplicated and neat. It seems to fit in well with the way information is processed by the brain. But as the market becomes more confusing with its violent upswings and downswings, what you see is ambiguous and complex. So your personal observations are dismissed in favor of the conventional opinions of others. In the face of this overwhelming consensus, it's far too difficult to form a personal or contrarian viewpoint, because you're constrained by the crowd, where the simplest explanation for market activity is the one that everybody agrees must be the simplest explanation.

Nevertheless, even when based on rigorous analytical thinking that everyone agrees will lead to investment success, the simplest explanation may be a total misdirection. There is a lovely story told of Lewis Carroll, the author of *Alice in Wonderland* who was also a university lecturer of mathematics. One day he set his students a problem that went something like this: if it takes 10 men 10 hours to build a wall 20 meters long and 10 meters high, how long would it take 60,000 men to build the wall? You can imagine the students all eagerly giving the answer based on simple arithmetic and thinking that old Mr. Carroll must have forgotten they were graduate students capable of sophisticated thinking. But after hearing several answers, Carroll waved the other students down. 'The answer,' he explained, smiling, 'is that it's impossible to get 60,000 men near the face of the wall at the same time. And even if you could get some of them there, fights would probably break out among the rest in an attempt to move forward.'

What Lewis Carroll was trying to instill in his students was that it's important to think beyond the confines of what everyone agrees is the way to proceed. Contrarian thinking would have allowed this because it would have shown that there's a point at which the simplest approach – in this case a mathematical one – only gives an absurd answer. In a similar way, many investors primed with the accepted investor mindset slavishly apply methods that they've learned and swallowed as being the simplest way to spot market opportunities or make investment decisions. Moreover, they find it incredibly hard to alter long-held beliefs, even when confronted with overwhelming evidence that they should, which leads them to keep applying the same logic.

Conformity and contrarianism

The usefulness of a truly contrarian approach notwithstanding, many investors feel that when the market is selling they should be buying, and vice versa. But, by thinking in emotional terms rather than financial, when every investor acts in the same contrarian manner they are, paradoxically, following the herd, and in the process creating greater trading pressure and market volatility. This is all a recipe for disaster, as it takes no account of fundamental valuations, the market itself, or the economic backdrop.

After the Asian markets fell in October 1997, the most worrying aspect was the way large numbers of experts fueled investor sentiment by predicting the turnaround of these economies and claiming that the moment to invest had arrived. I'm not suggesting that these economies won't rebound, but it will take time. They have wide-scale social and economic problems that need to be addressed before they return to profitability, including overcapacity in industrial production and heavy international debts, as well as mass unemployment. As if in answer to this concern, the market prices of many financial institutions and industries that have links to these countries fell over the next several months, even as the media pundits were still explaining what a marvelous opportunity it all was. By the end of August 1998, when the Dow Jones index nose-dived more than 850 points in three days' trading, concern over the Asian markets was again happily trotted out as a substantial reason for the decline.

☞ What should you do to profit?

Decide very carefully whether you want to go in the same direction as the investment herd, and don't let the crowd mentality force you to think in a way that will lose you money. Accomplish this financial goal by reducing uncertainty, ambiguity and complexity about the course of market events and your choice of investment. In other words, before you take a contrarian stand, make sure that you weigh up all the pros and cons in a realistic light, using appropriate information and without being unduly pressured to conform to a trend, media opinions, your emotions or an investment fashion. Most importantly, remember that experts are not always correct and that real profit can lie in challenging their estimates or appraisals on the basis of knowledge and experience.

The pressure to find an edge

We are talking about an edge over and above what can be achieved by index investing or average performance, and both private and professional investors are constantly on the lookout to achieve this extra icing on the cake. In the process, their increased trading size and frequency cause changes to general investor sentiment and greater market volatility.

A startling fact emerges when historical comparisons are made between particular investments and the theoretical perfect investor who

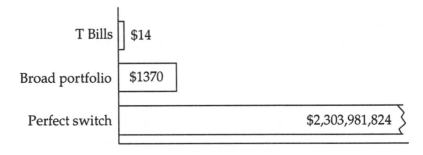

Figure 8 *Comparison of performance over 71 years (income reinvested)*
Source: Data based on Lo and MacKinlay, 1997

has perfect foresight. This investor always switches between investments at exactly the right time and thereby maximizes her profit. For example, she regularly moves between Treasury bills and a broad-based portfolio of stocks. By doing this, a $1 investment begun in January 1926 would in December 1996 have been worth a massive $2,303,981,824 (Figure 8).

Even the Buffetts of this world don't get it right that much because, of course, no one has perfect foresight. But getting it right some of the time would still produce a very handsome profit. And while greed plays a role, this thinking underlies the edge sought by many investors and creates trading pressure.

Perfect foresight apart, the vast army of securities analysts employed by major banks and brokerage houses are constantly on the lookout for a dealing advantage. Indeed, high profit is about getting it right, on balance, more than getting it wrong. To this end, analysts churn out, on a daily basis, figures supporting their views on the growth prospects of a range of industries, sectors and individual stocks. Obviously, they believe that, though not always perfect, forecasts are important and can be made with a degree of accuracy to gain an edge over the randomized averages.

It could be argued, however, that such research has more to do with sunk cost than usefulness. After all, analysis is a multimillion-dollar business, it keeps the market oiled, and a great many people make a very good living out of it. Nevertheless, securities analysts often build up an instinctive feel for where prices are heading, so they do justify their role and produce some very useful material.

But analysts can still be prone to the same characteristics as the rest of us. For example, they may specialize in a specific sector and focus on stocks above a particular capitalization, because their main clients are institutions who need to minimize their risk for their pension and insurance schemes. With visits to the companies, talks to management and a great deal of time spent on research, big, fashionable stocks are focused on at the expense of upcoming or out-of-favor stocks. Consequently, analysts can get very excited about earnings potential and performance, and may predict straight-line growth into the future. The opposite is also true and if they see problems ahead, they'll predict straight-line negative performance. In other words, they also overreact and underreact to information. Many behavioral finance researchers suggest that it is precisely this behavior that causes earnings surprises to have such a powerful effect on the market, leaving the way clear for value investors to make substantial profits.

A problem that feeds into this is that the more securities analysts there are who focus on a stock, the more the stock price is affected and the more dealing pressure it causes in the market. This is known as *analyst's irony*, since they themselves cause a change to what they are measuring. This makes sense, because they're recommending the stock and more investors are buying to an increasing level. According to Lang Wheeler of Numeric Investors, a stock followed by 30 analysts is going to sell for 50 percent more than one followed by 15 analysts.

Tying down this phenomenon a little more, work by Bruce Branson and Donald Pagach at North Carolina University and Daryl Guffey at East Carolina University suggests that when an analyst initiates coverage of an unfollowed stock, investors react positively. In this instance, the stock jumps about 3.1 percent relative to the market. But when the stock is already covered by three to six analysts, investors have got the confirmation they crave and pile in, with the stock jumping 6 to 7 percent relative to the market. Interestingly, with more than six analysts the researchers found that the jump in the stock price was weaker – possibly because more analysts' views don't necessarily bring much more hard information to prompt investors to act. Whether such specific figures can be applied is debatable, but it is certain that the more analysts say a stock is a buy, the more potential there is for mispricing.

Another point to keep in mind is that what analysts make available to the public may not be identical to what they believe. The so-called *whispering price* among these experts may be a more accurate reflection of true worth. There may be a variety of reasons for this secondary price, such as protecting the investment interests of their institution or simply buying cheaply and supporting an out-of-favor sector when there is no real reason for its decline in popularity, but again this changes volatility and market pressures.

☞ What should you do to profit?

Watch, listen and try to assess the weight of opinion in newspapers, articles and reports. This will tell you whether analysts are driving stocks or making systematic errors in combination. Nevertheless, this assessment should be done together with your analysis of financial fundamentals to get a clear picture of the extent to which prices have diverged from being realistic.

How the characteristics of the market create pressure

The investment market works like one very big, worldwide group. It has entrance requirements and rules of operation. Joining is easy. As long as you've got the money, you're in – and therein lies the problem. Because it's so simple to become part of the market – a great many people will be only too happy to accept your dealing orders – the group processes involved that can affect your decisions are easily misunderstood. And once you occupy a certain position in the market group, it's not so easy to give up and get out. Being part of a group, where you're part of a trade, means being part of a relationship.

The result is that the pressures of the group act to reinforce its existence. When you've traded once through a broker, you'll inevitably get a call telling you about another great deal. But more likely, having tasted the benefits or comforts of being one of the 'select few' who are members of the investing fraternity, there is a psychological tendency in many investors to want to remain part of this group. Although you may get sidetracked and miss the best opportunities, your behavior often serves to satisfy a variety of personal needs. Group processes then act to magnify or reinforce these needs.

There are two main components to group processes with respect to investment, the structure of the market and the way in which market membership operates. Human relationships always involve some kind of structure, with a variety of associated ways of interacting. Tables 4 and 5 show how these group processes exert pressure and produce particular trading results.

Table 4 *How the market is structured*

Ordered

The component parts of financial markets – different sectors, different instruments – maintain a degree of integrity and boundary, allowing investors to trade in a variety of ways according to their purpose, sentiment and propensity for risk.

Result

The market continues to work regardless of its participating investors. There can be a total change in the constituent investors – old investors leave and new investors enter – but the operation of the market remains intact.

Subgroups

The investment market consists of many groups, some big, some small; some private, some professional. Each has its own agenda. The position and group affiliations define the investor's actions. Hence, responsibilities differ. Traders are responsible to their clients or their companies while private investors are responsible to their interest group or co-members – such as in an investment club. This is a situation in which groups *within* the markets interact.

Result

You may make decisions due to group pressure that are different to the way you would have acted on your own. This can work the other way too, and you may try to influence the group with your own point of view.

Group constraints

The structure of the market determines investor behavior. Institutional and professional traders behave differently to private investors due to their capacity to affect the market by their levels of trading. And regardless of which trader in a company is trading the same limitations apply – the structural position being accessed in the market is more important than the investor.

Result

The market has formal and informal rules governing investor behavior, which are there to protect your interests and to ensure that no one gets an unfair advantage, for example that holdings above a certain size must be declared. Different group affiliations are also allowed for, such as Chinese walls, where institutions involved with new offers don't divulge information between departments.

Consistency

The structural patterns of markets are stable over time. Stock exchanges are constant entities regardless of who is selling – or the numbers of investors who want to trade. Constituent sectors and industries may alter, but we still recognize an exchange for what it is.

Result

① The personalities of investors may dictate wide variations in index levels over different time periods, but the market remains a market, while indexes themselves are only a yardstick – compare the high index number of the Hang Seng to the FT.

② There is no reason for you to think that because a successful investor has made a major deal, there won't be any opportunities in the future.

Table 5 *What membership of the market means*

Membership levels

All types of investors have their place in the market, from the professional to the occasional investor. Their level of membership is dictated by trading size and frequency.

Result

Entrance to market trading is easy, as is the ability to move to a higher level of membership – provided that you have sufficient financial resources and are trading successfully.

Expectations of behavior

There are rules and standards governing investor behavior, some formal and some informal. The higher the level of your membership – with the associated power to influence markets – the greater the potential sanctions for failure to keep to the rules. These sanctions may be from the market's self-regulatory bodies or by legal process.

Result

Higher levels of membership appear complicated to new investors. This serves to increase the mystique of professional fund managers and big investors.

Group reliance

This varies from low reliance to high reliance. You will be attracted by how much you like trading in the markets and being associated with other market individuals. Low-reliant investors have alternative interests and choose whether or not to trade. High-reliant investors have no alternative group to attach themselves to and no other interests.

Result

① Low-reliant investors are less easily influenced by market pressures to trade than are high-reliant investors.
② High-reliant investors can become very resentful when trades go badly, blaming the markets and everything else rather than taking responsibility for their own actions.

Marginality

Marginal members are non-members who want to be members but don't fulfill all the entrance requirements – for example, they don't earn enough or can't get a broker. They crave acceptance and will take any action to secure it. Marginality also applies to members who want to move to a higher level of membership within the market, but cannot do so due to lack of money, inexperience or a poor track record.

Result

'Wannabe' investors may borrow heavily, getting into debt or trading without sufficient funds to cover themselves. They may also take inappropriate risks in specialist market areas, such as options, in an attempt to get rich quick.

Non-members

These individuals are not part of the market and may even be actively opposed to it, for example because of political affiliations that downrate the importance of a market-led economy. However, they can represent an external source of pressure on prices.

Result

News and rumor due to non-member activity influence investor behavior and create volatility – for example media stories suggesting breakthroughs in technology; animal rights groups affecting company performance; wars and civil or political unrest in other countries.

Reference groups

Many investors belong to groups that lie outside the market, whether work, family or a social outlet. These reference groups provide a focus for you to identify with or promote your point of view with like-minded people. In fact, you don't even have to be a member to identify with the values of these groups. This is known as psychological membership. For example, you may be a firm opponent of smoking, yet not be part of any pressure group. The key reference group is the one with which you identify most strongly.

Result

① Your choice of investment is often in accordance with the values of your key reference group, rather than the values of the market itself. So even if it isn't the most profitable approach, you may specialize in a particular sector. For example, if you're a scientist, you may go for technology or industrial stocks. Similarly, if you identify with people promoting ethical behavior, you may refuse to invest in multinationals that use child labor or pay pittance wages.
② The amount of money you invest, and the amount of risk you will accept, can be moderated by your key reference group. For example, if you are a parent with a large family, you will be looking primarily to secure your family's future. Speculation is – or should be – a secondary concern.

When market pressures escalate

In a sense, the market is a living entity. It is a composite of a multitude of different investors' thoughts, feelings, behaviors and attitudes, and so is far, far more than the sum of its parts.

The result is that we can think of the market as a psychonomic system with inputs and outputs. The inputs into the market include money, investor actions, corporate behavior and external pressures, such as political and economic change; the outputs include profit, loss and investor response. As a system, the investment market's inherent, quasi-life is in constant motion – relationships are formed and broken, interactions are made, and the relative positions of investors and groups within the system can fluctuate.

In fact, the concept of a psychonomic system accounts for the way in which different parts that are autonomous on their own behave differently when working together. Hence, the behavior of an individual investor *changes* as a result of being a component of the group system.

Let's imagine the stock market as a psychonomic system with only two people, Bob and Ruth. There is only one stock in this market and the assets and performance of that company remain unchanged. All the market influences on Bob and Ruth are from each other – including personal and group pressures – and external sources. The more prices change, the more aggressive the price changes become, while the relative positions of Bob and Ruth change as they move in and out of the market from the vantage point of their key reference group (KRG) – the group with which they identify most strongly.

It is the constant movement of Bob and Ruth between parts of the psychonomic system that creates the market (Figure 9). As they move from one part to another, trading backwards and forwards, prices alter. The external pressures acting on the system reinforce this effect. If the market was not constructed in this way with a variety of groups and subgroups between which Bob and Ruth can easily move, or by which they can be influenced, prices would be static and there would be no real market.

In reality, investors may hold more than one stock – or take a stronger position in a stock – but the same concept applies. All that

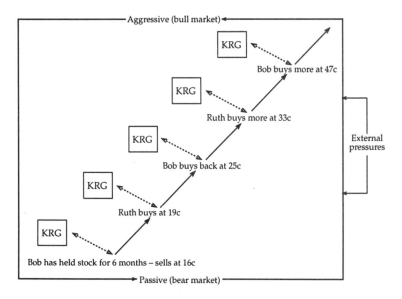

Figure 9 *The Bob and Ruth stock market*

happens is that the more stocks are held, the greater is the affiliation to the market and vice versa.

The equilibrium assumption

One of the properties of systems is their tendency to restore themselves to a steady state. In your body, you have many biological systems that are self-regulating. Oxygen and carbon dioxide, for example, are exchanged through the lungs at a constant rate by the process of homeostasis. If you need more oxygen because you're doing some heavy exercise, you breathe faster. Your body will return to its former state when the extra requirement has ended.

Social systems also operate at a state of equilibrium. If a wife suddenly becomes a high wage earner, this can alter the relative positions of family members. New roles may be taken on, friction caused, and different timetables instituted. The point is that as long as the system remains intact, a new state of equilibrium will be found.

There is an unconscious assumption that stock-market behavior mirrors natural behavior. Investors attempt to use the stock market as if it were a system that can always be brought back to the same point of equilibrium. They assume that the steady state is one of non-movement. It is only when you take a step back and look at the market's performance over the long term that a clearer picture emerges. Historically, markets rise. This means that long-term investment over several years, in good-quality stocks, produces good-quality returns. In other words, there is a state of equilibrium, but it is a dynamic equilibrium and one of self-adjusting increases in value.

One way to think of dynamic equilibrium is to imagine that you're flying on a plane and throwing a very bouncy rubber ball towards the cockpit. As the ball bounces backwards and forwards along the length of the cabin, it is moving between two fixed points, the walls of the cabin. But the plane is moving continually forward, so the ball is doing likewise. It's only when you are able to analyze the situation from a different vantage point that you realize that even if the rubber ball moves backwards, overall it is moving forwards. In a similar way, even when a decline in the market occurs and sparks a degree of panic selling, the general background trend over the long term can be upwards.

Another error that investors often make is to think that prices are just prices, something connected to worth but of no real significance. What they forget is that in a trade the psychonomic relationship is with another investor, not simply with a price. It is the other investor that affects the price, just as Bob affects Ruth and Ruth affects Bob and hence the price changes. Each of these investors is looking to impose their own state of equilibrium on the market – and then to get out when they believe it is at an optimum level. Because they never really know in the short term where this equilibrium is, they trade in and out until one of them decides that their stock is overvalued. One result is that the state of equilibrium is slightly different for different investors. Therefore markets can never really stand still. A bull market will eventually turn into a bear market, which in turn will become a bull market again – and on it goes in a continuous cycle.

☞ What should you do to profit?

Be completely honest with yourself about your position in the market, your relationship to other investors, and at what points you are interacting with the market in a self-reinforcing manner – where the market and you are feeding off each other to create an upward or downward spiral of trading pressure. This is really the essence of the previous section. Through this psychonomic approach – taking into account the structure of the market as well as your membership affiliation – you'll be more likely to understand the relevance of your particular reference groups and your true motivations for investing. You'll also be aware of how the variety of external pressures are operating to change mass sentiment. Hence, you'll be far less likely to act out of panic when these pressures are psychologically driven.

When market pressures lead to corporate crash

Clearly, the way in which investors interact and form relationships with each other, individually or within groups, underlies market pressure by changing general sentiment. However, investors don't always identify with the group that is going to bring them the greatest financial reward; they identify with a group to which they feel bound, or have a need for, in some deeper way. Furthermore, high-reliant individuals have less social capital – a measure of the complex web of social interactions, affiliations and trust between people within groups, organizations or companies that affects financial performance.

If for any reason there is an inability to determine the true psychonomic worth of weightless factors or there is an increase in psychological misperception of corporate performance – from both potential investors and from within companies themselves – then investor uncertainty increases along with market volatility, while at the same time bad management or plain corporate stupidity can be displayed. Hence, from the point of view of the company, either a key reference group (KRG) with its own set of values is exerting too strong an influence or social capital is reduced. In essence, *market pressures, both internal and external, are totally unbalanced.* At these times, speculation eventually leads to an investment crisis.

You can see this psychonomic model at work in many organizations. Take as an example one of the companies that suffered during the Asian economic meltdown in 1997. Let's imagine that over a period of years the managers have begun to feel very secure in their position. They have produced a good product that has sold well, unions are under control – or nonexistent – and workers are in almost full employment. Managers feel that they can improve performance and begin to recruit more senior managers among their circle of acquaintances. They are a well-educated and professional elite. Next, they want to expand the company into foreign markets. And again, in their circle, there are other individuals who are in senior venture capital or banking positions. It's all a safe prospect, as loans are made on the basis of the company's capital worth, with the bank becoming a stockholder.

At this point the KRG *is* the company, and the relationships between individuals, as well as divisions and departments, are strong. Hence, the psychonomic relationships, including the quality and extent of social capital, are optimal and the company is enjoying the fruits of its economic success. As long as there are markets for its products or services, and the value of its fundamental assets bears some relationship to any money being raised, then weightless value also increases.

But when the elite becomes entrenched through cronyism, protectionism and collusion, it begins to misperceive its own importance as personal merit and excellence are inflated. This psychological overreaction then outweighs the intrinsic value of the company, as managers fail to take account of any escalating situation that they and their workers are facing. In essence, the elite becomes the KRG at the expense of the company and social capital reduces as performance declines. Moreover, with this complex system of relationships skewed to a new KRG, the weightless value of individuals, in terms of personal contribution, individual and unique potential and commitment, is minimized. At this point, no one listens to realistic advice any more if it doesn't come from within the elite or from a source of equal status.

So begins the slide: with a falling demand for the company's product or services, trust and other factors such as job security break down. This has a reinforcing effect, as employees feel disinclined to work hard for an organization that doesn't care about them. The whole process is exacerbated when the company's cozy relationship with the banks is strained as loan repayment schedules cannot be met and businesses become overextended. Ironically, at these times, managers often take a

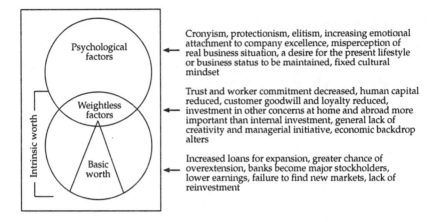

Figure 10 *Psychonomic model of financial breakdown*

head-in-the-sand attitude, absolutely convinced that by cutting prices they will undoubtedly increase margins. With this in mind, refinancing, money from stockholders, or further loans are sought for radical expansion programs to increase production. These individuals have an emotional investment in their company and personal bias, along with influence from their KRG, drives their actions at the expense of rationality.

However, as time passes, the company becomes even more over-extended in its loans, its exposure to international currency fluctuations increases, earnings don't meet projections, and there is overcapacity, with supply outstripping demand. At this stage, psychological variables account for nearly all the intrinsic value, along with decreased tangible and weightless assets. Although in the past it may have been a profitable company – and even though stock prices may have been bid up to astronomical heights – once the real situation is known in the public domain, investors bail out and the bubble bursts.

Magnify this effect among many companies where this type of behavior and mindset has become the cultural norm, and eventually the economy breaks down. Why, you may ask, don't politicians or leaders realize what's about to happen and take decisive steps to stop it? The answer is that they are part of this process too. While money is pouring in, even this sham economy continues to work. Either the elite has a vested interest in particular businesses, or they just don't accept that the gravy-train will end.

☞ *What should you do to profit?*

Table 6 represents a few of the signs that occur when psychonomic relationships break down, due to one group or set of individuals seeking to maintain its continuity at the expense of the common good. Bear in mind that an economy is only strong when there are relationships or affiliations with many different groups. Several Asian countries, such as South Korea, Thailand and Malaysia, are now in this worsening situation. The signs have been there for a long time but many investors dismissed them through their own self-interest. Some of these signs are also evident in eastern Europe where, after the collapse of communism, countries such as Romania and Hungary are beginning to wake up to the delights of free enterprise. For investors wanting to enter hazardous emerging markets, the question is always: to what extent do these psychonomic signs overshadow the normal risk associated with any economy or business going through a period of change or development?

Table 6 *Signs of psychonomic breakdown indicating weak investment opportunities*

1 **Denial**: A false belief that any corporate or economic problems are short term and can be waited out or toughed out. There is no identification with the company as a KRG.

2 **Delusion**: Personal prestige or honor staked on delivering high growth, while failing to address budgeting concerns or excesses of spending. (In Asia, 'saving face' has high cultural significance – a strong KRG. In other places, it may be due to pride or a reluctance to accept that mistakes have been made.)

3 **Foolish decisions**: Big marketing or research projects funded at the expense of corporate or industrial restructuring. This can be due to a type of one-upmanship among the elite, which has become the main KRG.

4 **Cronyism**: Poorly performing companies propped up by politicians or members of an old-boy network elite because of 'connections'. Companies are then said to be vital to the national interest.

5 **Escalating bias**: Ever bigger loans are given due to comparisons being made with previous loans; the perceived requirement escalates in the minds

of bank officials and corporate leaders. But the chances of default also increase if loan repayments cannot be met.

6 **Protectionism**: Government offices are given as favors to 'old friends' or members of the elite – even though they may have a severe conflict of interest; again, a strong KRG that overrides the corporate one. For example, the position may carry responsibility for economic development or financial regulation, but the individual may be a bank executive responsible for handling loans to insolvent companies. Or they may have been given the position as a reward for financing a politician's grandiose project.

Markets are complex systems

During a dramatic rise or fall in a financial market – locally or internationally – the crowd exerts a strong pull, because when things are moving rapidly, there is little possibility of identifying some underlying pattern. Moreover, the crowd is not simply emotionally driven in a unitary style, it is multi-sided. The actions of individual investors become blurred with corporate behavior and the mass response of the market in an escalating and self-reinforcing manner.

If you attempt to work out what's happening, it's easy to get confused. One moment a factor may be important, the next it isn't. And a moment later a new factor emerges that takes precedence. The relative importance of one factor over another is constantly changing and you cannot possibly hope to capture all the factors and make sense out of them. In the face of this maelstrom of activity, you're more likely to conform to the behavior of the crowd – and more likely to lose money.

Treating the market as a psychonomic system made up of groups, all with their own individual relationships, will help you to avoid making systematic errors at these highly pressured moments. You will become more aware of how the system operates – its structures, its interactions, and so forth – and why the market, or stock prices, are moving as they are.

5

Hunting for Profits

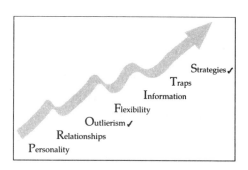

Strategies ✓
Traps
Information
Flexibility
Outlierism ✓
Relationships
Personality

Traditionally, the most effective method of investing has
been to use objective financial measures. The reality, however,
is that for the psychological reasons you've already seen, many
investors fail to use these strategies – or begin to use them with good
intentions and then panic. In order to overcome this difficulty, computerized trading systems are often used by large brokerage houses. The
human element is factored out, although not entirely because some situations call for a different or modified strategy.

And therein lies the problem: eradicating the human element is
counterproductive to achieving high profits, because then there's little
chance of finding the unexpected major opportunity. Furthermore,
being mechanically objective doesn't mean that risk is eliminated, nor
does it mean that there's the certainty of a higher return. Indeed,
investors often make poor returns, or lose, in seemingly good companies, usually because their timing is off or the investment is overvalued.
For these reasons, objective assessment is only part of the method
needed to sift out the good companies and opportunities from the bad
ones. Consequently, a psychonomic approach requires that you don't
factor out your subjective evaluation entirely; otherwise, although you'll
make some profit, you'll be following the crowd as everyone applies the
same criteria. There is therefore a complex relationship between sub-
jectivity, objectivity, and profitable returns.

Subjective assessment and intrinsic value

Figure 11 sums up the different components of a realistic assessment of an investment, which will be looked at in greater detail in the rest of this chapter. Overall, what you are attempting to do is find stocks that haven't diverged too far from their real value, due to investors piling in and inflating the price by overreaction. These fairly priced stocks have greater profit potential locked into them.

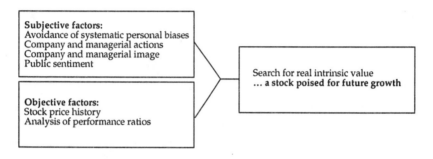

Figure 11 *Psychonomic evaluation of investments*

Your subjective evaluation, of course, begins with your internal market, spotlighting your private psychological world. In this way, you will be able to ignore the hype surrounding glamor or heavily promoted stocks. *You* have to make an unbiased subjective assessment – not swallow one being pushed by brokerage houses or individuals with their own agenda.

Similarly, there are stocks that have fallen from their position of glamor and are depressed in price. Yet these too begin to be hyped as bargains by brokers, on the assumption that things must turn around; another example of inaccurate contrarianism. That's not to say that the stock might not be good again, but it's important to check out the real picture before you invest any money. Very often, there is a good reason that other investors haven't ploughed in to push the stock back up to its former heights.

Nevertheless, with some investors constantly on the prowl for bargains – or what they perceive to be bargains – a depressed stock may suddenly reenergize with what's known as a *dead cat bounce*. The stock starts to climb rapidly in price and looks extremely tempting, but abruptly it reverses and drops to its former level or below. As before, a realistic subjective assessment means focusing on any emotional tendency you might have to get caught up in the hype and buy for anything other than a sound financial reason. Likewise, just because something is cheap doesn't mean that it's a bargain.

> *It's what you know, not what you feel, that will make you a successful investor.*

Your subjective evaluation must then turn outwards to the external market and weightless factors. You could look at the way a company's brand image is perceived by the general public; or whether the company is run by sincere, committed, honest and able people. If you couldn't make up your mind whether to buy Coca-Cola or GlaxoWellcome, you might consider what people really think about these companies. To what extent, for example, do they like the company's products and buy them? And if you like computer software companies and are awe struck by Microsoft, you could give some thought to how much further it could penetrate the software market. The answers to these types of questions, rather than a feeling, are the basis of outlierism. Once all the facts have been considered, then – and only then – is your decision down to gut instinct.

Let's place these different elements in context by looking again at the psychonomic model of a stock price you met earlier, this time in greater detail (Figure 12).

Weightless assets

Fundamental assets can be easily quantified, but moving from the left to the right of the model, measurement becomes far more subjective. If you look at Microsoft's balance sheet, for example, you'll see that only around 6 percent of its assets is accounted for by its market price. The other 94 percent just isn't there. Yet, though more difficult to evaluate, the non-financial components of its stock price are a far better indicator of its true value and future potential.

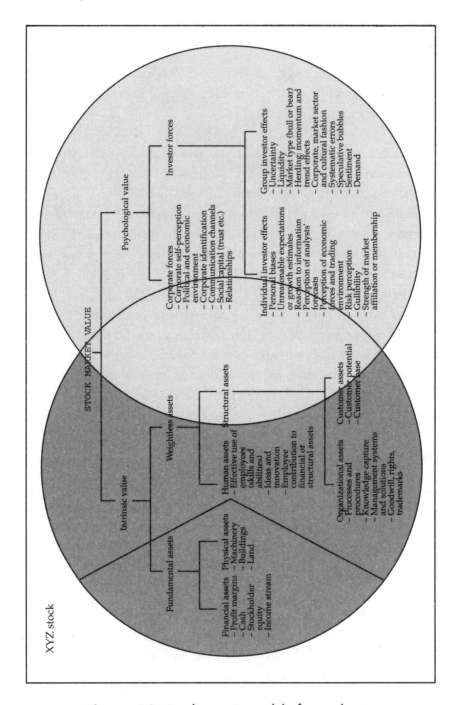

Figure 12 *Psychonomic model of a stock price*

Successful investors are good at what they do because they're able to determine *weightless value* more accurately while minimizing the chances of making mistakes. Moreover, these analyses that were previously carried out in a somewhat loose or inexact manner are now becoming a major focus of research. The insurance giant Skandia has developed methods to quantify intellectual capital, which it does, for example, by assessing the number of satisfied customers representing repeat business; the ratio of sales leads to sales closed; employee satisfaction, empowerment and retention ratings; and costs of production or managerial foul-ups in relation to lost revenues.

Weightless value is made up of *human* and *structural assets*. The structural assets of a company are said to be all the non-financial assets that are left when the employees go home. In this definition, a company's energies should be placed in transforming human assets, such as creative ideas, into structural assets, such as procedures, new products and customer loyalty. The idea is that a company can grow in size, not only from larger profits or increased sales, but also from developing the quality of its employees, its internal structures and so forth. As an investor, what you should be assessing is how well the company achieves this transformation, because it eventually translates into financial assets along with a raised stock market value.

The analysis of weightless assets – and, hence, a stock's real value – is an area that is subject to a high level of psychological misperception. This is caused not only by investors acting within the crowd and individually, or by interaction between these investor forces, but also by companies themselves. For example, managers may fail to accept that they have a communication problem between departments, procedures become slack, trust breaks down, or there is poor use of financial capital. Or if management decisions are taken with long-term aims, they are subject to media coverage, social pressure and investor sentiment as the market responds. The real situation may therefore be far different – worse or better – than management believes; and, indeed, than that stated in the financial reports or reflected in the current price.

The trick is to analyze performance by a method that accurately reflects a company's health and potential and then translates this into a financial value. However, few companies are going to release much of the necessary

information willingly and neither are you likely to find non-financial figures on any balance sheet – yet. So, to simplify matters, it comes down to
asking the right questions, while keeping your personal biases in check.

If a company is doing well, over time its weightless and fundamental
assets will reflect this and performance will steadily improve. So, for
example, *weightless goodwill* will increase as it breaks into new sales markets with successful products or services, as opposed to accounting goodwill in a balance sheet that depreciates over time. Accounting goodwill is
usually taken to be a value attributed to the company based on a brand
name or other intangible asset for which someone would pay over the
basic asset value should the company be liquidated. For our purposes this
is totally unhelpful, as it means depreciating an asset, based on a notional
sale, that is consistently adding value and likely to keep on doing so.

Take two chocolate mint companies that have the same production
costs, put the same number of chocolates in their boxes, and use the
same ingredients. Company A sells its chocolates for $1, while
Company B, using a secret process, sells its chocolates for $1.20. The
secret process used represents a weightless asset for Company B,
because more customers are prepared to pay extra for the enjoyable
taste it produces. In this case – though it won't always be so easy to
attach a figure – the subjective factor of taste reflects the value of the
weightless asset and can be quantified at $0.20 a unit sale. Only by care-
ful research would you be able to find this out.

But don't just consider past or even present performance. Ask yourself the overriding question of whether the company is poised for future
growth – because that is where the profit is going to be. Table 7 outlines
a few points to consider when applying your subjective analysis.

Table 7 *Assessing weightless factors*

❏ Does the company produce a useful and well-finished range of products
or services? Or is it a company with a short shelf-life item, catering to a
fad?

❏ Does the company have a clearly defined brand image with positive
customer recognition?

❏ Does the company demonstrate good, solid research and development that is likely to lead to new and useful products or services – not necessarily exciting, cutting-edge technology?

❏ What's it like being a user of the product or service? (Ask people. Try being a secret shopper. Call the company and see how long it takes to put you through to the person you want and whether they're knowledgeable and helpful. Look out for clues that indicate poor communication and relationships between employees or departments.)

❏ What is the attitude of the company to employee representation and its relationship with unions?

❏ What is the position of the company compared to similar companies and competitors in the same sector?

❏ Does the company have good long-term prospects with respect to future market share and penetration, goodwill built up from previous customers or clients, brand loyalty, or high-quality products or services that are in demand?

❏ Do the chairman's statements, AGMs and company reports demonstrate a full and open disclosure of the performance of divisions, management remuneration packages, objectives, successes and failures? Is the information upbeat or downbeat? Is it acceptable to you? Is it understandable? Or do you feel that the company's management is playing a game for its own ends and something is being hidden?

❏ Do managers have a *head-in-the-sand* attitude: not being mindful of any employee disenchantment or concern; heedlessly believing everyone will always work hard for the company; new stockholders will always be available; and they don't need to innovate because what they've done in the past has always been profitable? (This attitude is especially telling when margins are squeezed.)

❏ Does the company generate cash that is passed on to stockholders in the form of dividends or used for important projects? Or does it borrow money more expensively from institutions for futile pet projects, where little or nothing gets passed on to stockholders?

❏ Has the company shown a steady increase in performance covering previous economic cycles for at least five years?

❏ When changes are implemented, do managers demonstrate the ability to think for themselves in an original and creative way, or do they mindlessly appear to follow the actions of similar companies in their business crowd because it seems the best thing to do?

You may not be able to find out the answers to all these questions – although a watchful eye on newspapers, business magazines and the media will furnish considerable qualitative information, as will financial press-cutting services available by subscription or through your broker (Macarthy Information in the UK, for example). But knowing even some answers will give a good indication of the health of the company's weightless assets and whether these are likely to increase or decrease in the future. Many of these points, as well as others looked at in the rest of the chapter, can be used in a practical way (see the Psychonomic Value Inventory that starts on page 258).

Enlarging your investment focus

A stock price will rise above its intrinsic value if investors like the company and it will fall to the floor if they don't. That may sound obvious, but as you've seen, checking out weightless factors requires more than believing the profit figures in the company's balance sheet and then listening to what you think is sound intuition or your gut. Indeed, many companies have consistently good earnings but poorly performing stock prices – or prices that are falling relative to a market index. Does this mean that they're bad companies? Or perhaps you've come across that wonder stock that everyone else has missed? At these times, it's easy to become captivated with the power of your own limited, financial skills and rush headlong into the market to deal. But quality stock picking is more intricate than that.

When applying a psychonomic approach, one factor alone – a weightless asset, earnings or anything else – is not enough to base an assessment on. Nevertheless, many investors will continue to attempt to find that single, fantastic measure that will guarantee them vast rewards.

The honey factor

If you're flexible in your thinking and take a wide perspective, then you stand a much greater chance of making high profits. How do you do this? In addition to assessing weightless factors and basic fundamental data, you can look at company managers themselves, as they are often the ones behind any change in a company's fortunes. How, for example, has a particular manager performed over a period of, say, six or more years in relation to a company's stock price? If the manager hasn't been with the company for very long, find out where they were before and how they performed there. Remember, however, that this isn't to be done on its own but together with other methods. It takes time to do this type of homework, but it's worth it.

Graph the performance of your chosen company and mark any points where, for example, there was a change in leadership, company policy or type of business. Consider also whether the company has grown in size and real value over the time period you are looking at, or whether it is just perceived worth that has been increasing. The movement in the stock price in comparison to the movement in earnings gives an indication of this and shows just how well managers have been doing for their company's stockholders. Overall, the information is telling you what the market sentiment is about the company.

Keep in mind that clever accounting practices can inflate earnings when there has been no real increase in company growth. A variation of this measure, therefore, is to use the stock price in relation to return on equity – the ratio of net earnings to shareholders' equity – which gives a truer picture of how well managers have performed for the company. This measure, which centers on efficiency, is discussed in greater detail later.

The *honey factor* refers to a manager's consistent, positive achievements in raising the real, intrinsic value – not the perceived value – of their company in line with a rising stock price. The honey should stick to wherever the manager's financial and business efforts have been placed. Table 8 gives a few more points to think about when you look at a manager's performance.

Table 8 *Assessing the manager's honey factor*

☐ Managers should have a good track record, either with the company or in similar companies, since they gained senior positions.

☐ The manager's primary concern should be to raise the intrinsic value of the company for the benefit of its stockholders – not simply to raise its perceived worth to make it an attractive takeover proposition.

❐ Does the manager have a history of company hopping, leaving as soon as they get stock options?

❐ When the manager left a company, how did the stock price react? Did it remain stable or did it plummet? Did they leave with a good job well done and some honey behind them? Or was the person more important than the position?

❐ Is the company holding on to a manager because it knows that as soon as the manager goes this will send ripples through the market and create negative sentiment (one particular trick here is to move an important manager to a different company in the same group to support the stock price artificially)?

❐ Is the manager highly thought of by co-workers – and not simply a media darling?

Objective assessment and intrinsic value

Let's now turn to objective financial yardsticks in assessing intrinsic worth. These yardsticks provide a way to assess fundamental value and decide whether a stock is over- or undervalued in comparison to its present market price – although as will become apparent, sentiment also plays a big part in the way these various yardsticks work.

Looking back to the psychonomic model, you can see how psychological value can displace fundamental value, as well as weightless value, when investors make systematic errors. To overcome this, it is quality you should be looking for: companies that are strong and likely to remain strong with a long history of increasing earnings and dividends, and little or no debt.

To make profitable trades – as well as minimizing any tendency to be influenced by your emotions and behave irrationally or follow the herd – there are several measures you should look at, including:

❐ capitalization
❐ dividend yield

❏ relative strength
❏ price to book ratio
❏ price to sales ratio
❏ price to earnings ratio
❏ PEG ratio
❏ return on equity.

All these yardsticks can be applied to a variety of stocks and markets with different levels of associated risk, providing you with many diverse opportunities to explore. In addition, they will help you to identify anomalies in market pricing.

Capitalization

Is there an optimum size that a company should be to produce the best return? If you were to take a scattergun approach, you would buy the index. This contains a mixture of small and large capitalization companies. However, large and small are relative terms in the investment markets. The smaller companies that fund managers are offloading at the end of the year are not the minnows of the market. Those that are with average capitalizations of, say, under $20 million – known as micro cap stocks – are going to be the ones avoided by managers. These stocks may represent excellent value to the private investor, but to unit trusts and small capitalization mutual funds they are too small to allow either widespread buying or a valid weighting in their portfolios.

One interesting result of this is that funds that produce sales literature to entice you to invest with them often do so by graphs and tables that show how much better small capitalization companies fare compared to large companies. Yet they cannot take positions in these same companies that may indeed perform best in the future.

So, should you buy small capitalization stocks? If you choose right – and there are many good tipsheets to help you – some amazing gains are possible. The problem is wading through all the possibilities to find the stock that everyone else has yet to come round to. There are several thousand such companies and it is a mammoth task, which is why investors who specialize in this area rarely make the gains they'd hoped for. For the same reasons, fund managers of major portfolios are going to avoid these types of companies in favor of stocks that have lower risk and in which they can easily trade.

However, the average return of a quality small capitalization index is superior to that of the main market indexes, which makes these stocks very attractive. But as far as buying a wide cross-section of small or micro capitalization companies is concerned, again the problem is the sheer number of stocks to choose from. You could put together your own index-weighted portfolio and hope that some are potential high fliers. But this is risky, expensive, and beyond the reach of most private investors.

The biggest and the best?

Which would you rather have: a suit of designer clothes for $250 or a huge, bulk supply of ordinary clothes for $300? The extent to which you like clothes – and the amount of clothes you own – will obviously inform your choice, but many people will automatically choose the bigger supply because it appears to provide them with more. Greed overtakes their true needs and they make a decision that isn't in their best interests. A big trade is confused with a good one.

Many advisers will tell you that you can't go wrong buying well-known, large capitalization stocks. Their very fame and size are somehow meant to reassure you that they're worth the money and that you will profit. However, good large stocks – with market capitalizations between $500 million and $1 billion – *may* provide a small profit, but they don't provide the fantastic gains that you're really after in comparison to very small capitalization companies that carry the greatest risk. IBM, for example, is unlikely to triple its stock price at a rapid rate. In fact, although risk is attached, medium-sized companies with capitalizations between $150 million and $500 million are more likely to beat the S&P index on a consistent basis.

If it sounds simple just to choose companies in that range, why don't more investors do so? Bearing in mind what I've said about momentum and the tendency to confuse big deals, and big companies, with good ones, many investors will be looking at these medium-sized stocks when they're going through a relatively quiet phase with no big rises or falls. At times like these, the chances are that you'll wait to see what happens: which way is the price going to go? When there's a surprise and the price jumps, investors will begin to act – and you'll try to get on the bandwagon.

A surprise is just that, a surprise. Therefore, it's worth remembering that sudden earnings surprises are not confined to companies of a particular size, they can happen anywhere in the market, more or less on a random basis, which tends to obscure where the best, and most forecastable, opportunities lie. Nevertheless, information about many companies' future performance is already in the public domain. With this in mind, investors will be attracted to particular stocks if they believe that the outlook is promising or they hear a good story. Hence, investors generally act when they think they're going to make a profit in the short term, and don't want to wait around for something that is vaguely expected to occur at some future time. This is the way in which fashion dictates you should think – to be a really successful investor, you need to go against this outlook and behave in a contrarian manner.

The fact that capitalization may be a good measure of potential is only useful in this scenario if you're already holding the stock, otherwise you'll miss the best opportunities or pay more – you've got to get in and buy before the market comes round to it. The value inherent in medium capitalization, quality companies may just take longer to materialize and you need to be prepared to wait. If you take a wider psychonomic perspective of the market – not simply focusing on those stocks that suddenly begin to rise by momentum – your strategy will be improved if you understand how companies of different sizes are likely to perform over different time frames.

Dividend yield

One of the first questions that financial advisers ask clients is: 'Are you looking for income or capital growth?' The first time I ever heard the question, I automatically answered: 'Both.' Most investors would like the ability to make money in two ways from an investment, but it's not always possible. Some stocks are known for their high yields but don't perform in terms of capital appreciation as well as other stocks with lower yields. How can you get the best of both worlds?

The dividend yield itself is often published in the financial press next to the price and is expressed as a percentage. A good dividend record is an indication that the company has substance and is well run. In good years dividends will go up, while in bad years the company can stop the dividend altogether. The ideal is where there is a sustained year-on-year increase, the bad years only showing a slowdown due to, say, trading, market or general economic conditions.

The safest and most successful way of getting a good return with the possibility of some capital appreciation is to invest in high-yield, good-quality, well-known companies. These medium to large capitalization companies are able to pay dividends because their balance sheets are strong and they have a reputation to uphold. They may be, for example, market leaders with brand names.

Some companies increase their dividend when there is little possibility of increased earnings, while other companies keep the dividend unchanged. Under these circumstances, it is virtually impossible to predict which companies are going to have a higher yield in the future. Nevertheless, many investors try. They assume that an increase in dividend is signaling better prospects, so they stay in a losing situation. One reason is that investors become overconfident: they base their decisions on limited information, but they believe that they have all the information they need.

What you can believe, however, is that very small companies that have high yields may be keeping their dividends at this level artificially because they want to entice you to remain a stockholder. In psychonomic terms, this relates to corporate psychological misperception. Managers pay insufficient attention to increasing intrinsic value and their energies are instead devoted to inflating market value. In reality, few risky growth stocks ever have a sustained dividend policy. And in a situation where prices have fallen, it is important to be financially realistic.

Yet, once they have made an investment, people are often unwilling to get out when they should. This is another example of sunk cost bias, because once you've paid money for something, you don't want to waste it. Furthermore, according to Hersh Shefrin and Meir Statman at Santa Clara University, there seems to be an unreasonable preference on the part of investors to perceive dividends as a better source of cash than capital gains. So older investors who are no longer in salaried employment may place more importance on this source of income because it pays for their daily needs. They are therefore more likely to have a higher proportion of dividend-producing income stocks. Couple this to the fact that investors often plough into fashionable high-dividend stocks without fully assessing the merits of the company, and you can more easily see why these stocks may outperform the market at certain times.

Caution is always advised to avoid chasing heavily hyped stocks. If you realistically compare dividend yield, price and the company's prospects, you'll have a better idea of whether the company is heading up to the heights above or down to the rocks below, and whether you should stay put or trade out.

Relative strength

Relative strength (RS) is found by dividing the latest stock price by the stock price a year ago. So, if ABC Industries closed today at $3 and it was $1 a year ago, then its relative strength is 3.

RS relies on momentum. As more investors buy, for whatever reason, the price is pushed higher and higher. It's impossible to fight it – and you shouldn't try. Eventually, when an equilibrium is reached, the price will peak. Until then, if you buy at the right time, you can make a good profit. Furthermore, you shouldn't assume that other investors' actions are irrational and only your own financial outlook is rational – they may be buying for very good financial reasons. RS is therefore a good measure of potential; and a good stock that shows an excellent one-year performance is likely to do well in the future. Here, the rule is to ride the winner because it's likely to keep on winning.

This approach goes against all the preconceptions of 'random walk' and 'efficient market' theorists. According to their view, you shouldn't be able to use past prices to predict future prices. Additionally, because of the underpinning of investor sentiment, RS moves by momentum and is often independent of financial factors. Whatever the theorists believe, it seems that the market itself knows a sure bet when it sees one. And just so that no one forgets, sayings abound: 'Make the trend your friend.' 'Don't fight the tape.'

The main problem with a relative strength strategy is that prices are volatile. Investors are likely to buy on a hot tip or limited information as relative performance rapidly increases. Their thinking is short term and in reality they are following the crowd. As the price swings up and then down, investors believe that they are losing money heavily. This feeling is made worse if a bull market dominates. They believe that they should be making money – everyone else seems to be – but the evidence they have suggests otherwise. So they sell – at which point the price rebounds.

Relative strength is a very good predictor of a profitable stock, but to hang on in there in the face of such volatility is incredibly hard and psychologically draining. The only way to accomplish it is to be aware of the personality factors that underlie your behavior and to understand the principles behind the market's operation. There will be more on this in Part Two.

Price to book ratio

The price to book ratio (PBR) is the market price of the stock divided by its book value or net assets per share – tangible assets less any liabilities and depreciation. Book value can also be a stock's basic worth if the company is liquidated.

$$\text{Price to book ratio} = \frac{\text{Price}}{\text{Book value per share}}$$

The ratio of the two prices provides a measure of investor sentiment, that is, how much investors are willing to pay over assets. Many investors believe this value to be a more reliable measure because earnings can be discounted in their analysis. For those investors who don't trust published company accounts, and who say that unscrupulous finance controllers could manipulate the figures, there is some validity in this point of view.

A low PBR is generally a better predictor of long-term performance for good investments, while a high PBR indicates less likelihood of beating the market. What should be kept in mind, however, is that a high PBR is a sign of a growth stock. So a high ratio on its own shouldn't stop you from entering the market if other predictors are good.

Price to sales ratio

The price to sales ratio (PSR) is the market price of the stock divided by the company's annual sales figure. PSRs are a popular yardstick for many investors, who believe they give a more accurate assessment of how well a business is performing.

$$\text{Price to sales ratio} = \frac{\text{Price}}{\text{Sales per share}}$$

Because PSR is so tied in to the perception of performance, it is also a good indicator of investor sentiment; a high PSR stock rests on the belief that investors have in its future potential. Until hard financial information hits the public arena, investors are buying in for purely psychological reasons, in other words hope, expectation and perhaps a little greed.

One interesting characteristic of PSRs is that because they are a reflection of mass investor opinion, they are quite sensitive to market forces. Although a low PSR stock generally has more potential, research suggests that in bull markets that show rapid gains on sector constituents and new issues, the balance changes slightly. In these instances where the markets are more speculative, the higher-rated PSR stocks seem to perform slightly better, as they have become a measure of growth stock potential.

Nevertheless, low PSR stocks can beat the market on a consistent basis in passive and speculative markets; over the long term they perform better than high PSR stocks. And they should form part of your overall assessment.

Price to earnings ratio

A particularly well-known financial yardstick, the price to earnings (PE) ratio – or multiple, as it's also called – is often published in the financial newspapers alongside a company's current daily price. The PE ratio is given by the price of the stock divided by the earnings.

$$\text{Price to earnings ratio} = \frac{\text{Price}}{\text{Earnings per share}}$$

So, if the price of a stock is \$10 and the stated earnings per stock are \$1, the PE is 10. This multiple gives an indication of how cheap or expensive a stock is. On the whole, low PE stocks have greater potential than high PE stocks and often do better than the market.

The PE ratio is a good measure of investor sentiment, as it indicates the premium that investors are willing to pay for the stock or whether it is undervalued and trading at a discount. But where many investors go wrong is in assuming that if it has a low PE it must be a value stock and should eventually come right. Not all low PE stocks are good and, similarly, although the really high multiple stocks of, say, over 30 should be avoided, this may not always be the case. A ratio in itself means nothing, it is simply a number. This is true even when projected earnings, based on analysts' forecasts, are used as the earnings figure. This information only makes real sense when you compare the PE to the sector average PE for a range of similar stocks.

It's at this point, when the stock is being held, that investors will justify their decisions in their own mind. 'It's a good stock', 'It'll come right in the end,' or simply 'It's not expensive at all,' they'll convince themselves – even if there's abundant information to the contrary that should make them cut their loss and sell.

PEG ratio

A fairly recent development in hunting for value stocks, the PEG ratio is the PE ratio divided by the prospective growth.

$$\text{PEG ratio} = \frac{\text{PE}}{\text{Prospective growth}}$$

The prospective growth is taken from analysts' forecasts. Where the PE equals the growth rate – say the PE is 20 and the growth rate is 20 percent – the ratio is 1. This represents a fully valued stock, where market sentiment is saying that we already know what's going to happen and have built this into the price. Of course, unexpected news may totally throw this assessment and analysts would then be forced to revalue the stock.

In general, however, a PEG of 0.7 or under suggests an undervalued stock that is likely to do better, while a PEG between 0.7 and 1.0 is a stock to watch.

One problem with PEGs is that because they are so mechanical, any analysis of the market tends to throw up the same few stocks, which are pushed by various investment experts. It's important, therefore, to use other criteria as well, otherwise you'll just be following the herd.

Additionally, at the top of a bull market, it becomes harder to find these sorts of stocks, as valuations have all risen. Indexes are high and the market is at its weakest, with the greatest chance of its reversing on itself. At these times, analysts and market players have already piled in. Although they may have contributed to the overreaction in their hunt for bargains, you don't want to be following them and paying over the odds. The stock itself may be very good, but caution is needed.

Return on equity

One of the main evaluation measures favored by Warren Buffett, return on equity (RoE) can be used to compare companies in a like-for-like manner. If ABC Industries and DEF Associates both have the same market capitalization and profit margin, it allows you to assess which one is the better company on the basis of their efficiency, that is, how much return they generate for shareholders. When good companies have good earnings that are likely to be sustained and make efficient use of their capital, there is a better chance of profiting.

To work out RoE, you'll need to look at figures in the published accounts, although some companies are now beginning to include this value in their reports. As mentioned earlier in the chapter, RoE is the ratio of net earnings to shareholder equity and is expressed as a percentage or yield. So, if ABC Industries has net earnings of $0.31 and shareholder equity of $1.46:

$$RoE = \frac{0.31}{1.46} \times 100 = 21.23\%$$

Consequently, for every $100 of equity funds that ABC has, it generates $21.23 for its shareholders. Table 9 shows how several companies can be compared. Note that PEs are generally much lower in the UK than they are in the US.

Table 9 *Comparing RoE*

Company	Market capitalization ($bn)	Market price ($)	RoE (%)	PE ratio
ABC Industries	87.4	11.2	21.23	36
DEF Associates	87.4	21.3	22.40	48
HIJ Electronics	56.0	10.6	16.10	12
KLM Partners	120.3	33.5	9.60	52

What we're seeing here is that both ABC Industries and DEF Associates, for the same capitalization, are making good use of their equity, with DEF doing slightly better. HIJ Electronics also appears to have a good return. KLM Partners is a large company heavily hyped in the news but with a fairly low RoE in comparison to the other stocks.

However, to ascertain which is the best buy, you need to look at the PE, or some of the other ratios previously discussed, in conjunction with the RoE. Then you realize that HIJ's PE is well below the sector average (this value is found in the financial newspapers). Investor sentiment is saying that the outlook is poor and that the earnings are likely to drop along with the RoE in the coming months. KLM Partners' market price may have soared recently reflecting the media hype, with its PE around twice the sector average, but it isn't making efficient use of its equity. DEF is doing well and its RoE reflects this, as does its PE, which is way above the sector average. Investors have realized that DEF is a good company and have bid it up to expensive levels. On the other hand, ABC Industries not only has a good RoE but a PE slightly below the sector average, which makes it a good potential bet.

The other associated use of RoE is for predictive valuation. In essence, using efficiency as its starting point, this approach is saying that a company's basic worth is not simply its tangible assets but also the amount of compounded earnings – the income stream – that it will generate in the forthcoming years. Each year, therefore, a well-run company will retain some earnings, adding it to its equity base for development and reinvestment, or kept as cash reserves, and will give the rest over to its stockholders in the form of dividends. Consequently, using our example of ABC Industries, we see that 60 percent ($0.19) of earnings is retained and 40 percent ($0.12) is paid as dividends. The earnings retained is the part we're interested in and using this figure we find that the adjusted RoE is equal to 13 percent ($(0.19/1.46) \times 100$).

If we assume that the company will continue to grow its earnings at a constant rate – which is a logical assumption if it is a good company – then the equity base will increase year-on-year by a 13 percent compounded rate. In this way we can project our estimates of equity growth and earnings into the future. So, in any future year:

$$\text{shareholder's equity compounded at } 13\% \times \text{RoE}$$
$$= \text{projected earnings}$$

In year one:
$$(1.46 \times 1.13) \times 21.23/100 = \$0.35$$

… and in year five:

$$2.38 \times 21.23\% = \$0.51$$

To project the price of the stock, two ways are conventionally used for a simple acid test. The first is to multiply the projected earnings by the average historic PE for the last several years – if you're projecting forwards five years then you would go back five years and average this value. The second way is to multiply the projected earnings by the value of the inverse of government bond yields. So, if the current rate is 5 percent, the inverse would be 1/5 percent, which is 20. The reason for doing this is to provide a benchmark comparison. It's a bit like saying: what profit might you expect from your stock in several years' time if it rose in value at the same rate as a bond?

Note, too, that a comparison figure for the present value of the company against market value can be worked out by using historic earnings. Although this may allow you to buy at a reasonable price, bear in mind that any real profit comes from future price performance.

It is worth mentioning that there is an argument in favor of companies retaining most, if not all, of their earnings and paying a reduced dividend. This can inflate the RoE, which is another reason that using one assessment measure alone is unwise. If the company has good plans that the market likes, that's excellent news and a smaller dividend may not be such a bad thing. It therefore depends on what the company wants to do with any cash reserves it builds up – sitting on the cash mountain, as some large companies do, only adds to market speculation that the company lacks direction or that it's looking for juicy takeover targets.

I have discussed RoE and earnings in some detail, because it draws attention to an important point: in any attempt to forecast, all that can be said with any accuracy is that, all things being equal, the company *could* achieve this level of performance. To find out if such performance is probable in the coming years, you would need to look at weightless factors and how the company is run. After all, managers may not meet earnings expectations due to psychological and corporate forces. Besides which, a great deal can happen in the economy to change trading conditions, while international sales markets could also change in profile or in their demands for goods and services. A number of computer makers and allied companies making components or peripherals, for example, saw their profits slump in the months after the Asian markets fell apart in 1998. Moreover, as these effects materialize, investors

Can you trust published earnings figures?

Companies have several ways of inflating their reported earnings. Lying, of course, is illegal, as it constitutes fraud. Nevertheless, it doesn't stop unscrupulous individuals from trying. Cendent Corporation, for example, recently accused some former executives of a company it acquired of booking fictitious revenues to inflate earnings by $500 million.

More usually it's accounting tricks such as:

❏ Revenue recognition – booking earnings too soon on incomplete sales or on contracts that may extend over several years.
❏ Stock option disclosure – this may be hidden somewhere in the report, but it doesn't form a charge to earnings; nor is there a full indication of the effects on earnings if all options were exercised.
❏ Pooling – assets and liabilities of merging companies are combined at book value, which eliminates goodwill depreciation.
❏ Restructuring reserves – combining several years of forecasted expenses into a one-time-only charge.
❏ In-process R&D charges – an estimated value by a buying company of incomplete R&D of a company taken over.

What the last two tricks have in common is that they allow companies to write off charges or expenses in an early year, which inflates earnings in the following years. For some reason, investors often ignore one-time-only or restructuring charges – they appear to be very forgiving and may even assume that companies are simply getting on with taking the harsh medicine. Hence, it provides misperceived confirmation to the investor that the company is taking the right actions. Alternatively, as time passes, investors simply forget about the charge, which they wouldn't do if they saw a depreciation to earnings every year.

This is not all accounting sleight-of-hand, however. There may be a valid reason for charges being taken early on. And, when it comes to R&D or the acquisition of technology and information-based businesses, companies themselves may not know how to value weightless assets appropriately. In turn, this creates a greater incentive to make the most out of what they can measure and report to stockholders, that is, tangible assets and earnings.

may value the stock with greater personal bias, pushing it down as a market 'dog' or up as a highly rated 'glamor' stock.

In addition, not all companies are the same in the way they operate. Warren Buffett is known for his view that companies are either 'commodity' or 'consumer' stocks. Commodity stocks are those that are virtually indistinguishable from their competitors, such as oil and gas companies. These businesses find it hard to increase their customer base and can only compete on price. Consumer stocks, on the other hand – such as financials and food producers – have an expanding market, an above-average return on equity, high customer loyalty, and a degree of pricing flexibility. A prime example is Coca-Cola.

Another difficulty with RoE in relation to earnings projections is that the profile of companies is changing as we develop information- and technology-based industry. The factory model, where raw materials go in one end and a product comes out the other, is not relevant to these new industries – their raw materials are ideas, data, and so forth. The upshot is that companies can no longer easily be categorized into commodity or consumer – although there are still many bargains to be had if you look. Buffett himself is aware of this problem and has stated that he steers clear of these types of businesses, such as Microsoft, as he has little idea how to value them using traditional measures.

Nevertheless, Internet companies, as well as a host of research, computer, and information businesses, are here to stay and many are quality companies with very strong investment potential. As mentioned previously, the defining characteristic of these companies is their high weightless assets in relation to fundamental assets. The key to success, therefore, is to make your own unbiased evaluation of the company on a long-term basis and to examine weightless factors – in addition to applying performance measures – to the best of your ability.

Time to trade

Because the market is efficient some of the time, any formulaic valuation that looks to determine an intrinsic value of a stock can only be applied to a certain extent. After a while, although you can still find bargains, high returns are likely to decrease towards the index averages. The reason is that widespread use of these methods by analysts, brokers and investors eventually wipes out the systematic edge that originally produced the extreme profits. In other words, try as you may, it will become increasingly difficult to do better than a passive approach with a broad-based portfolio of stocks. The only way to get round this problem is not to become wedded to one financial school of thought or viewpoint, but instead to keep looking for quality investments by a mixture of objective fundamental assessment and subjective evaluation, and to be ready to change tack when the moment arises.

6

Reacting to Information

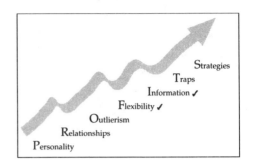

Strategies
Traps
Information ✓
Flexibility ✓
Outlierism
Relationships
Personality

PRIVATE AND PROFESSIONAL INVESTORS HAVE A VARIETY OF REASONS for investing. These reasons may be financially sound, emotionally driven, or based on personal views about anticipated prospects of their favorite companies, but they all cause trading effects to escalate. As a result, prices diverge from what they would be if the market were wholly rational and efficient, with subsequent prices being driven to new highs or lows. Information drives this process along and when profit announcements, earnings surprises, exciting stories, or any other piece of important news hit the market, investors, analysts and brokers all rush to act.

Is it your price or the market's?

Suppose you bought stocks in two different companies. They have the same current value, future earnings potential and market position. Yet for one you paid $1 per stock and for the other you paid $2.

The price difference results from your internal market and the external market making you subjective in your analysis of what you hear and see. In addition to fundamental value, psychonomics shows that some of the price component in terms of excess price is going to be influenced by any tendency you have to over- or underreact to news and information.

Consequently, with many investors all taking similar action, stocks don't trade at the correct price – they trade at the price the market *believes* is correct at any given moment.

Let's see how this comes about. You may hear information from a variety of sources:

- ❑ annual reports
- ❑ earnings announcements or surprises
- ❑ TV coverage
- ❑ newspaper or magazine articles
- ❑ 'hot tip'
- ❑ broker's recommendation
- ❑ analyst's coverage and forecasts
- ❑ specialist investment publications
- ❑ economic reviews
- ❑ market rumor
- ❑ industry and sector surveys
- ❑ Internet
- ❑ tip sheets
- ❑ the guy at the bar.

Now, what do you do with this information? The likelihood is that you will interpret the information and act in your own subjective way. There is a mismatch between what you hear and how you react. News is the fuse that lights the touch paper. Yet the company itself stays the same: if it is a good company, however the stock price is moving, it will remain a good company; if it is a bad company, it will remain a bad company.

Are you listening?

You hear the information, but are you really listening to it? Those successful investors who are listening are interpreting what they hear on the basis of their own considered assessment. Those who are not listening are being influenced by other investors or their own personalities.

Table 10 gives a few common examples of how an unjustified interpretation of what you hear leads to poor investment decisions.

Table 10 *Not listening leads to poor investment decisions*

What you hear	How you interpret it
'Record year for ABC Industries.'	'Last year was good, next year will be even better.'
'The market is heavily overpriced and is due for a correction.'	The market's going to drop and never recover. But I'll wait and get out at the top.'
'This bear market is likely to continue for some time to come.'	'This bear market will never end. My investments are worthless. I'll sell out and cut my losses.'
'DEF Associates is a fast-growing company. As a growth stock, the high PE is justified. Investors can do extremely well over the coming months.'	'These experts must know what they're talking about – and I don't understand ratios anyway – I'll buy.'
'It's a great stock,' says your broker. 'I'm putting all my clients in this – you can't lose.'	'I'll be rich! What a wonderful broker I've got.'
'Panic swept through Wall Street today as the market plummeted 674 points, its biggest one-day fall in many years. Major markets around the world reacted with heavy losses of their own.'	'The market is disintegrating. Sell! Sell everything! I've got to get out. Now!'

Overreacting to information

The most obvious way in which investors react to news is to *over*react. Behavioral finance has shown that investors become excessively optimistic or pessimistic about a company. Hence, they drive prices up or down as they get on the bandwagon. Everybody else seems to be making money from XYZ Stock, so you buy in too. But the wagon is going faster and faster and you don't know where it will stop. Deep down you may realize what you're doing, but money is money and if it's there to be picked up, you don't want to miss out.

In a similar way, you overreact when prices have peaked and you want to get off the bandwagon. Down the price begins to slide and without really understanding the processes involved, you interpret the news that you're getting on the basis of other people's reactions and you sell.

Market fluctuation due to investor misreaction can be demonstrated by taking a handful of stocks and separating them according to whether they can be classified as 'growth' stocks or 'value' stocks on the basis of their price to earnings ratios. Over a five-year period, value stocks produce about 8 percent greater return than growth stocks, while using price to book ratios gives value stocks a 10 percent greater return. But good stocks are sold every day for no better reason than impatience and most investors have overreacted and traded long before five years are up.

At the extreme, when too many investors are overreacting to news, the market is either hitting bottom with a large number of underrated value stocks – and investors wary of entering a bear market – or it's full of glamor stocks all vying for attention. There's always somebody out there singing the praises of some type of investment, whether it's IBM or the little minnow that makes the gizmo that's this year's latest fad.

Although you are bombarded with news throughout this process, it's important to ignore the media hype. The choices you're faced with are to buy, sell or hold, depending on your circumstances. For whatever reasons you tend to overreact, pause and ask yourself the question: is this a good stock that's worth the market price? In other words, even though the market may be going through some volatile movements, would you still be a buyer or a seller?

Overreaction and changing investor sensitivity

The market environment continually responds to news, which alters its liquidity and stability. If other investors react to news and buy stocks in a particular sector, then it's very likely that you will too. Sensitivity to news, therefore, can promote bull and bear markets.

However, as a bull market surges forward, news is interpreted differently. Stanley Schachter of Columbia University found that during the profitable bull market years from 1950 to 1966, investors became more self-satisfied and tended to ignore hard economic news, as well as news in general such as presidential elections or aircraft disasters. Prices were perceived as being stable but became increasingly driven by emotional misperception to unrealistic levels, way above intrinsic value. In contrast, in the years following 1966, when the bear market had arrived along with economic instability, investors become far more sensitive to news, hot tips and 'expert' advice, which had a knock-on effect on the volume of stock traded.

Financial behavior such as this illustrates the psychonomic disharmony that can arise between an investor's internal and external markets when information is used to justify dealing decisions or hopes about the future direction of trends. Investors tend to switch between overreaction to news due to market-led uncertainty when markets are falling and overreaction to news due to personal bias when markets are rising. Consequently, in bear markets any seemingly plausible external explanation is sought to account for poor performance, while in a bull market internal, personal reasons, fueled by hope, are relied on to account for success and everything else is, consciously or subconsciously, dismissed as irrelevant.

Underreacting to information

Suppose that you've just heard that DEF Associates has done better than expected during the last six months. You might act straight away and buy the stock, but not everybody will. Some investors will take longer to decide whether it's for them or not. As a result, though the news may be good, it can still take several months for the price to reach what it should have been at the time the company announcement was made.

Similarly with bad news, investors can also be slow to act. A cut in the dividend may signal a change in the company's fortunes, but it can still take several months for the price to drift to a level that is reflective of the company's performance and revised price fundamentals.

News causing overreaction is understandable. Less understandable is why it is news or information rather than any other external factor that prompts underreaction, resulting in stock mispricing. Yet this phenomenon has been known for some time and is exploited by followers of behavioral finance.

Victor Bernard and Jacob Thomas at Columbia University examined the effect by grouping stocks according to the size of earnings surprises that companies had produced in recent reports. One of the ways they did this was by measuring the surprise against analysts' expectations. They ended up with two portfolios, one made up of good earnings surprises – the good news portfolio – and the other of bad earnings surprises – the bad news portfolio.

What they found after tracking these portfolios for a period was that it took six months for changes to become apparent. At this point, however, the good news portfolio outperformed the bad news portfolio by an average of 6 percent. This is surprising, because logically you would think that investors would act on good and bad news straight away; that is the rational expectation of an efficient market. But it appears that investors don't always act immediately but take time to digest the information. Their personalities, the amount of information they have, their attitudes and the type of investor they are will dictate the degree of the time lag.

Dovetailing with this is whether investors perceive the news to be related to value or momentum growth potential. Good news may cause good stocks to rise slowly or more rapidly as the market comes round to them but, according to David Dremen who analyzed 67,000 consensus earnings forecasts made between 1973 and 1990, bad news can 'blow sexy stocks out of the water'. What's happening is that momentum stocks are often highly sensitive to hype or a story due to the short-term views of the market. With value stocks, however, negative surprises are more likely to cause investors to react tentatively.

Watching out for misreaction

What can you do about over- and underreaction? The answer lies in knowing when your investment behavior passes out of your real control and comes under the influence of personal biases or the power of the investment crowd. These influences may act together, but they are all fed by the overwhelming force of media information, news, hype, statistical data or stories. Before I show you some of the underlying psychonomic mechanisms that promote this type of activity, here are some pointers to keep in mind:

❒ Don't automatically accept that it's time to buy or sell because the media or other investors say it is.

❒ Give thought to whether news stories are leading you to be excessively pessimistic or optimistic about an opportunity. In other words, are your expectations being unreasonably changed?

❒ Remember that just because everyone says a stock is a 'loser' doesn't mean it is – you should always check the stock out before you buy and not base your decision on media-fueled contrarianism.

❒ When an exceptional news story hits the headlines and you're tempted to plunge into a trade, ask yourself whether anything besides the price – such as fundamentals – has really altered.

❒ Be prepared to buy for the long term in good companies.

❒ If there's a good financial reason to stay put in an investment, don't be panicked into selling through fear, hype or market sentiment.

❒ Remember that momentum delays or lingering effects, as a result of general investor response to good and bad news, provide a window of opportunity for profit – either by spotting value early or by disengaging from an investment that is likely to perform poorly.

❒ Consider – with absolute self-honesty – whether the current bull or bear market is causing your decision to be emotionally driven or whether your decision is firmly based on solid economic news.

❒ When a market rise occurs, and the media explain it with only 'good' news, ask yourself what 'bad' news is also available.

❒ Faced with a difficult investment choice, consider how you would respond in the absence of news.

Good news and bad news can make you over- or underreact. Consequently, your particular investment behavior is dependent on your outlook and how you perceive the market at any given moment through your information sources. If you're in control of your investment behavior and are decisive, these effects underlie the profitable implementation of a variety of strategies. Nevertheless, gaining control, against the backdrop of a constantly changing market, is a major obstacle to overcome.

Why investors interpret information the way they do

Why do investors misinterpret information and over- or underreact? Following the herd is one reason; in the face of a multitude of news items and media coverage, this translates into an information cascade, which most investors will not try to stand against. It is easier to swim with the tide.

This tendency is compounded when TV reports and newspapers are full of experts talking about how well a company is performing. You start believing that there's a limited opportunity to make a profit before all the other investors get in on the act. So you trade fast because you don't want to miss out.

Aggressive financial reporting can also change your expectations of what is a reasonable return by centering lead stories on exciting, 'glamor' stocks. You come to believe that the large gains from these high fliers represent the norm. This is known as *recallability bias* – when you hear another story about a similarly rising stock, you recall the previous story you heard, which distorts your viewpoint about the price rises likely to materialize in the future. On this basis, unrealistic action is taken. Although other stocks may have better long-term prospects, they are dismissed simply because they haven't soared so high, so rapidly.

Media hype and information often reinforce each other. According to Paul Andreassen, a psychologist at Harvard University, when an event hits the market there are usually two sets of facts that accompany it: one suggests that the event should have occurred and the other suggests that it shouldn't. The media tends to focus on the former while ignoring the latter, using good news to explain a rise in the market and bad news to explain a decline, even though both forms of news are available. Investors can therefore easily misread market and investment fundamentals or feel a heightened sense of expectation that a changed situation will persist.

Andreassen's work is interesting because it sheds light on how news causes investors to behave irrationally. In a series of experiments, groups of student investors were placed under simulated market conditions. In the group that was given no news to explain market events, the investors generally bought as prices fell and sold as prices rose. In this scenario, it appears there were no conflicting factors to cause uncertainty in the minds of the investors, who traded at the most opportune moments. However, in the group that was given news stories that could have explained the price changes, investors drove rising stocks higher and sold out of losing ones far too early, before these investments had begun to rebound. The upshot of this behavior was that hardly any investors using 'news' made a profit.

The notion that ignoring the media can be a profitable approach is a sobering thought for anyone tending to be obsessive about collecting huge amounts of data or constantly watching the market. Add to this the fact that with several small successes it's easy to fall into the trap of overconfidence, where you believe that it was your skill in information assessment, rather than natural market movement, that gave you those high returns. Investors, therefore, often get caught up in the cycle of their past investment style and miss the best opportunities. Their thinking is: if I used this information before in a particular way and it worked, it will work again. This can cause you to misreact to new information – even though market conditions have altered.

Linked to this is the way in which investors often make unreasonable predictions about future stock performance based on a small amount of information – the *representativeness fallacy*. So, when a series of limited news items are heard, investors project this new data into the future, believing that good news repeatedly heard will lead to more good news. Somehow, this gives an extra dose of courage to take fast decisions. Similarly, bad news heard is also projected forwards in the belief that the bad news will continue. This causes investors to act fast and incautiously, but this time out of pessimism and fear.

They mean what they say and say what they mean – don't they?

Markets have their own language. When an investor lacks knowledge about what the financial experts mean when they say certain things – coupled with the false belief that experts always know what they're talking about – it's easy to be confused and to misinterpret events while being swept along with the momentum of the crowd. Consider the way in which many terms can be used to say the same thing:

This stock is...
- ☐ cheap
- ☐ a 'value' stock
- ☐ oversold
- ☐ a bargain
- ☐ low priced
- ☐ at a discount
- ☐ a 'loser'
- ☐ underrated

- ☐ expensive
- ☐ a 'glamor' or 'growth' stock
- ☐ overbought
- ☐ a poor use of capital
- ☐ high priced
- ☐ at a premium
- ☐ a 'winner'
- ☐ overrated

To confuse matters even more, a stock might be presented in one way under one set of economic circumstances and in another way under a different set of circumstances. Additionally, it depends on who's talking about the particular stock and their personal beliefs about its future. Therefore, a 'glamor' stock might be presented as a profitable investment at one point by a particular expert, and at another point as a poor return on capital.

Previous experience and outlook produce an added effect: the tendency for investors to hear only what they want to hear. You've already seen how it's possible to misinterpret information you're presented with by not fully listening. In addition, there is a tendency to discard information entirely, centering on what your perception tells you is the most salient feature and dismissing the rest. You may also weight what you hear by subconsciously maximizing or minimizing its importance.

A particular term will have different meanings for different people. Hearing an investment called a 'glamor' stock, for example, may have a more powerful effect on your decision than hearing the same stock called a 'growth' or premium stock, simply because you could have a greater psychological association with one word than the other.

When you misreact too fast or too slow

As news changes, perception – as well as behavior – is itself altered by the changed perception in an escalating and self-reinforcing manner. Many investors therefore fluctuate between states of overreaction and underreaction, sometimes fast to act and sometimes slow. Figure 13 shows how this works. As the characteristics on the left increase, the tendency to overreact grows and investors will make trading decisions more quickly, jumping into the market to buy or dumping stock. Similarly, as the characteristics on the right increase, investors will tend to underreact and make trading decisions more slowly, procrastinating or simply waiting and watching before they buy.

Note that the opposite effect of the characteristic will occur in the other section. So, for example, if you become more sensitive to news or more confident with a resulting tendency to overreact, becoming less

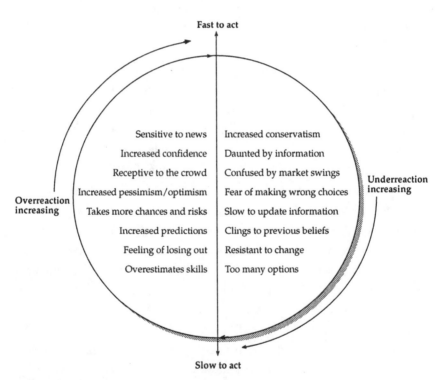

Figure 13 *Most investors misreact at some time*

sensitive to news or less confident will result in a tendency to under-react. Besides biasing effects, two other effects are important when it comes to how investors switch between over- and underreaction – and, indeed, switch between a rational reaction and a misreaction. These are your capacity to handle information and any tendency you have to look for an easy way to profit or find the 'sure thing'. In the rest of this chap-ter, you'll see the way these effects exert their controlling influence and how you can sidestep the psychological traps they produce.

How investors are biased

You misreact to information because it has become part of your nature to behave in this way. Therefore your biases make you repeat the same old mistakes. Here are three common investor biases highlighted by behavioral finance research.

You remember your successes and forget your failures

You're at your favorite bar drowning the day's work in a beer. The guy next to you starts talking about his problems and, before long, you find you've got a lot in common with him. Then the conversation turns to money. He tells you about this real sweet thing he's into and, pausing just long enough, asks, 'Had any luck yourself?'

'Sure,' you say, 'I've had a few winners in my time' – after all, you've got dealing experience, so you might as well promote it. Besides, you hope he'll spill the name of the company. With another beer down him, he does. And off you run to call your broker.

☞ *What's the reality?*

You've had a lot more failures than successes and if you weren't so single-minded about your desire for wealth, you'd realize just how much money you've lost by lack of knowledge and poor analysis of investments. But these facts pale into insignificance at the prospect of suddenly striking 'gold'. Known as *hindsight bias*, in your mind you magnify your few successes and dismiss your failures. You believe your-self to be better at investing than you are – the only extra ingredient you tell yourself you need is the right expert information or that 'hot tip'.

You hear selectively

Dinner at a restaurant seems like a good idea. The *Places to Eat* guide you're flicking through has two possibilities. Restaurant A has: 'Real food in a beautiful rustic setting. The large dining room demonstrates some of the finest examples of ironwork and woodcarving to be seen for miles around. The menu is a rare and special treat for everyone who enjoys traditional homestyle cooking. Our delicious specialties include smoked ribs, quarter pound burgers, fried chicken and Porterhouse steaks.'

Restaurant B is described as: 'A traditional country eatery for those who like excellent food – and lots of it – in a warm and friendly atmos-phere. We have the longest oak bar in the county dating back to the 1850s. Our classic menu includes a wide variety of mouthwatering soups, Bar-B-Q chicken wings and a range of beef and lamb dishes with spicy sauces.'

Which restaurant would you choose? It's difficult, because the descriptions are almost identical. What makes you decide is your own particular biases.

At Cornell University, J Edward Russo gave a similar restaurant description to groups of students, who found no real difference between the two places. But when the features were revealed one pair at a time – a traditional country eatery; a beautiful rustic setting – the students showed a distinct preference. In fact, 84 percent selected the restaurant they liked after hearing the first pair of features; everything else, as far as their decision was then concerned, became immaterial.

☞ What's the reality?

You're faced with deciding between two mutual funds. They invest in the same area of the market and their performance over the last five years is similar. How do you choose? Most people will pick up on some feature that may have nothing to do with the fund itself but everything to do with clever product marketing. That's why investment companies love to bombard potential clients with sales literature.

When you have your own specific preferences and then hear a set of features or characteristics, it's easier to distort the information to fit your preferences and to dismiss any other information that doesn't fit.

This effect has been termed *preferential bias*. If something about an investment catches your attention, that's when your preferences kick in. It could be the way the investment is presented, the fact that it's in your local area, an unshakable belief that this is the one that's going to make you rich, slightly above-average performance, or anything else.

So powerful is this effect that once your preferences have been accessed, it becomes easier to ignore all the important facts that would hold you back or at least make you pause and consider whether the investment is actually as good as it first appears. This is why many investors ignore exorbitant sales charges and commissions on buying investments or extra fees on mortgages when buying a family home.

You're locked into a routine

Many investors believe themselves to be flexible thinkers and receptive to new ideas. When asked, for example, whether they're a good driver, most people say they are. Yet it is patently not the case that everyone's a good driver – if it were true, there would be far fewer accidents. People tend to believe they can change, but in a situation that calls for change, they stick resolutely to their previous behavioral style.

Why do people resist change? They like to keep things as they are. It's familiar and it's comfortable. It's an example of *status quo bias*, and accounts for why people often end up paying more for financial services than they should. Changing a bank or a broker might save you a considerable amount of money, but you've been with the particular adviser or financial institution for a long time and it's easier to carry on with them than to move. This is not about loyalty or even laziness, but about a misperceived sense of security born out of habit. It also accounts for why many people often fail to claim tax rebates when they're entitled to them.

Secondly, when faced with a choice between different options, people tend to worry that they will make the wrong decision, so they end up not deciding at all. This is *choice conflict*, which works as follows.

Imagine that you want buy a new compact disc player but are not sure which make to buy. On your way home from work you pass a major store selling a Sony model at a significant discount to the list price. Would you buy the CD player or would you wait to learn about some of the other models available around town?

Take the same situation, only this time the store is also selling an Aiwa model at well below the list price. What would you do now? Would you buy the Sony, the Aiwa, or would you wait to learn more about what's available?

When the first situation was presented to a group of people by the psychologists Eldar Shafir and Amos Twerski, more than two-thirds said that they'd buy the Sony disc player. But when asked to choose between the Sony and the Aiwa, nearly half the group said that they'd wait and think about it.

In the same way, investors feel psychological discomfort if they try to sort out too many alternatives at the same time. Choosing between different investment opportunities is too confusing, especially when the market is causing the investment to rise and fall on a regular basis. They are concerned that a wrong choice will be made and money will be lost, so it is easier to leave things as they are.

☞ What's the reality?

You know that you should sort out your investment portfolio, but you keep putting it off. Everything seems to be OK. Maybe you should be checking out your pension arrangements: you've been paying your contributions in regularly for the last 15 years, but now that you're changing jobs, things could do with an overhaul. Your cousin, Will, is an accountant and has a look at things every now and then. Even so, it's been about two and a half years since he last looked at your financial affairs.

Although it may be easier to do nothing, if you don't know your financial situation then it's about time you found out. You don't necessarily have to change anything, but you must know where you stand so you are sure that you're making the most of any investment opportunities. Keeping to the status quo will not make you wealthy. It's a sad fact that most people don't know, even in approximate figures, how much their assets are worth, although they know they would like to have more money and be more able to handle their finances more effectively.

However, if you do want to do something but don't know where to start – for example, you want to choose a mutual fund or unit trust from the thousands available – you need to make a concerted effort to get advice and whittle the choices down to something manageable and understandable. At times like this, employing a well-thought-out strategy can be extremely beneficial. Even if the worst happens and you make the wrong choice, don't be deterred. On the contrary, by dealing with setbacks you will be learning from your mistakes.

When investors convince themselves to act on news

As news changes, private and professional investors need to develop a flexible response in order to be successful. What was a good decision last month, or five minutes ago, may not be so now. Below are a few common ways for investors to think when they receive new information. They find it hard to alter their outlook and end up rationalizing their actions.

Consider, as you go through this list, whether the situation would prompt you to be a buyer, seller or holder. How would your reaction change – if at all – when you asked yourself the right question?

☐ **You convince yourself:** If everyone says it's a bull market, it is.
   You should ask yourself: Is it a bull market only because everyone says it's a bull market? Do I fight it or run with it? How do I know the bull hasn't run its course?
☐ **You convince yourself:** It's not a crash, it's a correction.
   You should ask yourself: Is this just experts or colleagues playing with semantics? Do I have enough information to agree with this analysis accurately?
☐ **You convince yourself:** These investment tips worked before, even if I left it too long to get out afterwards.

You should ask yourself: Did I really get it right before? Does this mean that the information will work again?

☐ You convince yourself: The series of bad news announcements from ABC Industries overshadows the good research and development work that the company's doing – and its stock price has risen, so it's better than it appears.

You should ask yourself: Have I checked out the research and its commercial implications thoroughly?

☐ You convince yourself: Even though there's no apparent reason for the dramatic fall in the stock price of DEF Associates, something must be wrong.

You should ask yourself: Have I checked the company's recent fundamentals? What about the trading background? Could this be market jitters?

☐ You convince yourself: I don't have time to check this tip out, but I've heard it's a rising glamor stock.

You should ask yourself: How likely am I to profit if I base my investments on market rumor?

☐ You convince yourself: HIJ Partners produced a dramatic increase in profits during the last year. The high rating must be justified.

You should ask yourself: Why am I so attracted to HIJ Partners? Have I checked them out thoroughly?

☐ You convince yourself: Stock picking? I could do better than those experts. After all, everyone knew the market was going to fall.

You should ask yourself: Did I really know the market was going to fall? Am I looking at the information with the benefit of hindsight?

☐ You convince yourself: My favorite stock's fallen by 12 percent – what a great opportunity to buy more!

You should ask yourself: Are there fundamental reasons for buying this stock now or has the real situation changed and I should cut my losses?

☐ You convince yourself: The high rating of KLM Securities isn't important. It's still rising, so I'll wait to see how far it'll go before selling.

You should ask yourself: Why am I hanging on? Is KLM's price warranted?

It's easy to get sucked into trading when you believe that previous actions worked or everyone else is making money. Other investors may well be reacting to news with financial rationality, but you need to be sufficiently aware of what's really happening so that you can decide what to do without any personal biases affecting your analysis.

However, even with a highly developed psychonomically rational outlook and the ability to suppress your biases, it is still sometimes difficult to make sense of the information you're getting.

Information overload

Every moment of every day, news is hitting people squarely in the face. A national disaster, political uncertainty, changes to an industrial sector or company reports, it makes no difference. If it has relevance to investment, the markets move.

The problem is that the more information pours out from the various sources – TV, radio, newspapers, Web pages, Reuters screens and so forth – the more people have to process it, finding some way to integrate it into their world view. Each person's capacity to do this is different. Those who can't keep up, or have taken a conscious decision not to partake of this constant bombardment, are in some way considered unfit or strange. And it is wrongly assumed that everyone needs this mass of information to live effectively.

How much information do you really need?

Investors get caught up in the same ideology. 'You need information' is the litany taught by investment gurus. *The Financial Times*, *The Wall Street Journal*, *Barron's*, *Investors' Chronicle*, *Time*, *Newsweek*, *Money*, as well as a host of brokers' reports and financial statistics – these are what will give you the edge, or so they tell you.

What they don't tell you is that every time a publication is read and the information acted on, either a sale is made or a commission generated for the broker or financial reporter who produced it. They have a vested interest in making sure that you continue to read their recommendations.

As access to vast databases on the Internet is gaining public attention, the culture is changing to one that is information driven. Now, not only do you 'need' technical reports and constant TV coverage of financial topics, you also 'need' the latest and most powerful system you can lay your hands on. You believe that downloading enough of the *right* information will provide you with that critical edge you're searching for.

Less is more!

Knowing which piece of investment information is most relevant is like identifying a diamond in a case full of cut-glass crystals. Although it isn't an impossibility, it's easy to be confused and to get sidetracked. But if you knew the diamond was definitely there, what would you do? In all probability, you'd take the whole case. Similarly, most investors use a scattergun approach, trying to take in as much data as they can.

But rather than being useful, the high quantity of information ends up being counterproductive. There is simply too much to make sense of. The human mind will only sort and classify data if it can make a connection or it already has some reference point on which to hang the new data, otherwise it all becomes a confusing muddle. A change in the stock market index may signal a change in the economy, but you would only know this by taking other factors into account; it might merely be a market anomaly. Similarly, statistical or graphical data about XYZ Industries may suggest a wonderful buying opportunity, but in itself the information may not be sufficient for you make a considered judgment. The pattern is not clear. Therefore, when the connections are difficult to understand, interpret, reconcile, quantify, or conflict, the natural inclination of many investors is to put the information to one side and forget about it.

Don't get bogged down in data

To cut through this mass of information requires a common-sense approach. Following a few simple hints will make this easier. It also feeds into the way you use investment strategies effectively.

Table 11 *Hints for using information successfully*

- ☐ Do your research.
- ☐ Beware any bargains you are offered – there's no such thing as a free lunch!
- ☐ Never let new information push you into trading.
- ☐ Search for companies poised for growth by examining their fundamentals.
- ☐ Be wary of 'hot tips'.
- ☐ Never trust an advert.
- ☐ Never trust a graph.
- ☐ Be wary of investments offering above-average returns.
- ☐ Use the quality newspapers and magazines that have a high standard of financial journalism.
- ☐ Analysis of real and statistical information is useful, but be selective.
- ☐ Information provided from brokers that's not asked for is of less value than information actively sought by you – brokers tend to send information that is part of the marketing of a product rather than useful material.
- ☐ Don't be panicked by media coverage of stock market rises and falls.
- ☐ Know your sources, where to find them and the type of information they provide.
- ☐ Be cautious of management statements.
- ☐ When reading information, always consider: who else benefits from your trade?
- ☐ Learn how to be discerning about the information you use – decide which bit is the most important.
- ☐ When watching daily price changes, understand that short-term volatility is normal.
- ☐ When deciding on a course of action, assess the weight of expert opinion that agrees or disagrees.
- ☐ Listen to financial experts on TV, but make up your own mind.
- ☐ Learn how to read the relevant parts of company reports – fast.
- ☐ It's amazing how many once-in-a-lifetime opportunities there are. If it quacks like a duck, it probably is one!
- ☐ Learn to skim-read articles.
- ☐ Be consistent in your analysis of, approach to and strategy for investment decisions.

- [ ] Don't sweat the math – if the math is complicated it's a virtual certainty that someone hasn't got a clue what they're recommending.
- [ ] Avoid paying large sums for reports and data.
- [ ] Don't become a collector of data for the sake of it.
- [ ] If you're going to be contrarian and go against prevailing opinion, make sure that you understand all the above recommendations.

Looking for the 'sure thing'!

At some point, most investors ask themselves: who's in the know? After all, checking out the quality financial press and doing your own research can be difficult and time consuming. It's inevitable, therefore, that you'll investigate those who have made it their business to keep informed. You believe this will enable you to achieve better results, faster. So you turn to the most readily available source – tipsheets.

Tipsheets often spring into existence at the first sign of a burgeoning bull market, only to disappear as the buying frenzy abates. These short-lived publications are to be avoided. They'll only take your money for information you could have easily obtained elsewhere, a great deal more cheaply.

However, some tipsheets do a good job in analyzing investment opportunities. And there are several reasonably priced ones that have been around for many years. They have a track record and they make clear recommendations. But how do they compare to other sources of financial information?

The London Business School carried out a survey some years ago of New Year recommendations published in a variety of newspapers and magazines, such as *The Economist*, the *Daily Telegraph* and the *Sunday Times*, and a variety of well-known, quality tipsheets. It found that the tipsheets fared about the same as the tipsters in the newspapers. Leaving aside the fact that it's easier to make recommendations in a bull market, more recent surveys in the US and the UK have also found that quality tipsheets exceed the market averages around 20 percent of the time. Most of these recommendations perform only slightly better than the market, with just a very few doing exceptionally better. All these publications, therefore, can be cautiously viewed as alternative sources of useful information and advice.

But it's important to remember that tipsheets and tipsters play on investors' psychological weaknesses, such as believing that everyone else is an expert. The message is: if you'd taken our advice, you could have made a fortune. To back this up, their advertising will show a performance table with a selection of their favorite stock choices during the previous months. ABC up 24 percent, DEF up 33 percent and so on.

One reason that tipsheets work is because of information cascade – or the *snowball effect*. A result of the way people behave in herds, it accounts for the transmission of behavior and how such behavior begins. You can see this at work in many everyday situations: women's fashions that suddenly dictate lower necklines or platform shoes; or the latest trendy nightspot where you just have to be seen. A few people start it and soon the effect is multiplying exponentially as others take it on. Similarly, the actions of a few investors lead other investors to copy them.

With tipsheets the snowball effect happens very fast because the tipsters like to recommend companies that are relatively small, second-line contenders. They may be value stocks, but they may also be fairly inactive and trade in a thin market, where there's a limited supply of available shares. As a result, it doesn't take many investors to cause a change. The stock is potentially volatile, and as soon as there's some sustained buying, up the price shoots. The opposite can also happen; as soon as buying slows, the price can drop back down.

Those investors who move fast enough can profit. But by the time you hear about a stock, it's often too late: the price has already moved up significantly.

For example, Henry gets his tipsheet in the mail every Saturday morning. He reads it carefully and occasionally, if something catches his interest, he'll buy the recommendation. In the past, Henry has made a few dollars out of this particular tipsheet and feels that the only reason he didn't make more money is that he left buying till too late in the week. This time, he thinks, he'll do it differently.

At 8 a.m. on Monday, Henry's on the phone to his broker, Jeanette. 'Buy XYZ Industries as soon as the market opens,' he instructs her. The tipsheet quotes a price around $2 1/4 a share.

At 9 a.m., Jeanette calls back. 'Got you the stock,' she says, 'had to pay a bit more though, $2 3/8.'

Henry sighs. It's more than he wanted to pay. The stock might continue to rise, he hopes, but there's still the nagging feeling that he hasn't got his dealing quite right yet.

What Henry doesn't realize is that it didn't take many investors to get the snowball rolling. By the simple rules of supply and demand, there's not much stock on offer and there are other Henrys all doing the same thing at the same time on Monday morning. As a result, it's virtually impossible to buy in at a reasonable price. Indeed, the price Henry paid reflects more than the fundamental value, with part now reflecting buying pressure. This doesn't mean that it's not a good stock, simply that Henry has paid more than he should.

In fairness, good tipsheets and tipsters ensure that their tips are not used by people who have access to the information before you, such as proofreaders, contributors and printers, which could start the price rising. The logic is that everyone should have an equal chance to make a profit. Most importantly, they often tell you to wait a while and buy within a particular price range, once the Monday morning effect has subsided.

Nevertheless, once there's movement in the stock, it's hard to sit on the sidelines and do nothing when you believe you're watching a profitable opportunity slip away. As the days go by and the price rises steadily, it becomes increasingly difficult to stop yourself getting pulled into trading. The chances are, however, that you'll be buying in at the top of the market.

If you're going to use tipsters or tipsheets, a certain amount of caution is always advised. You can make money from their advice, but never rush into dealing without considering why a particular stock is being recommended, how much profit you're likely to make and who's most likely to benefit from your buying.

Ultimately, ask yourself this: if the stock is so good, why don't the providers of the tip keep it to themselves? Are they so altruistic that they're simply giving you the tip on a silver platter out of the goodness of their heart? The world doesn't work like that.

Straight from the horse's mouth!

You heard it from a man who heard it from a guy who's definitely in the know. That's the action you wanted: a real hot tip.

But such tips may not be what they seem. If you're financially realistic, you'll realize that though there might be a grain of truth in the story somewhere along the line, by the time you hear about it, it's likely that other investors have already acted on the information.

Stocks go up because more people are buying them. If a tip is doing the rounds, it's highly probable someone is trying to make the 'snowball' roll. Why do they – whoever they are – want to do this? There are two possibilities:

❏ They want to unload stock that is likely to perform badly during the next few months.
❏ They're holding a good stock, but no one knows it's a good stock, so the price has been static.

'Where there's a tip there's a tap,' goes the stock market saying. Either way, the effect is that there's available stock, somewhere in the market, looking for ready buyers. Let's take a closer look at what happens.

Dayna has just received a reliable tip that GHI Electronics is going to announce profits considerably above expectations in a few days' time. The source, from what she's able to make out from a friend of hers, is a former personal assistant to the chief financial officer who left the company after a disastrous relationship with her boss. The assistant has no axe to grind with the company, but feels she has no allegiance to it now and might as well use the information to her benefit.

So Dayna buys GHI stock. A week later, the annual report is published and, as predicted, profits have doubled and the dividend has been raised. Yet when Dayna checks the price, she sees that it's fallen by $1/4 from its high. Confused, Dayna wonders what could have happened.

What's happened is that smart investors had anticipated the health of GHI. These investors had carefully weighed up the real and fundamental information and knew what GHI should be worth and the level to which the price was likely to rise. The price just before the annual report already reflected the good news. When it reached or exceeded this price, these investors didn't wait but traded out. Hence, the price fell on the company's earnings announcement.

Another way to look at this is to keep in mind that up to the point of the annual general meeting and the announcement of the report, the price of the stock reflects the company's performance during the last year (or half year). But once the profit or loss information becomes public, the price reflects the hoped-for performance of the year to come. As this is not yet known, the game starts again.

Rumor spreads like wildfire

As well as information known in the market prior to public announcements, freshly planted news items allow companies to manipulate their stock price. You'll either hear a rumor directly from the company or read something in the financial press. The trick is to decide whether there's any truth in the rumor or whether it's been started by speculators – who could be connected to the company in some way. For example:

❏ There's about to be a takeover.
❏ There's about to be a merger or acquisition.
❏ Corporate restructuring is on the agenda for the coming year.
❏ Major overseas markets are buying the company's products or services.
❏ Downsizing is on the cards for a large number of the workforce.
❏ A new product license is likely to be granted very soon.
❏ A major scientific breakthrough is just around the corner.
❏ An innovative drug is now going through its final testing phase.
❏ A new chief executive, who has a great record with a variety of well-known public companies, is believed to be joining.

Generally, if the market likes what the rumor suggests, the price will rise. If it's subsequently found to be inaccurate, the price will fall; as it will also do if the market doesn't like what the rumor indicates.

If you're uncertain what the information means, then be cautious. Never follow a tip or a rumor without considering whether it makes sense or how it will affect the company's performance in the future. There are unscrupulous people out there – beware.

The market is a harsh mistress

Information can include solid, real facts about changes in a company's approach or status, statistical data, expert advice, tips or market rumor, among a variety of other pieces of news and reports. When attempting to price an investment, what is important is to decide what information is relevant and how much you need. In this way, you're less likely to get bogged down in unimportant facts. Furthermore, you'll stand a far better chance of making a clear and unbiased analysis of your information sources and what the market data really means, before you react and trade.

If you misinterpret the information you're getting and make the wrong decision, the market will see to it that you lose money. But if you make the right decision, the financial rewards will be yours. To put it more prosaically: wherever you hear your information, always consider which end of the horse is really talking!

Part Two

Investment Psychology and Self-awareness

7

Becoming a Successful Investor

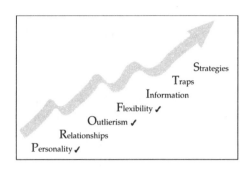

INVESTMENT INVOLVES DEALING WITH MONEY – MOVING IT, RECEIVING it, trading it. And whenever people and money come together, strange things begin to happen. Egos blossom, perceptions become warped, realism takes a back seat. The ability to make rational decisions disappears, forced out of existence by unresolved motives such as greed and fear, or a need for self-worth, image enhancement, happiness, status or power. Controlling these motives is the only way to ensure that any negative personality characteristics you have are factored out of the investment equation.

You may feel that some of the characteristics of psychonomic rationality could be developed in your own approach. But how are you going to achieve this? In this chapter, we'll look at the specific steps you can take to utilize your internal market to the full and gain the maximum possible return.

Deciding on your investment goals

Three fundamental questions need to be considered:

❏ Where are *you* now?
❏ Where do *you* want to be?
❏ How are *you* going to get there?

Where are *you* now?

Before you launch into the variety of available sources that advise on financial planning or investment procedures, you need to assess your life situation realistically. This is where most of these sources fall short, however good their advice is. They will help you to analyze your financial situation and goals, and the type of investment instruments that would be useful, but they don't help you to change your mindset. That it is your psychological perspective that's important when you assess your financial situation can be illustrated by considering whether there would be any point in suggesting to a confirmed shopaholic that they should make regular contributions to a savings plan. They would not be able to handle the discipline of saving – nor, for that matter, the discipline of controlling their desire to spend spontaneously when they have money in their pocket.

Step 1: Learn to reflect

Consider your investment situation. Do this in relation to other things going on in your life. Remember, if you're depressed or stuck in a rut, it stands to reason that this is going to affect your psychological outlook, your behavior, and your ability to make rational investment decisions. Which of the following, therefore, might apply to you?

❏ Investor wanting to improve on previous small successes.
❏ Investor with continual heavy losses who's out of control.
❏ Investor with heavy losses or debts after initial high success.
❏ Investor of several years' experience, with average or mediocre performance, but with available funds.
❏ Professional trader good at work with other people's money but bad with your own investments.
❏ Investor who got burnt once and is reluctant to invest again.
❏ Investor trying to make a move from stocks to derivatives.
❏ Investor who gets all the information available and still doesn't make a good profit.
❏ Investor who wants to assess professional advice more effectively.

❏ Financial expert or consultant wanting to learn more about what drives your clients.

❏ Fund manager hitting a bad patch.

❏ New investor, with time to spare, who wants to learn the techniques of successful investing.

Now relate the following to your overall situation. Of course, you may be in one of the financial situations above because of a reason shown below, or being in an investment situation may have led to a personal situation. So keep in mind that it works both ways. You may be:

❏ depressed or fed up

❏ having family problems

❏ having work problems

❏ seeing a therapist to help you with personality development – to be more assertive, to be more decisive, to be more fulfilled, to have a better self-image...

❏ someone with no outlets, interests or hobbies – only work, work, work...

❏ undergoing problems with substance abuse such as alcohol or drugs

❏ having financial problems, such as debt, legal proceedings pending, inability to deal with household budgeting, expensive spending habits

❏ in an unrewarding relationship

❏ suffering a sudden loss of libido (sexual drive)

❏ lacking a good social life – going out with friends, meeting the opposite sex

❏ in poor health

❏ undergoing a sudden life change, such as retirement, children leaving home, divorce...

When your life situation affects successful investment

Learning to reflect means being realistic about your situation and accepting the need to change. Let's take a look at an example that demonstrates how these two lists are linked.

Sam is 32 and works as a computer programmer at a busy engineering firm. The work, though exciting when an interesting project comes along, is generally mundane. Sam has little commitment to the job and knows that he has to make a change. But without good contacts and some extra funds, it's not likely to happen soon. He could obtain extra funds by reorganizing his portfolio of investments and buying some new stocks. Sam knows it needs to be done, but is reluctant to change anything, feeling locked in and not competent to take matters in hand. Giving the management of the investments over to professional advisers is not an idea that Sam likes either, as the portfolio was a present from his grandparents and, deep down, he believes it's better to leave things alone. Sam also doesn't feel that he knows anything about choosing good advisers, the investment market or the way this will all affect his portfolio.

As this snippet of overheard conversation at the office he works indicates, Sam's feeling quite run down:

'Are you coming to the theater with us tomorrow?' asked Sharon, a colleague seated nearby.

'No, I... I have something on.'

'You always do, it seems. Why don't you do something different for a change? You never know, you might have a good time!'

What should Sam do?

Sam's main difficulties are a lack of confidence and an inflexible outlook. He is procrastinating in many areas of his life, including his general attitude and handling of investments. Sam needs to make a concerted effort to try different things. In this way he will begin to see situations as challenges and opportunities and his investment approach will improve. At the moment, he's too focused and not receptive to the range of investment possibilities.

It's hard to change your outlook suddenly and it takes a degree of courage. But Sam has sufficient realism and intelligence to know that he must make the attempt, otherwise he'll remain stuck in a rut and out of funds. So, after finally talking to friends and giving serious thought to his situation, Sam decides on a plan of action:

1 *Look at other more interesting career opportunities with better wages.*
2 *Set one hour aside, at regular intervals every few days, to analyze previous investment performance.*
3 *Make a list of investment goals and what needs to be done to achieve them.*
4 *Go out with friends when they ask – without thinking that it's a waste of money and time.*
5 *Examine my investment portfolio – what I actually own and the returns I'm getting.*

Facing up to the fact that your life situation has seriously affected your wealth goes some way towards achieving a realistic investment approach. Now, you need to gain greater control over your financial situation. But, like Sam, you may not be sure how to begin. The next step demonstrates practical techniques to help you.

Step 2: Analyze your financial self

Investment history

Find a quiet moment on your own and draw up a table with columns similar to Table 12. Give thought to your investment performance for the past several years. It's likely that the way in which you perform was fixed a long time ago and the cycle has been maintained. In addition to your own unique experiences that formed your outlook and behavior, you may also approach investing as a result of the way your parents treated money and investments and picked up habits from them. And, as discussed above, you may have started to approach investment differently due to some personal situation you were facing at the time. So, go back as far as you feel able and keep in mind the question of what made you invest in a particular way, and whether it was useful or not. Check old receipts from brokers and banks and any stock certificates you may have. In the investment history below, the first couple of entries have been done as an example.

If you are a professional trader or investor – investing clients' money or managing an institutional portfolio – check your records and keep in mind that the key here is simplicity, to strip down what you did to its barest essentials. However, your analysis shouldn't be confined to your professional life but should also include any personal investments, so that you gain a summary of your total financial performance.

If you think you have no investment history, remember that an ordinary bank or building society account can be an investment. Consider what it enabled you to do and whether it made financial sense.

Table 12 *Investment history*

Date	Successful investments and strategies	Grade term	Unsuccessful investments and strategies
12.7.83	Increased contributions to occupational pension scheme	C	
6.10.96		F	Bought XYZ stock then sold two months later at a loss, only to see it double in price

Apply the grade term that most sums up your performance (or use one of your own terms):

S – Stupid, F – Futile, I – Impulsive, M – Mediocre
E – Effective, P – Profitable, C – Clever, A – Amazing

Investment dialogue

This is another technique that can be used to examine investment performance. Here, you imagine Investment as a real person whom you're interviewing or having a conversation with. Either write down or record the dialogue. If you prefer, you can treat a specific stock, company or your savings as the individual.

As trivial as it appears, it has a serious side, as it will enable you to view your financial behavior from a different perspective. It's not for every investor, but many find it useful.

Let's say that some of your previous investments have been impulsive. What would Investment feel? What would Investment say to you? Investment might say: 'You don't think about me enough any more.' Or: 'Why didn't you realize you were turning me into something cheap and valueless?' If you've made some particularly bad or stupid investments, Investment might say: 'Why didn't you check things out by doing your research?' Or: 'Why did you throw me away? What are you trying to prove to yourself, that you're a great investor? Don't you know you had to work hard to get the money to buy me?' And if you've had some amazing investments, Investment might give you indications of why you did well. For example: 'I was good as ABC Industries. By doing your homework and getting in when you did, I've multiplied significantly.'

This technique goes beyond looking at personal investment performance. It can be applied to your attitude to market volatility and fluctuations. Legendary investment figure Ben Graham characterized the investment market as a remarkably obliging fellow called Mr. Market. His approach was this: Mr. Market is your partner in business and every day he appears and names a price at which he will buy your investment or sell you his. Yet even though the business may be very good, Mr. Market's quotations won't be. Because unfortunately, Mr. Market has incurable emotional problems and is somewhat unstable. Sometimes he's uncontrollably excited about the business and sets a high price, while at other times he gets very depressed and sees only doom and gloom ahead for stock prices and the world in general. At these times, his prices are very low.

But overall, however manic depressive Mr. Market gets, you should remember that he is there to serve you, not to guide you. Foolishness and not wisdom is his stock in trade, and you are free to either ignore him or take advantage of him. At times when the market is going through some highly volatile gyrations, having a dialogue with Mr. Market to find out what he's really up to may be quite enlightening.

Sam's dialogue with Investment

INVESTMENT: You've been ignoring me for a long time now.

SAM: I couldn't bring myself to deal with you. You're just too much work.

INVESTMENT: If you want to live well and take care of your future, I'm the way to do it. So put in the work.

SAM: You don't understand. My portfolio was left to me in my grandparents' will. It's just too much of an emotional tug for me to get down to it. And I want to change jobs. I thought that takes precedence.

INVESTMENT: Changing jobs is very good, I'm all for that – especially if there's more money coming in to spend on me – but you must deal with all the things in your life, and I'm looking after your interests. If you forget about me, things will only get harder for you, not easier.

Where do *you* want to be?

Step 1: Decide on the purpose of your investments

Consider what you really want to gain from the investment. This may seem obvious: to make money. But not everyone does want to achieve this to the same degree. Some people are happy making smaller returns when they know they can make enough to be comfortable. Their needs are less, and that is fine. Their approach is consistent and there is no conflict as they know what they want.

The difficulty for many investors, however, is that the line between profitable investment and the desire for wealth blurs. Investment becomes synonymous with making money, rather than a way to achieve personal success through a structured approach. By virtue of this, many people look for short-term gratification – a quick buck – rather than a solid investment that may take longer to materialize. They cannot differentiate between good and the bad investments: greed takes over, and logical judgment vanishes. The behavior of these people becomes inconsistent and their desires conflict.

Moreover, when people say they want to be wealthy, what does this actually mean? How wealthy do they want to be? Is it some unclear notion or can it be quantified? Having a goal means at least having a ballpark figure, and a figure that – at least in the short term – is reasonably achievable.

Below are some possible reasons that people have for wanting to invest. Remember that these apply to deep-rooted desires and not simply to superficial reasons that might be used in ordinary conversation between friends. As you will see, most are related to the acquisition of wealth or luxury in some way. Do any of them apply to you? Consider also whether they are sufficient on their own, or in combination, to form the core of a rational investment outlook.

- ❑ I want to be rich.
- ❑ I want to pay off my credit cards.
- ❑ I need a new car.
- ❑ If I had the money I'd change my appearance – have a makeover, plastic surgery, buy designer clothes...
- ❑ I want to quit my job and tell the boss what she can do with the pittance she's paying me.
- ❑ I want to impress the opposite sex.
- ❑ I want respect.
- ❑ I want to be able to donate to charities and worthwhile causes.
- ❑ I want more time so that I can pursue different interests.
- ❑ I want to be happy.
- ❑ I want to be in control of my finances.
- ❑ I'm interested in the stock market.
- ❑ I want financial freedom without working.
- ❑ I want to make enough for a pleasant retirement.
- ❑ I want to get even with the people who kicked me when I was down.
- ❑ I want to make money easily.
- ❑ I want to make people envious by having them believe I know things about investment that they don't.
- ❑ I want to get the maximum benefit from my money and savings – I worked hard for it, I deserve it.
- ❑ I want the power that money and investment knowledge bring.
- ❑ I want to spend, spend, spend...

Step 2: Form a personal definition of 'success'

To say that you want success is, on its own, insufficient. You need to have some idea of the type of success you want and the level you aspire to. Furthermore, from a psychological perspective, success is a relative term. For everyone it's slightly different. But generally, people feel successful when they're in control of their behavior and actions, when they can't be influenced against their will. The problem for many investors is that they get swept along with the mass actions of people reacting to their own hopes, dreams and fantasies. The result is that your goals become clouded by theirs. Ultimately, this creates volatility in markets.

What is interesting is that the more an individual feels they are in control of their financial destiny, the less important it becomes to acquire money for the sake of it. Other factors in life begin to take on a new meaning. And because you will know the level of financial success you need to become satisfied, any investment gains above this are a pleasurable bonus. It becomes a way of keeping check on just how well your approach is working – and continues to work.

As people like Buffett put it: 'After a while it's about playing the game and keeping score.' Buffett in fact, is known for his frugal approach to life: his little economies, his wrinkled suits, and his passion for Cherry Coke rather than expensive wines. Yet with his own private jet, and a personal fortune totaling billions of dollars, he can well afford the best of everything. For men like Buffett, success is not measured just by their ability to buy ever more expensive items but by their ability to do the things they want and lead their lives in a way that gives them pleasure.

How are *you* going to get there?

Step 1: Develop good self-control

Some would-be investors are easily swayed away from psychonomic rationality when they see someone else displaying the fruits of success – the clothes, the fast cars, the lifestyle, the whole image. This is *negative emulation* or, if you prefer, just plain lust. I'll talk more about this in

Chapter 9, but for now remember that it has no real basis in knowledge or understanding and is purely superficial. Self-control here is about putting your thoughts and personal goals in order. There's nothing wrong in taking on the appearance of a successful investor, as long as appearance hasn't become more important than true success.

Negative emulation can dovetail with *found money*, that is, money that's been made without any hard work. Imagine you were unexpectedly given a gift of $5000: would you spend it or would you invest it? This seems a simple enough choice. Yet some individuals are in a more precarious position because they've got money in their pocket but are more likely to blow it all on a whim. Found money is 'easy come, easy go' – losing it doesn't matter very much. Self-control here is about respecting the value of money for what it can do for your future.

Self-control is also important when the moment to trade has arrived and there are profits to be made. A clear head and the ability to look realistically at the situation you're faced with are prerequisites if systematic investment errors are to be avoided. For example, it's no good procrastinating, panicking or believing that because everyone says it's a good investment, you should buy.

Having said that, it's often very difficult to take a step back and control your own biased thinking or not to follow the investment crowd. When new information emerges from a variety of sources – be it political, economic or otherwise – most investors get swept along on the wave of euphoria generated without fully understanding what lies behind the market's movements.

Understanding is nevertheless vital and these moments can be important opportunities for profit if you're really in control of your outlook. Truly successful investors, with strong clarity and self-control, may know the relevance of changed conditions before others do, making calculated decisions while the experts are still pondering what it all means. George Soros's famous currency deal that netted him over $1 billion is a prime example. He had the same information as everybody else – he just knew how to use it to greater advantage.

Step 2: Learn financial confidence

It is vital to have confidence in your investment decisions. Otherwise, opportunities will be missed or you'll change tack because you'll constantly be worried that your money should be invested elsewhere, or indeed that the investment was a mistake in the first place, which leads you to panic and trade at the wrong times.

When people lack the confidence that they can invest successfully, they don't take – and even resist – the opportunities that present themselves. Here are some examples of the way in which poor confidence can affect investment behavior. Consider what changes need to be made to each person's outlook:

- ❏ 'I've lost money every time I've made an investment.'
- ❏ 'Sure, if I had the knowledge the big players have, I'd also be rich!'
- ❏ 'It's a gamble, no one ever makes any real money.'
- ❏ 'It takes years of practice.'
- ❏ 'I'm working, I haven't got time to find out about something that is unlikely to help me retire comfortably.'
- ❏ 'It's all rigged!'
- ❏ 'The rich get richer and the poor get poorer – it's always been that way.'
- ❏ 'What's the use of investing my money, I'll only end up in debt.'
- ❏ 'I'm happy the way I am!'
- ❏ 'Everybody struggles to make ends meet – investing isn't going to help.'
- ❏ 'I can't even decide what shoes to wear in the morning, so how am I going to decide on suitable investments?'
- ❏ 'You need luck – I don't have it!'
- ❏ 'I bought, I sold. The only person to get rich was my broker.'
- ❏ 'I'd be better off becoming a broker and getting the commission.'
- ❏ 'If nobody else thinks my ideas are any good, maybe they're right – I'd only make lousy investment choices.'
- ❏ 'There's no money until the end of the month, so it's not worth thinking about investments now.'
- ❏ 'Proper investment is too complicated – and I don't have a decent computer system to work out all the information.'
- ❏ 'How to make a million: start off with two million and invest it!'

One way in which many successful investors develop their confidence is by making their goals reasonable. Their financial goals are high, but they don't overreach. They look for hurdles that can be surmounted with ease, not disproportionately high hurdles that they'll smash into, shattering their confidence as they fall to the ground.

In contrast, some people have got used to doing things the hard way. Somehow, the importance of learning something new or taking action increases in proportion to the effort required. Their thinking is: it must be right to do it this way because it's difficult! Furthermore, they look at other people, and when they see that these others are also going through the same process and having the same difficulties, it reinforces their irrational belief that they're going about things the right way.

For this reason, many people make the same mistakes when they invest. They get used to the feelings and emotions associated with poor dealing decisions. Their nature propels them time and again towards investments they are emotionally ill-prepared for and unable to handle rationally. They expect to feel bad when their poorly understood investment drops – and when it does, their misguided foresight is born out. Of course, they say to themselves, it's only to be expected, I'm never any good at investment. Rather than looking for investments that can be easily understood and handled, they continue to make the same errors. It's a self-fulfilling prophecy of dwindling confidence and a habitual cycle that is ever more difficult to break.

Step 3: Develop your financial outlook

Greed and fear can often drive people to make investment decisions, as can a range of other emotions. Professional traders and investors are just as prone to this as the private investor. But a rational financial outlook dictates that these emotions should be kept under control.

In general, successful professionals have learned to be more detached and maintain a rational perspective. This may be because they have seen so many of their clients or colleagues make disastrous decisions and realize the pitfalls. And working with large sums of money every day can produce a hardened response. After a while, it becomes ordinary; the money no longer has any real value, and it's not theirs in any case.

They may also have a greater incentive because it's their job and their livelihood is on the line if they don't perform at their best.

One approach that successful investors use to maintain control is to face any self-doubt or insecurity they may have. There can be many, for example: 'Have I used the right strategy?' 'Is this a solid investment?' 'Is the investment appropriate given the present economic situation?' 'Does it form the basis of good portfolio management?' 'How long should the investment be maintained for?' Bringing these feelings to the fore means that they can be more readily dealt with. It is a type of psychological and emotional honesty, while self-delusion is a stumbling block for many would-be successful investors.

Acquiring this detachment and self-honesty is a matter of experience. Successful investors know that self-confidence and the ability to master their emotions can help achieve this because they are linked to the development of an informed and logical approach. Moreover, self-honesty is a useful safeguard against obsession, which lies lurking round the corner if trading occurs too frequently. Investing for a purpose must override any feelings that could push you to make an investment because you're feeling lucky or it's a once-in-a-lifetime opportunity. It is important to question your personal motives continually. Remember, opportunities will be there another time and the markets will still exist tomorrow.

However, there is an element of hunter and prey in seeking the ultimate investment, the one that's going to soar and make you rich. There is a curious adrenalin rush when the money has been placed in a volatile investment and the price rises and falls, then rises and falls even more. You thought you had the markets and your investment worked out, but events appear to move against you. One moment you're mentally counting your new-found wealth – feeling dizzy with the thought of how much you're worth – and the next, you feel as if you've been punched. Neuro-chemicals are racing through your brain with all the concomitant physiological changes: sweating, shaking, changes in breathing. All your self-esteem collapses, to be replaced by self-doubt. Just like the flight or fight response that adrenalin would produce if you were confronted by a snarling wild animal, you want to get out quick, to run away, rather than stay and get financially mauled. Acting on impulse at this point is easy to do, but the result is likely to be a loss.

Psychonomic rationality is a matter of training. To maintain a realistic approach you have to make your instinctive behavior follow carefully integrated personal experience – not the other way round.

Step 4: Develop awareness

A concept from behavioral psychology is that if you can establish a new pattern of behavior, your thinking processes will eventually alter. The trick is to break old habits and establish new ones. These in turn will affect how you make investments.

Another component of a successful investment approach that we learn from psychology is that it is better to begin with small changes and work up to bigger ones. This concept is very much in keeping with the confident approach that highly successful investors use when they look for goals that are reasonably attainable. Suddenly deciding to invest all your money without deep consideration is even more counterproductive than not investing at all.

Begin by making small changes to your outlook and small changes to your investments. Then as things progress and you gain confidence, you can make bigger changes.

Step 5: Observe successful investors

Acquiring the attributes of success can seem like a lot of hard work, or in fact totally impossible, so many people don't really try or delude themselves that they're better at investing than they are. Yet a claim of many successful investors is that once they have learned how, it isn't difficult to make profitable investments and you don't need to do extraordinary things to achieve extraordinary results.

The information on which to base investment decisions is often just as freely available to the private investor as it is to institutional fund managers. The difference between skilled investors, such as Buffett and Soros, and mediocre investors is that the skilled investors use the information to far better effect.

You've seen how the P.R.O.F.I.T.S. framework underlies psychonomic rationality. Successful investors apply this framework through

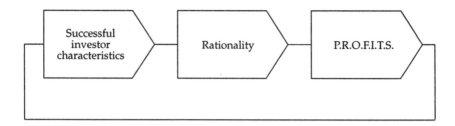

Figure 14 *Common characteristics feed into psychonomic rationality*

natural ability and experience. And research shows that they have certain characteristics in common that feed into their approach and, hence, their ability to find good opportunities repeatedly. Before we look at what these characteristics are, Figure 14 illustrates this process.

The process itself is dynamic. As investors continue to develop experience, rationality also improves. At the same time, there is a feedback effect when investors interact with the external world. For example, if a series of bad deals are made in the markets, this can affect future confidence. If information is misused, or an investor becomes less flexible in their thinking, they may become more reluctant to take a calculated risk.

What's happening is that rationality is easily thrown off track. Psychologists have found that people make decisions about alternative courses of actions on the basis of the future benefits they believe they will get, going for the alternative that gives the most benefit. This is known as *decision bias*. But this tendency is itself biased by past experience. If you're faced with a choice between two mutual funds – one invested in technology stocks and the other in blue chips – do you look only at the projected returns and go for the one with the higher figures, or do you recall how you fared previously in similar investments? It's possible to examine the opportunity both ways. Despite any issues about the quality of the fund's management or general market conditions, many investors will be prejudiced by their previous successes or failures and use the latter method, however irrational their eventual choice is.

There is a constant tug-of-war going on between what you think you might achieve and what you've already achieved. This *habituation effect* means that the more bad investment choices are made, the stronger the pull of these past experiences and the more likely you are to repeat your financial behavior. Conversely, the more success you have, the more this leads to future success.

What characteristics are useful in generating superior performance? Have a look at the list in Table 13, which shows that these successful investor characteristics are quite extensive. Take some time to study them and relate them to the way you handle investments. Which ones do you think you need to develop?

Table 13 *Successful investor characteristics*

☐ Clarity and acute realism – often seeing financial opportunities before others do.

☐ Forward looking – not letting past habits dominate future actions.

☐ The ability to start again – not allowing failure or defeat to get the better of them.

☐ Taking responsibility for their actions – both good and bad.

☐ High degree of self-respect.

☐ High level of commitment and motivation to succeed.

☐ Positive attitude – not negative about life and its associated problems.

☐ Not relying on luck, but a strategy consistently applied.

☐ Faith in their own decisions.

☐ Goal-oriented outlook.

☐ Good self-control – keeping in check any personal tendencies or characteristics that are counterproductive to success.

☐ High self-confidence.

☐ A fascination for numbers as applied to money and finance.

☐ A liking for investing, not simply for the money, but because it's enjoyable and holds their interest – it's a professional hobby!

☐ Not being easily influenced by other people or events.

☐ Often passionate about investing.

Anybody can become a successful investor by developing psychonomic rationality. The reason is simple: there are many routes to achieving an integrated and balanced outlook in life.

As you will see from Table 14, by making appropriate changes you can develop a range of useful investor characteristics. These are just a few suggestions from the many possibilities that might surround you.

Table 14 *Developing successful investor characteristics*

Becoming aware of your behavior	Characteristics developed
At home or at work, why are you doing what you are and what is the likely outcome?	Clarity and acute realism Flexibility in outlook
How motivated are you and how willing are you to put effort into learning new investment skills?	The ability to start over
How do you react to setbacks and how do they affect you emotionally?	The ability to start again, not letting failure or defeat get the better of you
How do you perceive situations around you – do events bear out your thinking, proving you right? Or do you constantly misperceive current events?	Flexibility in outlook Clarity
Do you argue with other people, trying to make your point heard? Or do you listen to what they say – without always feeling the need to respond – and continue to believe in your viewpoint?	Self-control Self-confidence Clarity Self-respect Contrariness
Are there things you really enjoy doing? If not, why not?	Goal directed Passionate about an interest

How do you react when you've made a mistake that costs you money, time or status? Are you easily flustered or do you roll with the punches?	Self-control Responsibility High sense of self-worth

Begin to take notice of the things you do in your everyday life and assess your reactions. Give serious thought to your current situation and the way in which the development of specific characteristics could improve your decision-making and investment skills.

Step 6: Implement successful investor characteristics

When useful characteristics are developed and internalized, new investments can be made without constantly looking over your shoulder to see how the other person's performing. You will be the one setting the standard by which you first judge yourself in order to get to your financial goal. Only then, without any undue influence, will you find it useful to make comparisons with the performance of other investors. It's a question of doing things the right way round, in effect imposing a structure that will give you more control over your actions. From a psychonomic perspective, you are seeking to integrate your internal market and to evolve your own style.

However, there are three characteristics based on the above lists that are especially prevalent among successful investors and that deserve special mention. These are motivation, contrarianism, and the ability to deal with defeat. You've met these in various forms already, but here we're interested in the underlying psychology that generates them.

Becoming motivated

We cannot know all the antecedent experiences that feed into a highly developed sense of realism about the world, causing certain individuals to become more keenly aware of investment opportunities, but we can say that these individuals are exceptionally motivated to accomplish their goal. According to the psychologist Abraham Maslow, 'Man is a wanting animal – and what he wants is more.' Additionally, needs and desires evolve over time. The result of all this is that success feeds on success. This is another cycle, but a positive one. What this means is that with the correct motivation, the correct behavior and action will follow. In other words, by forming a set of needs and desires that are appropriate to the development of financial action and success, the better and more experienced you become, and the more you can achieve.

One particular motivational drive is self-actualization. This is a psychological term often misused by those who want to legitimize their actions without regard for the feelings or needs of others. In reality, the self-actualized person is someone who seeks to achieve constructive personal development and mutual success in their dealings with others. Such people achieve success because they have confidence in themselves, a positive attitude and flexibility in outlook – they don't get bogged down in irrelevancies. Moreover, they are clear about their goals and don't get too emotionally involved with their situation. This is why they are able to deal with both good and bad investments, in a cool way, without becoming overly stressed or extremely elated. To this type of successful investor there is no one to blame if things go wrong – not even themselves – rather, the situation is a challenge, one to be resolved and learned from.

Understanding how contrarianism and success are linked

Taking action before other people involves going against accepted wisdom. Although this wisdom may turn out to be invalid – and could have its basis in nothing more than fashion – it takes a particular type of independent foresight to be able to assimilate and analyze new information, then act decisively. Contrariness involves having faith in your own decisions, where the confidence to take action is balanced with the psychonomic rationality to consider whether the choice is logical and makes sense. In this way, successful investors are often able to go against the herd mentality.

The contrarian perspective is a result of a number of psychological traits coming together and gives rise to the type of individualistic spirit you met in Chapter 4. In addition to acute awareness, confidence to take action, self-control and the ability to be realistic, a strong characteristic of successful investors is flexibility in outlook; they are self-actualizers, independent thinkers who are not easily influenced and who don't let past habits dominate future actions. The mere fact that an investment has been conducted in a certain way is no reason to carry on doing it that way. But, similarly, they don't go against a trend just for the sake of it.

In a sense, for these individuals, there is no real contrarianism; rather, their approach is simply a logical extension of their views based on their awareness of a multitude of facts and their model of the world. And if a successful investor decides that the time is right to get into a different market sector when the accepted view is that the sector is going nowhere, then their contrarian approach is dictated by their analysis and understanding of the facts as they see them at that moment. Their view may be correct and they profit substantially. If it is wrong, then they know that they've done all they can, to the best of their ability, but that they must move on to the next opportunity.

Learning to deal with defeat

How a person deals with setbacks is one of the most important facets of successful investing. As Niels Bohr said: 'An expert is a man who has made all the mistakes which can be made in a very narrow field.'

Highly successful investors may not publicize their disasters, but they have had them. George Soros, for example, decided to invest in property when the UK market was at the bottom of its cycle. His timing was way off, although the idea that the property market would eventually recover was held by many financial experts. What nobody knew was when.

So even the most successful investors can suffer defeat at some point. But rather than dwell on the loss, their attitude is forward looking. This involves a high degree of self-control to overcome the negative emotions that are the normal result of knowing that a bad decision has been made; as well as, of course, accepting the loss of invested money. Again, psychonomic rationality must impose itself on any personal tendencies or characteristics that are counterproductive to success. Learn from your mistakes, but have sufficient confidence to continue believing in your abilities and to plough back into the markets; wiser perhaps, but undeterred.

Step 7: Choose professionally managed investments with care

Although you may not want to handle the running of your investments yourself, judgment is still the watchword. Everyone else is not necessarily the expert they purport to be.

Investment managers, with billions under their control in the form of unit trusts, pension schemes, savings instruments and so forth, should have a better idea of how to make successful investments than the private investor. After all, that's what they get paid to do, and with their ear to the ground and all the information at their disposal from their research departments and outside sources, you would think this to be the case. However, the reality is that investment managers consider that the assets under their control are doing well if they exceed the interest available from fixed-rate deposits by a few percentage points, taking inflation into account. Or for those who manage to do a little better, a comparison is made against another yardstick such as the S&P 500 or FT All-Share index. As long as the fund is not doing worse, this 'outperformance' will be shoved in the face of every investor, or potential investor, who can read an article or glance at an advert.

Good investment managers will get it right most of the time; which is to say, more than they get it wrong. But they are human and subject to the same vagaries of fashion and whim as anyone else. If the expert consensus is that funds should have 10 percent of managed assets in Japanese growth stocks, then no self-respecting professional investment manager will try to spit in the wind. They too will follow their colleagues.

Sound economic reasons may lead a manager to choose an investment. But when a bull or bear market begins, the ensuing mood of the market will cause the professional investor to make the necessary provisions; safeguarding the fund's assets is a priority. But that is a phrase that's interpreted in an assortment of ways by different managers. It may be your life savings, but to them it may be nothing more than computer data. And as trends take hold, and the market picks up its own psychological momentum, even the most experienced fund manager can be gripped by the mass hysteria, forcing them to follow the herd. And when major funds sell or buy large holdings, stock prices are affected, causing the market to change even further.

Among all the advertising for a variety of funds specializing in every part of the market, and with a huge range of associated risk, how do you find the one with the best management? Table 15 offers a few factors to keep in mind when making your assessment.

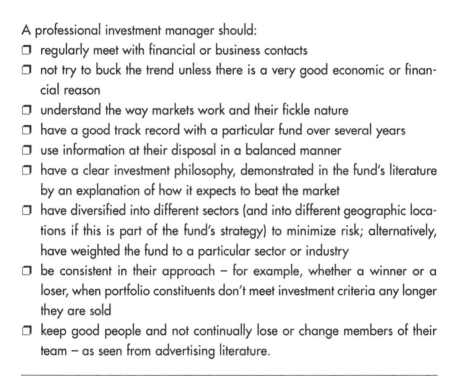

Table 15 *Tips for assessing professional investment managers*

A professional investment manager should:

- ☐ regularly meet with financial or business contacts
- ☐ not try to buck the trend unless there is a very good economic or financial reason
- ☐ understand the way markets work and their fickle nature
- ☐ have a good track record with a particular fund over several years
- ☐ use information at their disposal in a balanced manner
- ☐ have a clear investment philosophy, demonstrated in the fund's literature by an explanation of how it expects to beat the market
- ☐ have diversified into different sectors (and into different geographic locations if this is part of the fund's strategy) to minimize risk; alternatively, have weighted the fund to a particular sector or industry
- ☐ be consistent in their approach – for example, whether a winner or a loser, when portfolio constituents don't meet investment criteria any longer they are sold
- ☐ keep good people and not continually lose or change members of their team – as seen from advertising literature.

Another interesting point highlighted by behavioral finance is that pension fund and mutual fund managers are often promoted on the basis of their recent performance, even though a rising market may have given them an extra boost. It's important to assess the fund manager's accomplishments dispassionately, without giving way to your personal biases or the biases of the person who picked them. In this way, you will be cautious about the service or package being offered in its entirety and you'll be maximizing your chances of success. And remember, just because other investors have ploughed their money into the fund, or you like the manager's picture, is not a good enough reason to invest with them.

Investment and reward

By examining your financial situation realistically, you will have begun to structure your approach towards your financial goal. As psychonomics shows, all the internal and external factors in your life are connected, so altering one aspect of your life has a knock-on effect on others. If you get your structuring right and start to develop a real awareness of where you are now and where you'd like to be in the future, you can begin to see your life in a new light.

This is the start, and in the next chapter you'll see how to take the process of self-examination a stage further by looking at various personality styles that produce differences in investment performance. Knowing what type of investor you are will allow you to make decisions that are more likely to be profitable and that you'll be able to live with more comfortably.

Don't assume, however, that to be really successful is easy. Accomplishing it takes work and commitment, but it is worthwhile.

8

What Type of Investor Are You?

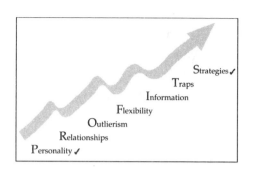

Strategies ✓
Traps
Information
Flexibility
Outlierism
Relationships
Personality ✓

W HETHER PRIVATE OR PROFESSIONAL, THERE ARE JUST A FEW categories of investor. This is because the movements of the markets can only elicit a finite number of responses: buying, selling or holding. Within these limits, investors will respond according to their individual natures. As most investors eventually find out, success is not only about buying the right investment but also about knowing *when* to buy, *when* to sell and *when* to hold.

If you are aware of the type of responses you're likely to make, you are more likely to maintain psychonomic harmony within your internal market, and less likely to make the wrong investment decisions due to systematic behavioral errors. In addition, those traits that are good for investment – such as the ability to listen carefully to what people are saying – can be developed, and bad ones – such as the tendency to panic – can be suppressed. Other important traits you might possess include:

- ❒ Ability to plan or think ahead.
- ❒ Being good with facts and figures.
- ❒ Commitment to what you have decided to undertake.
- ❒ Decisiveness.
- ❒ Ability or desire to gamble.
- ❒ Patience.
- ❒ Being technically minded.
- ❒ Capacity for self-reflection.
- ❒ Being responsible for your own actions.

Not just seemingly investment-driven personality traits but any trait that is part of your unique character will have an effect on your investment choices. Even how you socialize with other people will have a bearing on your ability to find or glean useful investment information. These and other traits, in their almost infinite combinations, underlie the type of investor you are.

Investor types

The categories of investor that will be discussed here are: Cautious, Emotional, Technical, Busy, Casual and Informed. As you read through this chapter, you're likely to find that your own investment behavior is similar to one of these types. If you want to take this further, you'll also get the opportunity later to make a deeper assessment of your profile and to discover how your risk tolerance can moderate your overall approach.

The cautious investor

For many investors, not liking or feeling comfortable with the possibility of financial loss means that they take time before making an investment to weigh up the chances of their personal funds being hit hard. These investors are very conscious of the value of their money, having worked or saved solidly for long periods, and will avoid placing their funds in jeopardy. Sometimes it's part of a person's nature to be cautious, but often a lack of understanding of the investment being considered – or a lack of quality information – leads to this type of behavior.

The cautious investor is not easily swayed by tips or press articles and prefers to make their own investigations. They are generally untrusting of professional advice – bank managers included – and will only invest when they are certain that the risk has been minimized. When they do seek professional advice, they can take a considerable amount of time to decide whether the adviser is right for their needs.

A problem with being cautious is that occasionally the time taken to decide whether or not to invest causes the moment to be lost, so that the maximum financial gain isn't obtained. And, once having chosen an investment, too much caution about selling may cause an unnecessary loss.

Cautious investors will tend to make large investments only in instruments where, if there is a loss, it is of a cyclical nature and likely to be recouped at a later date. Although an occasional small high-risk flutter may be undertaken, investments in derivatives or commodities would be avoided in favor of strongly performing blue-chip equities or other secure investment devices, such as guaranteed bonds, index funds and money market accounts.

☞ *Characteristics of cautious investors*

Cautious investors:
- ❑ won't rush headlong into an investment without careful thought
- ❑ don't like to lose even a small amount of money on an investment
- ❑ may dither occasionally
- ❑ can be short-term or long-term holders of investments
- ❑ are conservative about their choice of investments, steering clear of fashionable tips
- ❑ avoid professional advice, preferring to carry out their own research
- ❑ may wrongly attribute high risk to investments with medium or low risk
- ❑ may have a need for financial security due to family considerations
- ❑ avoid excitement and market volatility.

The emotional investor

This is someone who bases investment decisions on a personal perception rather than an informed choice – much like the guy who bets on a horse called Silver Lightning in the third race, because his mother always wore three silver bracelets and once got hit by lightning!

Emotional investors invest their money because something attracts them. It could be a fondness for a particular product made by a certain company, like a motorbike or a chocolate bar, or it could even be something as simple as a picture of the company's main office seen in a brochure. Emotional investors, who base their decisions on nothing more than a good story, are the most likely investor type to follow the herd – wherever it's heading.

At the other end of the scale, this type of investor's actions may have led to an investment of time and effort in research, or in some other way, making the personal attachment extremely powerful and hard to break. The danger is that these investors will trade only when their back is against the wall, or they won't trade out of the investment at all. By that time, of course, it's too late.

Sometimes emotions can prove to be a positive force in successful investment. Liking something – even having a passion for it – means that there is an extra ingredient in any investment choice. The proverbial gut feeling, which could be defined as emotion mixed with instinct and experience, can come about when an investor develops a deep interest in a specialist field. The stock market flotation of UK soccer clubs is an example of this. Investors may have a real love for a particular club or the sport in general. These investors are emotionally driven and want to put their money into their favorite pastime. They may feel their team is going places. But they have also built up a strong background knowledge about the sport, the players and the management. And because they have unwittingly internalized many of these nuances that can affect market performance, their personal perceptions and potential actions have been modified.

☞ Characteristics of emotional investors

Emotional investors:
- ❒ tend to act on a whim
- ❒ can become passionate about a particular interest that leads to investment decisions
- ❒ don't always consider the effects of political or economic changes
- ❒ may fail to obtain or use available information
- ❒ can build up a high degree of knowledge about a specialist field
- ❒ tend to remember successes and forget about past failures
- ❒ often believe in the power of luck or providence to safeguard things and may not keep a proper ongoing watch on the investment

❏ have difficulty in cutting losses when the investment begins to do badly – because there's an emotional investment, it's hard to break free

❏ are easily swayed by personal attitudes, gut feelings, tips or unsubstantiated advice

❏ believe that things will come right in the end.

The technical investor

Some investors get into the feel of things by having all the right equipment and obtaining all the statistical information they can lay their hands on. Although it is often useful, the information can take a long time to sift through. To help, the latest computer programs are used along with real-time updates from financial companies that specialize in online information services.

This type of set-up is also likely to be used in more risky investments where the chances of incurring losses are high, such as futures and options, and where heavy trading needs to be undertaken.

One particular type of technical investor is the chartist, who is not so concerned with getting all the right gear as much as making predictions about future price movements. Chartism, also known as technical analysis, is a branch of investment analysis, and its professional adherents can be found beavering away in major brokerage houses around the world.

A major premise of chartism is that certain types of market behaviors repeat, and that trends are identifiable and therefore predictable. It's all in the numbers, and all relevant market, political or economic information is reflected in the trend.

There is no doubt that technical or computerized analysis of price fluctuations and various factors, both internal to a company and external in the market sector, can provide an important edge. And computerized trading is widespread among major institutions – the stock market crash of Black Monday was partly attributable to this form of trading. However, armed with all this gear and information, how much better is the private investor doing than if they threw darts at the stock market page of the financial press? It is this type of question that you must continually ask yourself if you are going to beat the market.

☞ *Characteristics of technical investors*

Technical investors:
- believe in the immutability of facts and figures – numbers don't lie
- trade actively based on price movements
- spend hours watching the screen
- believe that the faster information is obtained, the better the chance of profit
- can become obsessional, needing to be continually in touch with market sources, through phone or laptop carried with them wherever they go
- often buy the latest electronic devices in the hope that this will provide a much desired edge.

The busy investor

Some people love the excitement of market investment, whether it's the stock market, currency speculation or anything else. It gives them a sense of belonging and they love to be involved. It provides them with their daily high – a buzz – when they check the latest price movements of their investments. For these people trading is the main fun; making money is just a close second and the extra icing on the cake.

Because of their need always to be busy, these investors cannot buy and then leave their investments alone. Their interest must be kept high. So investment facts are ravenously digested, and heavy trading takes place, until there is a degree of satiation. Interest then quickly passes to the next investment opportunity that presents itself.

☞ *Characteristics of busy investors*

Busy investors:
- constantly check prices – sometimes several times a day

- subscribe to a variety of financial publications
- have a working relationship with one or more brokers
- keep an ear to the ground for any tidbit of information
- may not fully appreciate the nature of the work carried out by a company they have invested in
- don't feel involved unless they are buying or selling
- may trade heavily on price fluctuations, market rumor or limited information
- are often short-term holders of investments.

The casual investor

However much effort is put into the initial choice of investment, there are people who tend to forget they've actually invested their money somewhere. Their choice may have been based on their own acquisition of information or professional advice, but as time goes by, strange as it seems, the investment is left unchecked and unattended. Initially, it may be the result of tendencies such as status quo bias that you have met earlier. After a while, however, the result is a 'leave it alone and let it ride' attitude, where eventually the investment is mentally written off. This often happens with pension schemes or savings, which are low risk but vitally important in an overall personal investment strategy. Consequently, contributions to pension schemes may be too low to provide sufficient retirement income when maturity is reached. And likewise, the number of bank and savings accounts that are dormant, with combined assets of many millions of dollars, runs into the thousands.

A casual investor may have acted on a tip from a friend and bought shares, or other investment instruments, and forgotten about them due to the pressures of work or family concerns. If their investment was recommended by a professional adviser, they may simply feel that they don't have the expertise to keep a check on things; they'll get around to it some time, but it's easier to procrastinate than actually to learn some basic facts about handling investments.

☞ *Characteristics of casual investors*

Casual investors:
- ☐ are often busy with work, family or traveling
- ☐ are hardworking, with the attitude that a good job or profession is the way to make money and that investment cannot provide a real income
- ☐ believe that once an investment is made it will take care of itself
- ☐ may miss the best opportunities through lack of action
- ☐ have a good income
- ☐ tend to be wasteful with money, not always knowing what it is spent on
- ☐ believe that professional advice that is paid for is good advice and doesn't need to be double-checked
- ☐ are often long-term holders of investments.

The informed investor

This type of investor knows where to obtain the information they need – and, more importantly, knows how to use it. Newspaper articles, press releases, TV items, statistical data, brokerage house analyses and even a word heard in the right bar, all come under careful scrutiny. The informed investor watches events and listens. In essence, they have many of the attributes of the other types of investor mentioned above, but their approach is more balanced and they are not obsessive.

Information can be found in a host of places and it is a question of being aware of changes around you and of attuning yourself. A clothes shop that suddenly opens branches in a remote part of the country where you took a holiday; efficient service from a company when the little rubber thing drops off the electrical gadget you bought from it six months previously; a phone call to a public company where you want to speak to Mrs. Smith in the research and development department and are passed from one person to another and end up half an hour later talking to the first person you spoke with. All of these situations provide potentially useful investment information.

Armed with all this information, which is still being continually updated, the informed investor then makes their investment decision.

Not only can a novice investor have this type of approach, but it is likely that a good professional fund manager will operate in a similar way. However, it is far more common than outsiders realize for fund managers to rely more on personal contacts and word of mouth over a good dinner than on pages of data, boardroom decisions and company reports.

One problem with being informed is that it is easy to become over-informed. Too much information can be overpowering, becoming difficult to wade through, and long hours in front of a computer screen, analyzing data, don't help. If the information is ambiguous or conflicting, matters are only complicated further. A prime example is when you feel that a stock in a particular sector is right to invest in. But the experts interviewed on the TV say: 'This market sector is overvalued and a correction is imminent', which is financial speak for: 'It's going to fall heavily and you'd be crazy to buy in.' Two hours later another expert says: 'This sector has a long way to go yet and definitely hasn't reached its peak in comparison to its European counterpart.' When this happens, it is difficult to decide which information is correct. It's a certainty that the experts don't know, but where does that leave you? The only way out is to make a choice, right or wrong, having faith in your own analysis of the situation.

☞ *Characteristics of informed investors*

Informed investors:
- ❒ use information from a variety of sources, both common and uncommon
- ❒ keep an ongoing watch on the investment, the markets and the economy
- ❒ listen carefully to other people's assessments
- ❒ only go against the market fashion after weighing up all the possible consequences
- ❒ may miss the best opportunities by taking too long to analyze all the information
- ❒ can be long-term or short-term holders of investments.

Keeping a flexible approach

The above categories of investor demonstrate where investors sometimes make errors in their approach. In reality, although some investors
may fall strongly into one particular category, there is also a degree of
overlap, so that a successful investor may have characteristics from
more than one category. These categories are also neutral, becoming
good or bad only when taken to extremes. Nevertheless, whatever category you fall into, there are occasions when investment can become
excessive and turn to obsession.

The obsessional investor

When investment takes over an individual's life, becoming an all-
consuming infatuation, then it has become an obsession. In common
with other obsessions, it isn't a healthy position to be in because it
becomes impossible to think about anything else when it isn't linked to
investment in some way. Even a simple act such as watching television
only has meaning when there is an important economic news item that
feeds into investment decisions. This is not to say that gleaning information from the news is bad. On the contrary, under normal circumstances it is very useful and certainly good practice. But when no
pleasure or enjoyment is taken from other TV programs or another
interest, investment needs to put into perspective. It is a hobby or a profession, it is enjoyable and it can make a great deal of profit, but it is not
the whole of existence.

One interesting point to remember is that an obsession is never truly
satisfying to the obsessional individual. They may feel forced to think or
compelled to act in a certain way, but their abilities eventually become
dulled. Balance is important in maintaining a healthy outlook on life,
and a variety of interests is more helpful in producing success in all
walks of life, not just in investment. Consider how many business deals
are done on the golf course or over a meal in a restaurant. Why?
Because a diversion is pleasurable and can sharpen the mind.

☞ Characteristics of obsessional investors

Obsessional investors:

- ☐ spend as many hours as possible checking price movements or analyzing computer stock quote data
- ☐ often forget to take meals and neglect personal hygiene
- ☐ let their family relationships suffer, accompanied by increased arguments
- ☐ falsely believe that they've identified a hidden trend by their technical prowess
- ☐ become social bores, only able to talk about their investment successes
- ☐ eventually withdraw from social contact, friends and former interests
- ☐ believe that the 'big breakthrough' is just around the corner
- ☐ after a while, don't take heed of investment information or advice and waste money, being unable to differentiate between good and bad investments.

Investor profile

Let's now look at the type of investor you are at a deeper level, how your individual traits feed into your investment decisions, and how you deal with security and risk.

A list of traits is provided to help, although there may be others that you feel should be included in any individual assessment. There is nothing immutable about the way these traits have been used; and this self-assessment profile is simply a guide, nothing more, to help you focus on ways to improve your handling of investment. The profile is meant for personal use only. For details about how to obtain a commercial, standardized version for use with clients, please see the Sources of Information section in Further Reading at the end of the book.

For each of the items in the Self-assessment Investor Profile, circle the number on the scale between 1 and 3 that you feel most closely reflects your tendency. If you feel that the question doesn't apply to you, or the answer is 'No', circle 0. Be honest with yourself and give careful thought before you answer.

Self-assessment investor profile				Part 1
	No or doesn't apply	**Slightly**	**Quite a bit**	**Very much**
Circle the number that most closely applies to you.				
Example:				
Do you like reading newspapers?	*0*	*1*	*(2)*	*3*
Now complete the following:				
1 Are you good at planning?	0	1	2	3
2 Are you a hardworking person?	0	1	2	3
3 Do you find numbers interesting?	0	1	2	3
4 How important is wealth to you?	0	1	2	3
5 Do you ever feel lucky?	0	1	2	3
6 Can you be decisive?	0	1	2	3
7 Are you a hoarder who hates to throw things out?	0	1	2	3
8 Do you commit heavily to what you do?	0	1	2	3
9 Are you a friendly person?	0	1	2	3
10 Do you ever do something without giving it much thought?	0	1	2	3
11 Are you interested in facts?	0	1	2	3
12 Are you good at dealing with money matters?	0	1	2	3
13 Are you controlling of situations?	0	1	2	3
14 Do you ever get nervous, stressed or edgy?	0	1	2	3
15 Do you like gadgets?	0	1	2	3
16 Do you tend to believe what people tell you?	0	1	2	3

17 Are you a patient person?	0	1	2	3
18 Do you like computers?	0	1	2	3
19 Do you ever take risks in anything you do (sports, friendships, etc.)?	0	1	2	3
20 Are you mechanically minded and able to fix things?	0	1	2	3
21 Are you hard to influence?	0	1	2	3
22 Do you prefer staying in with a good book to socializing?	0	1	2	3
23 Do you prefer short rapid tasks over longer ones?	0	1	2	3
24 Are you irritated by people who talk a lot but do little?	0	1	2	3
25 Are you a family person?	0	1	2	3
26 Do you like to gamble?	0	1	2	3
27 Do you find there are too few hours in the day?	0	1	2	3
28 Do you finish what you start?	0	1	2	3
29 Do you ever forget things?	0	1	2	3
30 Do you have a good income?	0	1	2	3

Below are a series of boxes for each investor category: Cautious, Emotional, Technical, Busy, Casual, Informed. Fill in your answers below the question numbers. Your total score can then be worked out for each category by adding up your responses. A hierarchy will be produced, with the highest score reflecting your strongest category, and the others in descending order of influence. You will then have a profile of the way in which you respond to investment decisions, and where – if at all – you need to make changes.

Cautious

Question no.:	4	7	12	14	17	21	24	28	
Response:									Total =

Emotional

Question no.:	5	9	10	14	16	19	22	25	
Response:									Total =

Technical

Question no.:	1	3	6	11	15	20	22	24	
Response:									Total =

Busy

Question no.:	6	9	11	14	19	23	26	27	
Response:									Total =

Casual

Question no.:	2	9	16	19	25	27	29	30	
Response:									Total =

Informed

Question no.:	1	4	8	11	17	18	21	28	
Response:									Total =

Interpreting your score

There is no significance in the exact totals, only in the spread and the order – your dominant category being the most important.

A good profile is one where categories are differentiated but not spaced widely apart. What this means is that under different circumstances you have the ability to draw on different personality traits, giving you a flexible outlook.

However, if you've scored the same for several categories and believe that this isn't reflective of your character, go through the questions again and think very hard about your responses. For example, in question 4 – How important is wealth to you? – many people will automatically say it is highly important. But consider whether there are things you value above wealth. If there are, then you would not circle '3'.

Overall, the important thing to remember is that these investor types are neither good nor bad but simply point the way to better-quality investing. So, for example, if you feel that you need to become more informed, make the effort to do so. If you're overly emotional as well, then try to think through your actions – or inaction – in a colder and more logical manner. If your main tendency is to be casual about investing, then go into something that carries lower risk and can be left alone for long periods under the guidance of a professional organization with good credentials.

Factoring in risk

It is also important to consider your propensity for risk. One of the problems with many investor classification systems is that risk is seen as an attribute of the type of investor you are. In reality, it's a little more complex. Two different investors who share a similar profile may feel comfortable with different amounts of risk. An investor who is cautious by nature may feel comfortable with either a low level, a medium level, or a high level of risk. If that seems strange, then recall how people are unique, with different biases, backgrounds, experiences and beliefs. All these factors feed into the perception of risk.

Here's a simple way to assess your risk level. The following questions center on your personal attitude to handling risk and your total score is used in conjunction with Part 1 of the Investor Profile.

How do you handle risk?				Part 2

Circle the number that most closely applies to your attitude to risk.

	Highly disagree	Slightly disagree	Makes no difference	Slightly agree	Highly agree
1 Personal wealth is not an issue and financial loss doesn't keep me awake	1	2	3	4	5
2 I'd rather be in one investment with the chance of a higher return than in a broad selection with less chance	1	2	3	4	5
3 If the market is volatile, it's not a worry – I'll still trade	1	2	3	4	5
4 I'm willing to take as much time as I need to oversee my investments	1	2	3	4	5
5 I enjoy the excitement of investment trading	1	2	3	4	5
6 Price swings in investments I own are of little concern	1	2	3	4	5
7 I don't need a steady dividend income and would rather have capital growth	1	2	3	4	5
8 It doesn't bother me that my investments are not easily tradeable	1	2	3	4	5

	Highly disagree	Slightly disagree	Makes no difference	Slightly agree	Highly agree
9 Investment in emerging markets or high-tech research is more appealing to me than traditional blue chips	1	2	3	4	5
10 I don't feel the need to check my portfolio frequently and can leave it alone for long periods	1	2	3	4	5
Now add up your total score for all the questions				Total =	

If you score below 25, your risk tolerance is low and you will feel comfortable with the least aggressive investment approach. A score between 25 and 40 indicates that your risk tolerance is medium. Over 40, your risk tolerance is high and a more aggressive investment approach can be taken.

Your investor type together with your propensity for risk will dictate certain classes of investment to choose or avoid. But if you don't want to take on the responsibility for managing your investments, then a passive approach – with fixed-rate deposits, or a quality unit trust or managed fund – is an avenue to explore. The next step up in risk is an active approach where you take responsibility for choosing your own investments. Here, value strategies can be highly profitable. At the extreme of risk tolerance are speculative investments such as small cap stocks, derivatives and commodities; while for the exceptionally wealthy, there are hedge funds.

Taking on too much risk that is unsuitable for you is a sure way to lose. If your dominant characteristic is cautious, emotional or casual and you have a low tolerance for risk, it would be folly to invest in highly speculative investments, such as looking for value stocks in emerging markets. Don't bite off more than you can chew!

Finding your best route to profit

Figure 15 shows the relationship between the type of investor you are, your current level of risk tolerance and some investment avenues to explore. Remember that your propensity for handling risk is not the same as the amount of risk inherent in an investment.

The examples of different investments are by no means exhaustive, nor do you have to stick to them. They are simply suggestions of where you might feel more comfortable putting your money.

Note as well that if your investor profile is undifferentiated for more than one dominant characteristic – for example, you have similar scores for cautious and technical – you will have more investment alternatives to explore, given the amount of risk that's most suitable for you.

In any financial planning strategy, a priority is always adequate provision for you and your family's future needs. So pensions and insurance management should always come first. For some investors, such as cautious ones, increasing contributions to private or occupational pensions and savings schemes can also be a useful way to develop your approach. Certainly, it can be a good place to start if you're uncertain about your ability in choosing investments.

After that, most professional advisers say that you should never invest more than you can afford to lose – good advice for even the most successful investors.

	Cautious	Emotional	Technical	Busy	Casual	Informed
Low risk propensity	Savings instruments Pensions Insurance Fixed-rate deposits CDs (US certificates of deposit)	Pensions Insurance Savings instruments Fixed-rate deposits	Blue chips Large and medium cap stocks Value stocks	Bonds Blue chips Unit trusts Mutual funds	Money market funds Savings schemes Pensions and insurance schemes CDs T Bills (US Treasury bills) and government bonds	Large cap stocks Unit trusts Mutual funds Fixed-rate deposits Blue chips Government and corporate bonds
Medium risk propensity	Money market deposits Indexed funds Blue chips Large cap stocks	Blue chips Unit trusts Mutual funds Government bonds	Momentum and growth stocks Speculative investment funds Real estate and property	Medium cap stocks Value stocks	Indexed funds Managed funds Unit trusts Mutual funds Blue chips	Medium cap stocks Specialist funds Value stocks
High risk propensity	Home investment funds Large specialist or sector-weighted funds Medium cap stocks	Managed funds Large cap stocks	Small cap stocks Micro cap stocks Derivatives and options Commodities	Real estate and property Speculative investment funds	Large cap stocks Offshore deposits Leading medium cap stocks	Momentum and growth stocks Small cap stocks Micro cap stocks Venture capital schemes Emerging markets Options and derivatives Hedge funds

Figure 15 *Investment avenues and strategies to explore*

9

It's Human Nature

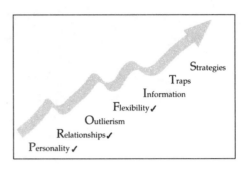

THERE'S AN ANCIENT FABLE ABOUT A FISH THAT ONE DAY LOOKS UP from the pool it's swimming in and sees a fox. Knowing that foxes aren't the greatest friends of fish, it's just about to dive down into safer depths when the fox says, 'Hey. Wait a moment. Before you go, I've got something to tell you.'

'Yeah, sure,' called back the fish. 'And if I wait here long enough you'll get closer and eat me!'

'No, really, I have got something to tell you,' said the fox. 'Look, if you're worried, I'll stay right here.'

That seemed acceptable to the fish. So it said, 'OK, go ahead, I'm listening.'

'Well,' said the fox, 'there's a much nicer pool on the other side of this river bank. The beautiful sparkling water is a wondrous sight to behold. It ripples in the sunlight and is so clear, you can see your reflection in it. On all sides, it's surrounded by lush vegetation. While within the pool, there is an abundance of good things to eat. For a fish like you, it's paradise on earth.'

'Why should I believe you?' the fish wanted to know.

'I have no reason to lie to you. By the way, did I tell you that there are some of the fattest and juiciest worms you've ever seen there?'

'Umm,' said the fish as it thought about those worms. 'That's all very well, but how am I going to get there? I've been in this pool since I was born and it's much too far to jump to the other pool.'

'I'll take you in my mouth, like I carry my children,' said the fox. 'And just as I would never harm my children, I give you my solemn word, I will not harm you.'

The picture conjured up by the fox's description was an overpowering lure for the fish and, thinking that it was worth the risk, it finally replied, 'All right, you've convinced me. Take me over there.'

The fox came down to the water's edge and gently scooped the fish up in its mouth. Several minutes into the journey the fish began to relax. But just then it felt a searing pain. Realizing it was dying from a mortal wound, the fish looked up into the fox's eyes. As its last breath ebbed away, it cried out, 'Why did you do that to me when you gave me your word?'

'I couldn't help it,' replied the fox. 'It's in my nature!'

Human beings are not blank pieces of paper. Just like the fish and the fox, we come into this world primed with a variety of instincts and traits. This gives us our nature. But unlike animals, we learn to control our instincts – we learn what's good for us and what's bad. Even so, when money enters the picture, it becomes harder to tell the difference, because people see money as a route to fulfilling desires and life goals. As a result, just as the fish sees only the juicy worms and the fox sees the fish as a meal, people revert to instinctive behavior rather than rational judgment. In this chapter, we'll look at how this comes about.

What can stop you becoming a successful investor?

I've discussed at some length how it's important to develop successful investor characteristics in order to get your internal market – the one inside your head – structured for the best chance of investment success. However, the negative, instinct-dependent characteristics that need modulating or controlling don't exist in a vacuum, they are driven. Think of it as a balancing act: on one side the useful characteristics and on the other the competing characteristics – attitudes, desires and so forth. As long as the balance between them is maintained, financial realism remains prominent and there is psychonomic harmony (Figure 16).

Let's now take a look at several of the factors that underlie an investor's outlook and can cloud your financial realism, forcing the competing characteristics to become stronger: desire for comfort, conflicting emotions, negative emulation, uncertainty about risk and market volatility, the effort needed to obtain reward, and susceptibility to influence.

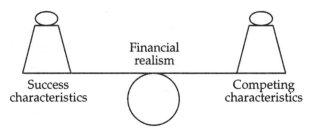

Figure 16 *Maintaining psychonomic harmony*

Desiring comfort

We all create a place for ourselves in which we feel relaxed, secure, comfortable and sheltered from the turmoil of the outside world. In a physical sense, it might be our home with comfortable armchairs, central heating and soft lighting. The relationships we have with other people also contribute to our sense of comfort. Generally, we gravitate towards people who have a similar outlook and life expectation to ours or a shared belief system.

In addition to these externally generated comfort zones, we have internal comfort zones. This is where we have developed attitudes, emotions or psychological mechanisms to deal with the problems of everyday life.

Some time ago I met a friend of mine at a party. I hadn't seen Judy for a while and wanted to catch up on how she and her family were doing. 'How's your Dad these days?' I asked.

Her eyebrows moved up and down and she sighed deeply. 'You know Dad. Business is bad, he eats... Business is good, he eats!'

Judy's father's response was the same whatever the circumstances. Food was his comfort. This was the activity that helped him feel most able to deal with the difficulties he faced in the running of his brokerage business. It was his reward for business well done and his refuge when business didn't go well. But potential clients would see him puff and blow as he slumped his overweight frame into his deep leather armchair and, unfair as it was, he still lost business.

It is no easy task to break away from your comfort zone. But you can begin by considering whether there are any behaviors or activities you enjoy so much that they are just as, or more, important to you than becoming a successful investor. What comfort is stopping you from developing a flexible outlook and taking a step into successful investment territory?

For example, many people take pleasure in lording it over others. They have a superiority complex and want to show how clever they are – an inflated sense of self-importance is their comfort zone. Usually, such people have inner doubts and insecurities that they are covering up. Or, as with many mediocre investors, they spend an inordinate amount of time pouring over piles of company documentation and reports, become overwhelmed, and miss vital information – although they can speak for ages about particular companies in great detail. Technical prowess is their comfort zone.

In a similar way, some investors see the highly successful few, like Buffett and Soros, and say to themselves: 'Why can't I be like them?' They fail to understand the work and approach that went into this type of success. Admiration turns to bitterness and they minimize the skill involved, putting it down to luck. And all these investors are left with is a warped comfort zone constituted of envy and greed.

If you have a true desire to develop your investment skills, you must first deal with any conflict of attitude that is leading you to act in an inconsistent or irrational manner. Decide what comforts, positive or negative, are trapping you. The alternative is simply to keep repeating the same behaviors.

Below are a few categories of comfort zones and the way in which they exhibit themselves. They are all refuge-seeking behavior of one sort or another. Do any of them reflect your own behavior?

- ☐ *Defensive*: 'I paid good money for the advice. I *know* I've got the right investment.'
- ☐ *Reinforcing*: 'I did all I could. Up 20 points, I sell. I didn't make a big profit, but so what? It's the way I always work.'
- ☐ *Delusional*: 'I'm the best investor I know. It was simply bad luck the directors got jailed for fraud!'
- ☐ *Stress reducing*: 'I can't deal with my dropping investment now – later, tomorrow, when I've been to the bar, had a hot bath, made a call, had a good sleep...'

The comfort of the familiar

Which would you rather have: an investment abroad or an investment in the city where you live? Refuge-seeking behavior can dominate an investor's outlook and lead you to make investments that you think you know something about, even if greater risk is attached. As a result, many investors will go for an investment in their home territory.

Investors think they know about the company because the familiar breeds confidence. It's familiar to them because it's in their backyard, they hear about it more and so feel they've a greater connection to it. Consider how many people approach celebrities and begin conversations as if they're an intimate friend – they may have never met the other person before and only ever seen them on TV, but they feel they know them.

As a result, overseas investment is still avoided by many investors, despite the fact that it's becoming increasingly easy to enter these markets, with more research now available and dealing costs dropping. Furthermore, such investments can represent good value and help in the management of portfolio risk through diversification. Nevertheless, even when it's a relatively safe investment of, say, US citizens buying leading UK domestic stocks or vice versa, investors still stay at home.

Research bears out just how insular investors can be. When US phone company AT&T split into seven small companies, Gur Huberman at Columbia Business School examined stockholding patterns of the new regional companies. Known as the Baby Bells, these became the main service supplier in each different geographic area. In line with the idea that people are comfortable with the familiar, Professor Huberman found that local investors in the Baby Bells accounted for greater stock ownership in comparison to other providers.

Retreating to the familiar allows investors to worry less about their money. In this way, internal conflict is reduced and they believe that their investment decision is rational and consistent. In reality, they may not know any more about the local company than any other one abroad.

Conflicting emotions

Few investors would ever admit to acting inconsistently – but have you ever placed money in a stock and then traded repeatedly, in and out, as the price fluctuates? It's illogical and it's irrational when common sense tells you that it's a good stock and you should leave well alone, but many people still trade unnecessarily. Or you may have researched an investment and are about to complete the deal when a friend tells you an important piece of information that you've overlooked and that should dissuade you from taking any action. You know they're right, but you still buy in.

Simply put, you act one way when you should act another. At the root of this inconsistent behavior may be unfulfilled desires or psychological needs, which conflict with the desire to be a successful investor. You think to yourself: 'I'm going to buy that stock and it's going to rise and rise – that'll wipe the smile off that smug boss's face'; or 'It's the story of my life. I should have got rid of that stock along with that excuse for a husband.' In the example above, you still buy into the bad investment, because otherwise you'd have to admit to yourself that someone else assessed the situation better than you. Yet rationality dictates that there is always someone better – just like the fastest gunslinger in the Wild West who falls to the ground in a shootout, mortally wounded but with a look of total surprise.

Experiences that have shaped your character, such as relationships, personal episodes or upbringing, are likely to be the reason for your psychological perceptions being out of kilter. For example, you believe that high investment returns will bring you security, independence, power or happiness. Rational thinking would tell you that money alone is not enough. But at particularly sensitive moments, your prior beliefs compensate for an area of your emotional life that's deficient.

To a large extent this is normal behavior; we all occasionally make the wrong decision. At times like these an understanding partner or friend can do wonders for the ego, and with self-reflection our rationality returns. It's when the root cause cannot be identified, when the reason for your strange behavior lies buried deep within your psyche, that the problem is more difficult to deal with.

Unresolved conflict

Some investors who think they want to profit become strangely apprehensive about success when prices are rising and feel guilt about losing when prices are falling. It's part of their dysfunctional psychological outlook – an unresolved part of their character – and they cannot help themselves. Rational action only produces the wrong emotions, such as anticlimax, dissatisfaction, depression or reduced self-esteem. Coupled with this are all their desires and predilections which come together and drive their behavior – envy, competitiveness, a pathological need for wealth, fast cars, status, control, to be the best and a host of other deep-rooted motives. There may also be a cultural component to this, such as the way wealth and success are viewed by our peers that has been overly internalized. These investors know they are taking the wrong course of action but something triggers the emotion, overwhelming their good judgment and compelling them. Inevitably, they make the wrong investment decisions.

For some, achieving success brings no satisfaction whatsoever. In fact – though they won't admit it to themselves – it makes them depressed. So they deal and deal and keep on dealing in a highly competitive frenzy, until they lose everything or burn out. Similarly, there are some investors who find loss strangely satisfying. It makes them happy, relaxed and somewhat euphoric. It is inconsistent with normal expected behavior. After all, they should feel good if they do well, but they certainly should feel bad when they lose.

The most worrying aspect for many of these investors – whether they have superficial conflicting emotions or deep-rooted ones – is that even with prior knowledge, when the same situation arises again, they make exactly the same mistakes. It's an unbreakable cycle. The only way to overcome it is to realize that you're in the cycle and to face it.

Breaking the cycle

How do you know when you're in the cycle? The chances are that you'll display defensive behavior or a psychological justification that in some way helps you get through the day.

Take a look at the list below and see whether you've ever said or done any of these things:

☐ You start watching videos all night to take your mind off things.

☐ You rationalize your losses. 'It's all a game, isn't it?' 'I'm not in it for the money.' 'It could have been worse.'

☐ You lose your temper easily over the smallest things, your anger being directed to any easy target.

☐ You want revenge. 'That damn market isn't going to beat me again!'

☐ You justify your losing stock because it's an ethical investment or it's in a business that's providing an important service.

☐ You become indecisive and keep calling your broker to change your dealing instructions. 'But I've just got this new information!' you yell down the phone when the broker gets irritated.

☐ You cover up your inner feelings. You laugh and tell jokes – you're the life and soul of your workplace.

☐ You procrastinate or get depressed, letting things slide – you'll go through that investment information tomorrow.

☐ You're losing heavily but can't bring yourself to change your investment situation – you're emotionally locked in.

☐ You tell your friends, family and neighbors about this great investment you have even though it's been steadily dropping – there's comfort in numbers. 'I'm the one to ask for expert advice,' you tell them.

☐ You pretend you never lost any money. When your spouse asks what happened with the investment you look surprised and say, 'What investment? Oh, I got out ages ago!'

☐ You minimize your loss to yourself and others. 'Me, get burnt? No way. Lost a bit, sure; anybody would have. But I managed to get out fast.'

☐ You shift the blame away from you. It was luck, it was providence, it was your broker's fault, you just couldn't compete with electronic trading systems.

☐ You know a decision has to be made, but your old football injury suddenly flares up and requires medical attention.

☐ You watch your bad investment drop as if on the sidelines. If it drops further, it's only proving your demoralized outlook correct. You say, 'Hell, I wasn't going to make any money out of that, anyway!'

If you see any of your own behaviors mirrored in the list, then you can take heart in knowing that at least you've begun to self-reflect. The process of change towards becoming a successful investor is not easy. If it was, there would be far more successful investors. It may also be painful; change often is. But the acquisition of psychonomic rationality is a worthwhile goal that can have repercussions in many areas of your life. Keep in mind that it is *you* who has to develop your investment approach. You can learn from other people, to see how they accomplish this, but you have to do more than just watch or admire them.

Negative emulation is counterproductive to success

Many people search for a role model, someone they can look up to and even copy. This happens frequently in adolescence, when teenagers are searching for an identity and copy pop stars and film stars. For others it is a means of bolstering a poor self-image or invigorating a humdrum life. They become 'wannabes'. 'If only I could be like that, everything would be great,' they say to themselves. But what they fail to realize – either in their youthful zeal for personal development or in their desire for accelerated social acceptance – is that what they see is often a contrived exterior for the benefit of adulating fans. The real personality may be considerably different from the one seen on stage or screen. And, moreover, far more work and intelligence may have gone into the production of this public image than is apparent.

Similarly, many people want to get rich quick. And what they see in successful businesspeople and investors is the persona of wealth. They emulate this in an attempt to show the world that they too are wealthy and successful. But it is negative emulation because there is nothing behind it – no real knowledge or carefully formulated approach to investment. It is all based on fancy, self-delusion, envy and greed. They rise fast and can fall just as fast, leaving a trail of debt and unhappiness behind them. They may have vainly tried to shore up the dam as their financial situation started to crumble, but they don't have expertise, only guile. In the extreme, these are people who carry out a con trick then disappear, only to reappear somewhere else where they are unknown.

Dealing with uncertainty

Many investors panic and make the wrong choices because they're anxious. And it's easy to become anxious when you're uncertain about how safe your investment is. Often, this results from an inability to make sense, or gain any feeling of control, of what's happening in the market. So you worry about whether you've invested too much money, whether you've got the right investment, and when the market begins to swing violently, affecting investments generally, whether it's all been worthwhile in the first place – or indeed, whether you're going to lose everything. Psychonomic harmony between your internal market and the external market is significantly reduced. At these moments, it's easy to panic and believe that it's better to cut your losses and get out. The risk of staying in is just too much to bear.

The greater the level of uncertainty you feel, the greater the chance that you'll misperceive risk. But what does risk actually mean to you? Are you facing real risk or only imagining you are? Table 16 gives a few ways in which different investors view risk.

Table 16 *What does risk mean to you?*

☐ Losing money.

☐ Not making money.

☐ Investing in something or in a way that makes you feel uncomfortable or unable to concentrate on anything other than your investment.

☐ Agitation over reduction in total portfolio value.

☐ Agitation when a single stock in a portfolio declines in value and the rest remains buoyant.

☐ Fear of being burned again. This is equated with high risk and leads many investors to avoid opportunities, even though they may have originally lost due to circumstances beyond their control such as a falling sector, bad advice or lack of quality information. The perceived risk is greater than the real risk.

☐ Perceived loss by amount rather than percentage. A fall of 5 percent is the same whatever the size of your holding. But if you think in amounts then your level of worry and perception of risk can increase immeasurably, as the sky's the limit – thousands, millions, billions...! (When was the last time you heard 'billions wiped of the stock market!' It has drama when the news reports talk about amounts as opposed to percentages.)

❑ A fear of the unknown. Inexperience and lack of knowledge lead many investors to dismiss opportunities as too risky when they may just be slightly more complicated.

❑ Nervousness when the investment has been doing well for some time. The perceived risk of greater loss increases the longer the holding period and the higher prices climb.

❑ For the professional, besides all the above, risk is also a quantifiable statistic known as *beta*, where the likelihood of portfolio returns is estimated in comparison to the market. (The S&P 500 has a beta coefficient of 1. A stock with a higher beta is more volatile than the market and so is considered to be more risky, while one with a lower beta will rise and fall with less volatility and is considered to be less risky.)

Handling risk is about handling worry and anxiety, dealing with fear of losing, and your ability to tolerate volatility in markets and prices. To a large extent, you can overcome your emotional responses by learning about the investment instruments you're proposing to get into, gaining experience, and keeping informed. Nevertheless, investors are prone to make repeated errors when it comes to risk. In the rest of this section, you'll see why this happens. After you've finished reading it, you might like to go back and redo the 'How do you handle risk?' part of the Investor Profile in the previous chapter to see whether your views have changed at all.

Pushing back the boundaries

The more risk there is financially and psychologically, the greater the chance of a higher return. Committed investors are often looking for ways to expand the boundaries of acceptable risk. If you understand what you're doing, that's fine. But if you don't, and your judgment is clouded, you'll land in trouble for not being adequately prepared to take on the extra risk. The desire for greater financial return causes you to make rash and risky decisions without careful forethought. And this is the important point: the inherent risk of an investment at any given time is stable or assessable, while perception of risk can fluctuate according to whim, bias, and external influence. To take on greater risk involves an appropriate modification in your tolerance to risk, otherwise you'll be baling out at the slightest price hiccup.

Table 17 shows the progression of investors' attitude to risk. Note that the risk here refers to the inherent risk of the investment vehicle in comparison to other investments. You may initially keep to deposits in banks, but having tasted greater returns from saving schemes and pensions, or hearing about dazzling high gains in other instruments from high-pressure marketing, you're more likely to move to more speculative investments. All these investments are useful – but only in the right context and with the right mental attitude.

Table 17 *The riskiness of an investment*

	Low inherent risk	Medium inherent risk	High inherent risk	Possible return
Banks and building societies	✔			low
Insurance, saving schemes and pensions	✔			low
Blue-chip equities		✔		medium
Property/real estate		✔		medium
Subsidiary markets (AIM, OFEX)			✔	high
Company start-up			✔	high
Derivatives (futures, options)			✔	high

The better you get, the more you sleep!

The sleep factor, as it has become known, is a way to assess whether you've invested carefully, being able to stand the amount of risk associated with the type of investment – and whether the amount invested is appropriate. Too much and you won't sleep; too little and you'll sleep but you won't make any money – which may ultimately keep you awake in any case!

It's a question of finding a comfortable balance between risk and security. If you imagine these on either side of a seesaw, different people will be able to cope with different amounts of each; the desire for low risk isn't just a characteristic of cautious investors. As a simple exercise, consider on a scale of one to ten how much risk you could tolerate and still get a good night's sleep.

Risk and self-delusion

Many people can't accept the need to change their minds once the choice has been made and money has been invested. They may reason as follows: 'I'm an intelligent person who's good with money and I only make good investments.' This flies in the face of evidence to the contrary when the investment goes wrong.

This type of behavior, where investors mentally justify their strongly held beliefs – even when they conflict – is known as *dissonance*. If they take positive action to safeguard their money, they have to accept that they were wrong, which is very hard for some people to do. Prior investment successes only add to the strength of the firmly held belief. Many investors entering the derivatives market are in this position. They may have made some good profits and feel that they understand the complexities of this type of trading. With each successive trade, they become more confident and more daring, sometimes with the blessing of their broker. When things go really bad – and the cold sweats in the middle of the night begin – they feel immobilized. They won't limit their losses by trading and they won't accept that they've made a mistake.

When the opportunity presents itself again, instead of having learned from the experience and starting from a carefully considered standpoint, they plough back in. In the most extreme cases, fortunes are lost.

Balancing risk with the avoidance of regret

If you have no trouble sleeping at night and are comfortable with a degree of risk, there are many small quoted companies that can be considered as investments. For the even more adventurous there are the so-called *dogs* of the stock market that have languished on the investment periphery for years, unloved and ignored. There may be a good reason for this, such as the fact that they may be on the verge of bankruptcy. But tales abound of the penny share that was used as a shell for a reverse takeover (a method by which companies can gain a stock market listing by taking over a languishing quoted company then injecting their own assets into it) and suddenly rose and rose... and rose.

Many investors dream of such things happening to them, of finding such a shell. They'll pour over specialist publications in the hope of getting in early on a situation of this type and finding the next Polly Peck. They know too that previously profitable companies show lower returns than is potentially obtainable from dogs. Investing in IBM or ICI is unlikely to allow you to double your money; all you can reasonably expect is a slowly increasing dividend and a small appreciation in capital.

Yet the fact is that few people prefer dogs to well-known companies. One reason is the fear of regret. Investing in ICI is conventional and safe. Investing in a dog isn't. If the dog drops heavily in value, you may kick yourself and wonder why on earth you put your hard-earned money into it. But if ICI drops, you'll think it was such an unlikely possibility – and all the experts surely didn't foresee this – that it's just a misfortune; even the will of providence. There is no feeling of responsibility and therefore no regret.

While large numbers of investors stay away from what they perceive to be risky stocks – even to the extent of missing quality bargains – other investors, choosing stocks with similar market risk characteristics, may leave themselves open to feelings of regret by inappropriate trading. Let's say you've had your money invested in ABC Industries for the last two years without much increase in value. You then hear about another investment on the television news, XYZ Electronics, a company that is heavily hyped and is said to be heading for a dramatic rerating. Not having sufficient funds for both, and without checking the fundamentals, you sell ABC Industries and buy XYZ Electronics. Six months later, XYZ Electronics has gone nowhere while ABC Industries has rocketed to three times its original value. With both investments the real risk may have been equal, but the intense pain of regret comes when you imagine what profit you would have made had you stayed in ABC Industries.

And the question is: what will you do next time you're faced with a similar situation?

Fear of loss

Now let's suppose that you have to make a choice between:

❏ a sure gain of $6000; and
❏ an 80 percent chance of gaining $8000, with a 20 percent chance of gaining nothing.

Which alternative do you think will give you the best chance to profit? *Prospect theory*, developed by Amos Twerski and Daniel Kahneman, shows that most people become risk averse when they're faced with the prospect of investment gains. Hence, they choose the first alternative, a risk-averse choice of a sure gain of $6000. This seems logical if you think that there's a good possibility of losing. But this choice was actually the less desirable one. If investors chose the second alternative their overall performance, on an aggregate basis, would be better because there is a greater chance of a higher return of $6400. The likely gain is given by the sum of the outcomes multiplied by their probabilities: $(8000 \times 0.8) + (0 \times 0.2) = 6400$.

If there is even the hint of a possibility that they are going to lose money, many investors will dismiss investment opportunities simply because they perceive them to be more risky. Successful investment is about getting it right most of the time. By focusing too narrowly on single stocks or events, fear of losing money is proportional to the desire to avoid risk. The reality, as the above example shows, may be quite different.

Risk-averse investors can also respond in the opposite extreme by buying large numbers of stocks for their portfolios. If it is a balanced portfolio, diversification may be prudent to spread the risk. At the same time, not only might these investors still be narrowly focused and misperceive the risk taken on, but it affords these investors less opportunity to earn much high returns from fewer, well-chosen stocks.

Many investors make the wrong choices, however, because they dislike losing more than they hate risk. On the face of it, it seems strange for risk to become a secondary consideration. But let me give you another example. Suppose you had a choice of either:

❐ a sure loss of $6000; or
❐ an 80 percent chance of losing $8000, with a 20 percent chance of losing nothing.

Which did you choose? Many people choose the second. On first glance this option appears to be less risky and more certain because you might not lose anything. But is it? In reality, it is more risky because you stand to lose more than $6000. The likely loss is given by the sum of the outcomes multiplied by their probabilities: $(8000 \times 0.8) + (0 \times 0.2) = 6400$.

Let's look at this a different way. Suppose I toss a coin and you have the choice of either:

❐ heads you win $300; or
❐ tails you lose $200.

Would you take the bet? Most people don't, although the risk is very good. The potential profit is 150 percent of the potential loss. Try it and see.

When investors believe that they are in an investment situation that has a low level of risk, they are certain – and have convinced themselves – that they've taken all the precautions available to allow them the maximum possible gain. What is often forgotten is that the low-risk investment may not be so low risk as first appears. And their choice may have more to do with minimizing their fear of loss.

Furthermore, this tendency dovetails not only with the inclination to avoid regret, due to the remorse that might be felt by losing, but also with sunk cost bias. Imagine that you've won a holiday in the Bahamas for you and a friend. The plane is about to leave from a fog-bound airport. The pilot warns you that though you should make it, it's likely to be a dangerous flight and the responsibility for your safety is your own. Would you take the chance?

Now consider the same situation but in this case you've paid $3000 and it's non-refundable. Would you take the chance under these circumstances?

According to behavioral finance researchers, people are more likely to take a risk if they have paid for it. It shouldn't make a difference, but it does, because once you've paid money for something, you feel unwilling to waste it.

The upshot of all this is that, although investors may generally try to avoid unnecessary risk when they're facing the prospect of a gain, when they're facing the prospect of a loss they can actually be drawn to make more risky investment choices. When this happens – strange as it appears – even good-risk investment situations may be overlooked or dismissed as being of poor value.

When investors get nervous about performance

When investors assess stocks or other investment instruments, they consider attributes such as past performance alongside what they believe to be their chances of loss. And as performance changes, there is greater uncertainty about the future. The more uncertainty, the more investors' emotions can rule their decisions. As a result, actions are taken out of fear rather than rationality.

Let's say that you've been buying small capitalization stocks rather than safe blue chips. If performance has been good for some time, with values soaring skywards, it's possible that you'll get anxious about the prospect of losing. The higher your potential profit, and the more volatile the stock, the more anxious you'll get.

Although it might be wiser to stay put, many investors will get out at this point. Not only do they want to avoid loss, they don't want anxiety to turn into panic by seeing their investment suddenly fall – they don't want to be in a position later where they're looking at what they did with hindsight and mentally kicking themselves for their lack of action. Again, investors want to avoid regret.

In an attempt to avoid early panic dealing, many investors use professional investment advisers. Often, however, the professional may understand the price and market movements much better than the client and know that it's wiser to stay in the investment. But when the client is constantly on the phone – wanting to know how to handle things, asking for advice, giving instructions – to keep the client happy, and not to get the blame if things do turn sour, they will advise selling. The adviser doesn't want to be faced with what's known as the 'Monday morning quarterbacking effect', where a client, again with the benefit of hindsight, will say: 'Anyone could have seen what was coming; I knew and you certainly should have!'

So much for when performance has been good. But what if investment performance has been poor for some time – say you're holding an unfashionable stock in an unfashionable sector? Fear of loss can also increase.

On the one hand, investors may procrastinate, believing that as long as they don't sell, there's no real risk because any loss hasn't been realized. Yet if they've really got a lemon on their hands, swift action would safeguard their finances. These investors are likely to justify their decision irrevocably and believe that things will get better. Instead of trading out of a bad situation, they hang on.

On the other hand, with reinforcement from media information and broker analyses, investors easily imagine that risk is increasing. The more they hear, the more they believe that things can only get worse. So they overreact. In this case, although the stock may be good, investors sell when they should hang on.

One investor's uncertainty is another investor's opportunity

In reality, real risk may be minimal and buying an unfashionable stock, at an unfashionable time, could be a good strategy. Successful investors, such as Warren Buffett, know the importance of this concept. To them, the overall picture needs to be considered – assets, management, product range, market penetration, potential earnings and so forth. The fact that it is only a value stock and not considered good by the market is neither here nor there. If it is a good stock, in their opinion, it is worth buying. Furthermore, the current market price is less important – a few points up or down is not a reason to delay buying. It is real value that is important – not perceived value – and it is this that should drive your investment decision.

Fear of volatility

Where investors hate risk, the most popular advice is to invest in bonds rather than stocks. Financial consultants will also often advise clients with a high proportion of stocks in their portfolios to balance the risk with a proportion of bonds. Similarly, young clients are viewed as inherently able to withstand greater risk and are advised to hold more stocks, while older clients are viewed as less able to tolerate risk and are advised to hold a higher proportion of bonds. Assessing clients in this way has little basis in fact. Age, for example, has little to do with the ability to tolerate risk. However, although a balanced portfolio with a mix of investment instruments is often the best way to proceed, the correct advice ends up being given for the wrong reasons.

Nevertheless, most of these financial advisers are basing their approach on accepted wisdom. Historically, stock prices fluctuate far more than bond prices. The theory is that because stocks are more volatile, they are riskier. Investors who bear this risk should be compensated, so the thinking goes, and therefore stocks and shares offer higher average returns. During the last 70 years, in the US and the UK, these average returns – including dividends – run at between about 6 and 7 percent a year on stocks compared to about 1 percent on bonds. This peculiar difference in returns is known as the *equity premium puzzle*.

In reality, stocks may be no riskier than bonds. They appear to be, because investors are focusing on individual events that are affecting their investments and causing stark rises and falls. Their investments appear unstable and there is reduced certainty about future performance. Many investors don't take well to this uncertainty and they become anxious, constantly worrying about fluctuating values. Under these circumstances it is easy to take a decision to buy or sell. Volatility causes more investors to act, driving the market further. It is a short-term viewpoint where, in order to profit, a successful investor needs to be able to ride the waves of uncertainty.

So why are short-term investors more likely to be holding stocks and why do they have to be compensated for tolerating greater risk? Furthermore, why are long-term investors more willing to hold bonds? Research in this area by Richard Thaler and Shlomo Benartzi has labeled this phenomenon *myopic loss aversion*. According to their theory, people are much more sensitive to losing money than to gaining it; losing $100 hurts twice as much as gaining $100 gives pleasure. The upshot of this is that the pain of loss is increased when investors make more frequent evaluations. In the short term, stocks can rise and fall on a daily basis, which enhances the effect. And in the long term, although stocks are likely to outperform bonds, these investors have left the opportunities behind them.

The explanation provided by Thaler and Benartzi's research is that loss-averse, long-term investors are evaluating their portfolios about every 13 months rather than every day, once a week or some other narrow timeframe. Therefore, stock returns are high to compensate those who get more anxious and count their money too often. The implication, too, is that for those who can develop patience, stocks represent excellent opportunity and good value.

This theory goes a long way to explaining the motivation behind many investors' actions. But it still doesn't fully cover why an intelligent investor, who is sufficiently aware that they know a long-term investment is profitable, may still make the wrong choices. Of course, lack of quality information may be a reason, as might be a timid attitude to what could be thought of as a gamble. An alternative is to consider whether the effort involved in making a decision, or assessing portfolio value, is a factor.

The reward–motivation equation

One characteristic of successful investors is to weigh up information. Their strong clarity then directs them to internalize the information if it is considered worthwhile. Similarly, it is a characteristic of most people to make a judgment based on potential reward. Economists refer to this effect as *utility*. However, psychological research shows that this is more intricate than a simple mental accounting procedure. It is balanced, for example, with how motivating the experience is to gain the benefit, or how boring it is.

Experiments have been conducted involving giving a task to an individual that is considerably tedious and repetitive, then seeing how they perform in comparison to someone else given the same task but with a reward – usually payment. After a while, even with a reward, unless the task is interesting there is little motivation to continue and the task is left. Even if there's a bigger reward, the same thing happens. In fact, there appears to be a cut-off point above which motivation is lost even more quickly. It's as if the person is saying to themselves: 'Hey, I'm only doing this for the money now and I'm not really committed any more.' This works with children as well. Provide a boring jigsaw, with a few dollars for every half an hour worked, and the child can still lose interest. The child will fiddle with something else on the table, sigh, yawn, get up from the table, walk around or find something else to play with in the room. The exception is when the task has a particular relevance to the person or they simply find it stimulating or challenging. In other words, they have to like what they're doing. Successful investors like to invest; it's their hobby, it's their passion – it's their motivation.

Investors may initially check their investments quite frequently in the published performance tables or with their advisers. But if there is no real interest or pleasure taken in the management or overseeing of the investment, involvement wanes along with motivation. The reward is in short-term gratification alone and these investors are likely to be quick in and quick out. They move rapidly on to the next opportunity or something of more relevance in their lives.

If for some reason they stay in the investment for the long term, their interest is minimal. They don't like to involve themselves in active management of their investments; they like to invest and forget about it. For this reason, more secure, less risky investments are recommended by advisers, bonds included. Yet the reality is that when the right mix of investments is made, these long-term investors can perform better than those who are in and out of particular investment vehicles all the time. But it is down to luck or the use of good advisers that produces this effect rather than any committed, wide-ranging approach. And for many investors, the investment was simply something that was done years ago. There is no thought, for example, that a yearly financial check-up or portfolio assessment needs to be undertaken. Simply put, they're just not motivated and even the thought of making money is not a sufficient reward for the effort involved in taking control of their finances.

Profit plus motivation equals investment success. Profit without motivation only allows for short-term gratification.

What this all means is that investment reward must have two main psychological components in order to be successful. First, there must be strong commitment. And initially – while experience is being gained – it must be without sky-high profits, which would act as a conflicting motivation, that is, it would interfere with the development of a real liking for investment and the formation of a structured approach. Profits need to be on a consistent basis, starting out at a manageable and conceivable level and then rising... and then rising further.

Secondly, there needs to be a feeling of ownership over investment choices. Investors need to feel – and get feedback – that it is what they're doing that is bringing the reward; not luck, but their research and their effort.

Susceptibility to influence

The problem is that the more effort you put into an interest, the more experience you gain, which means that you can be influenced by previous experience. Any investment decisions you then make can be irrational and biased, because you won't be making a true assessment of how things actually are. Furthermore, investors become more influenced the more information changes from being statistically based to being story based.

Suppose that you've just been asked to bet on the sport of applicants for an Olympic team position. The only information you're provided with is that out of last year's 50 applicants, 40 were field performers and 10 were track performers. Assuming only these two options and given the data, you'd probably say that it's likely that this year's candidates are in the same proportions, four field for every one track. Sounds a good bet?

Now suppose that you had a brief biography of some of the applicants. For example, Lauren is 26, married with two children and has eight years' competition experience. She owns and runs a restaurant and her hobbies include skin diving and mountaineering.

What would you bet the applicants are more likely to be now, field or track?

Many people will ignore the data in favor of real information. They're influenced by personal preferences and, in this instance, whether they believe it's more likely for field or track performers to have particular characteristics. So, even though they know what the applicant proportions are, if they *feel* that Lauren is a track performer, that's the way they'll bet.

In the same way, when there's a good story behind the change in a company's status or its reduced earnings, many investors take the wrong course of action, holding or buying when they should sell. For example, ABC Associates has just spent millions on researching a new drug for the common cold; DEF Industries reports that it has had to adjust to a change in the market sector; or GHI Electronics states that next year is definitely going to be better after restructuring and the new manager has settled in. All this information may be important, but you shouldn't base your investment decision on a personal preference for hearing certain types of corporate reasoning, or explanations about performance, at the expense of real hard facts; the company may just be making the noises that it wants people to hear.

The fact is that people love a good story. Human nature is sensitive to hearing about the highs and lows of others; that's why so many of us watch soap operas. And certainly, a story is much more interesting than analyzing statistical and financial data. The only way to make systematic gains is to ignore this tendency and only use information that is relevant.

But people want to remain true to their beliefs and attitudes. These are firmly linked to experience. By being consistent, investors reinforce their previous behavior. The reward is in the known outcome. Anything that deviates from this will cause psychological imbalance.

To take an example from the discussion of comfort zones, the reward is in a behavior that lowers stress. So investors revert to a financial strategy that engenders lower anxiety and, hence, is comfortable. The result is that when investors are likely to obtain greater reward – such as an enhanced comfort zone – this option will be taken rather than staying in the investment. The fact that it isn't profitable to do so is less important than the maintenance of the particular personal behavior. In this way, an investor can make the wrong choice when buying or selling stock. And, moreover, any market makers who alter the daily prices of these stocks are able to flush out the nervous traders. In effect, they are manipulating investors' actions.

The likelihood of making an investment decision is further enhanced by the perceived scarcity of an investment. 'It'll never be this price again,' says your broker. So, you act. Was it your decision or your broker's? Or a brokerage company sends you some shiny documentation about a particular investment vehicle they are only giving out to their important clients. In big letters on the front it states the closing date for applications. Of course, you feel good that they're taking the time to advise you of such an imminent and potentially lucrative opportunity. But the reality could be somewhat different. The investment may indeed be good, but you need to check it out. The closing date may not be the official one but the broker's. Commission charges may be less at another broker. The projections need to be checked for accuracy. And you need to know what your broker's involvement is with this investment – what's their link and their slice of the pie?

As you read the documentation, you are unaware that your broker is using sound psychological principles to market the investment. They know they have to provide a reason for you to justify to yourself that the investment is good. Hearing it from them is not sufficient, you have to believe it. You read the estimated projections in the slick tables next to the colorful pictures and think: 'Wow, I'd like some of that!' They've accessed your desires, but they've done it in such a way that only partial cues are provided. They've given you a specific amount of information that is limited in true content but designed to make you think that you have enough information on which to base a decision.

Then you get your follow-up call from your personal financial consultant to check whether you received the important information they sent. In other words, the most powerful tool they can employ is to make you believe that you only have a limited window of opportunity to compete for a scarce resource that is going to bring easy wealth, and they're doing you a big favor. They've pushed you out of a state of psychological and physiological equilibrium. You get worried and irritated with yourself about not acting, and feel compelled to make a decision. So you make a decision, not primarily because it's a good investment but because you have to get back to a state of equilibrium.

Controlling your investments

Managing the internal market inside your head is about developing self-awareness and financial realism in order to judge your personal actions with psychonomic rationality and take the guesswork out of attaining your goal. Hence, there is no secret to becoming a successful investor, and if you make use of the information outlined in this chapter, you can't go wrong. What should be apparent, therefore, is that you have a high degree of control over your investment decisions. Human nature – in the form of emotions, desires, propensity for risk or susceptibility to influence, as well as any other factor that motivates your behavior – can be overridden. And with experience, panic can be avoided.

10

Traps for the Unwary Investor

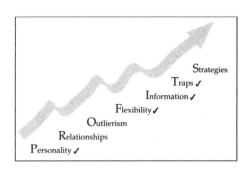

Strategies
Traps ✓
Information ✓
Flexibility ✓
Outlierism
Relationships
Personality ✓

Time and again, the world's craziest schemes attract attention and mobilize investors' propensity for greed. This is nothing new. For hundreds of years, investors have followed the crowd as if, somehow, there's financial safety in numbers. A few investors make money, but the vast majority lose their shirts as they mindlessly follow their fellows into financial oblivion.

Investors often have nobody to blame but themselves when things go wrong. They've overestimated their chance of making money in a madly volatile market or they've waited too long to trade out. If you've ever lost money this way – by attempting to build a palace on nothing more substantial than a rainbow – then it's unlikely that you timed your retreat with any accuracy.

Using the behavior of the herd to their own advantage, investment traps can be dreamed up by ruthless individuals to turn a fast buck. These people know how to capitalize on investors' natural inclination to be influenced by their personal biases – and by other investors – rather than by clear thinking. The irony is that fraudsters may be more in control of their own actions than inexperienced investors are of theirs. As a result, there are always a few investors ready to throw caution to the wind as greed takes over from good sense on what appears to be an extremely attractive proposition. The courtrooms of the world are, unfortunately, littered with investors who were suckered and got their fingers burned. But if you're knowledgeable and know what to look out for, you won't be duped.

Schemes and scams

Schemes and scams represent the vast majority of traps into which investors fall. The difference between them is really academic. If you're going to lose money, the important thing to know is how to avoid getting caught.

Nevertheless, schemes are often legal and money can be made. Investors run into problems when, for example, the scheme is badly managed or advertised in a way that suggests that it's a greater profit opportunity than it is. At times like these, it's easy to become susceptible to the sales patter you hear, and you need to maintain your financial realism in order to assess the true situation you're proposing to get into.

In the UK, Business Expansion Schemes were heavily pushed during the late 1980s. While these schemes were designed to enable small companies to raise money from private investment, they gave the investor the chance to get in early on an opportunity that might realize high gains and, as an incentive, were also a way of obtaining tax concessions. But as different business ventures and ideas sought easy funds, including light engineering, electronics and property, some of the companies were on very shaky ground and the opportunities became more risky. Investors kept piling in, however, in spite of the fact that they didn't fully understand the nature of the investments they were buying, the businesses' growth potential, the markets they operated in, or how to value the companies effectively. The result was that plenty of people found themselves with either a very small return or a loss.

Scams are dreamed up for the sole purpose of swindling the public out of its money. As we shall see, this doesn't always mean that they're illegal. Some of the most famous scams have passed into legend, including the many bubble companies that sprung up during the 1700s. Have things changed much since then? You'll have to be the judge of that.

But even if you can rationally assess the merits of an investment opportunity, it's still easy to be swayed into parting with your money when it's a professional who's managing your finances and you believe that you're getting the best possible advice. Unfortunately, this is not always the case.

How investors get caught

Successful investing is about not being duped into parting with your money unless there's a good chance of a decent profit. Yet the reality is that schemes and scams have been around since the invention of crude methods of exchange, and even before. There's always someone ready to take advantage of someone else. That, unfortunately, represents one of the worst sides of human nature. Sales and marketing methods simply capitalize on this propensity.

Through understanding your reactions, you can become more aware of when somebody else is attempting to exploit your desire to invest. Table 18 is a list of common mistakes that investors make.

Table 18 *Investors' mistakes*

Common mistakes	**Why you act**
A broker cold calls and convinces you to buy a hot stock	The sales patter is beguiling and you feel that you'll miss an opportunity if you don't act
You're influenced by news or information which constantly refers to the latest glamor sector, such as high-techs	'Everyone else is making money,' you think, 'why not me too?'
You forget that there's always a catch – even if they say there isn't	You believe that the scheme is an easy way to make a profit and want to get in before too many other investors find out about it
You're influenced by testimonials of happy and rich investors who previously entered the scheme	You see yourself in the role portrayed in the free video, successful and standing by a large house or car

You fail to check the facts before committing your money	The sales and marketing emphasize speed, while they also instill a feeling of guilt if you don't act fast to take advantage of the never-to-be-repeated offer
You confuse expert with slick and believe that the salesperson must know what they're talking about when all your questions elicit ready answers	You forget that the salesperson has the gift of convincing people to buy – or may be working from a prepared script

---

Whenever a slick salesperson or a fraudster dupes you, they are counting on your lack of financial awareness and any innate desire or need that you have. To some extent, therefore, you dupe yourself when you fall into a bad deal or trade at the wrong time. Similarly, at irrational moments like these, you enter the market along with the frenzied dash of everyone else. And once you are hooked, it's easy to believe that the speculative investment is going to bring you high rewards.

The trouble with bubbles

It is the investment bubble that speculators rise on. Bubbles form because of crowd behavior and the snowball effect. As increasing numbers of investors place more and more money into one particular investment, the price rises sharply. There is no relationship to fundamental valuation and, as a result, the bubble can burst just as quickly as it formed.

Once a bubble exists in the market it can cause ripples that do more than just inflate investor perception, where one investor causes others to act in concert towards psychonomic breakdown. As overinvestment increases, companies themselves begin to perceive their financial situation differently; believing, for example, that they're making more efficient use of their capital than if they chose an investment elsewhere with equal or less risk or, indeed, that their high market price reflects their asset value.

There is no doubt that it is mania that causes bubbles to inflate. And once the herd is moving, psychonomic momentum rapidly picks up in a self-reinforcing manner. But how do bubbles pop into existence in the first place? As I've previously intimated, they start either on their own or by someone attempting to capitalize on investors' predispositions. Either way, let's go back in time to see some remarkable examples.

Tulip mania

At the end of the sixteenth century, the tulip was first introduced from Turkey and soon became a popular flower throughout Europe. In Holland particularly, the tulip rose to prominence when wealthy Dutchmen bought them as a status symbol; much like owning the latest fast car or a set of designer clothes is a sign of prestige today.

Things would have stayed relatively quiet in this area except for the fact that a virus suddenly descended on the tulip bulbs. This didn't hurt the bulbs, but had the effect of producing colorful variations in the next generation's petals. Demand increased astronomically and Dutch flower producers and merchants found it difficult to keep up with orders.

In an attempt to control the supply of the new tulips and make some money, the merchants realized that pre-ordering the bulbs from the growers at the beginning of the planting season, or sitting on them for a while after delivery at harvest time, gave them a guaranteed profit when they sold. And that is when the price of the bulbs began to rocket. By 1634 everybody was speculating in tulip bulbs and the bubble was growing.

During the next two years, the bulb growers covered every angle and there were tulip bulb investments for everyone's taste. The most common was the Gouda, which doubled in value to three florins; a craftsman would earn this in about a week. The Centen rose from 40 to 350 florins, the value of a small house. And the rare Semper Augustus rose to 6000 florins, the equivalent today of about $820,000.

The word spread fast among the crowd that unimaginable gains could be made. And where there's money there are salespeople. They traveled around the country from village to village selling a variety of tulip investments to local people, who would often pawn their family heirlooms or mortgage their farms. There were tulip auctions where the prices of bulbs were bid up to stratospheric heights. And taverns organized discussion evenings where people could talk about tulips and the trading that went on in Amsterdam.

By the end of 1636, it seems that the Dutch population had gone tulip crazy, believing that what had previously risen would continue to rise. But prices bore no relationship to the real worth of a tulip bulb – even though it could be argued that the bulb had potential profit built in because it would be the progenitor of future generations of flowers and more bulbs.

With the mania at its height – and with terrible timing – Dutch government officials stepped in to dampen the market, believing that the wild speculation was a threat to the economy. On 2 February 1637, this action sparked a turn in prices. With their finger on the pulse of the market, the Dutch merchants decided that it was time they realized some of their profits and began to sell off their stockpiles of tulip bulbs. Within two days, the bubble burst and the market in tulip bulbs crashed.

This was inevitable, as the people who were speculating had little interest in the tulips. They simply wanted to buy the bulbs so that they could eventually sell them at a higher price.

Did investors learn the lessons of history? A little over 80 years later another bubble craze would inflate speculative investment to unprecedented heights.

The South Sea bubble

The South Sea Company, formed by John Blunt and his associates in 1720, proclaimed with 'confidence' that it would fund the UK's national war debt, amounting to around £31 million. Its business would be in trade goods, such as wool and cotton, and its markets would be in South America and the Latin countries. The likelihood of success was promoted on the basis of better political relations with Spain, due to a relatively quiet interval after years of periodic conflicts among various European countries. Trade routes would therefore open to this area of the world administered by Spain and the formation of trading links could begin. It all appeared plausible and a marvelous opportunity that shouldn't be missed.

The people liked the concept and so did the British parliament, which promptly passed a bill giving it formal approval. The stock, previously at £130, was now worth £300.

It seemed too good an opportunity to miss and investors wanted more, from George I and leading members of government down to ordinary people. So the company issued more stock... and more stock... and more stock. There was even an installment plan. Ten percent was required as a downpayment and the rest could be paid a year later. The price eventually peaked at £1000 a share. Then, the bubble burst.

A recipe for disaster in the making? Perhaps. But the end appears to have been precipitated by the directors themselves. They knew full well that the value of the company bore no relationship to its fundamentals and they quietly began dumping stock. News and rumor have a way of spreading and becoming public. The secret got out and as investors sold heavily, panic swept through the market, driving the price down through the floor. And that was the end of the South Sea Company.

We're far more experienced now – aren't we?

These historical financial events are some of the most colorful ever recorded. Perhaps the reason they occurred with such dramatic consequences is that the markets were still in their infancy. Overall, it forced the professionals and politicians of the day to face the realities of a market system and the need to change practices and introduce safeguards.

But if you think that the twentieth century has escaped by good sense and experience, here's just a sample of speculative bubbles to hit markets around the world, with the approximate year their cycle began:

☐ Florida real estate, 1923
☐ Stock market speculation, 1923 (ending in the Wall Street crash, 1929)
☐ Gold, 1978
☐ Rare stamps, 1979

❑ Japanese equities and property, 1982
❑ Jojoba beans, 1985
❑ UK housing, 1986
❑ New stock issues, 1986 (ending with the crash of Black Monday, October 1987)
❑ Lloyds Insurance underwriting, 1988
❑ Emerging Asian markets, 1991 (ending with global market correction, October 1997)
❑ New issues/Initial Public Offers of Internet companies, 1995

This last speculative craze to hit the market represents one corner of the technology sector that appears currently to hold a fascination for investors. If a company is connected to exciting, cutting-edge research in biotechnology, medicine, computing or electronics, there's a steady flow of enthusiastic buyers.

During 1995 and 1996, the whole Internet sector was buzzing and new stock was being snapped up before the IPO application forms had even hit the doormats of prospective applicants. These new companies proceeded to make some of the most spectacular gains the market had ever seen. Yahoo!, for example, was issued in April 1996 at $13. It opened on its first day of trading in the market at $24.50 and continued rising to $43. This represented a gain of 231 percent, with the stock trading at 77 times predicted earnings for 1997.

Was it sustainable? Many financial experts thought so and fueled the risk-taking binge, promoting these speculative stocks even as the bubble expanded. The attitude was: in the same way that the railroads of a century ago created change, these are innovative companies responsible for the coming revolution in the way we live and work, and so important that they must form part of a comprehensive investment strategy. Emotive stuff for sure, and with sector prices scaling new heights every day, and the general public's eagerness to buy technologically driven companies, the brokers didn't have to try too hard.

At the same time, however, reality was beginning to rear its head. There was uncertainty about achieving the physical Internet hook-up of users to access all the commercial possibilities; no one knows what the Internet's ultimate potential is; and so far, many of these companies suffer from a serious lack of earnings, as well as needing to sustain a massive capital outlay for an increasing customer base. Several months later, matters came to a head as short-term investors began bailing out. Yahoo! slid to $28, while other Internet companies fared worse. CompuServe, for example, issued at $30, had reached a high of $36 and then fallen back to $9; an overall loss, to any unlucky buyer who entered the market at its top, of 75 percent.

Nevertheless, however crazy this market is, for those who bought the initial Yahoo! issue and sold at the height of the 1998 US bull run, a handsome profit has been made. At $148 this represents a gain of 1038 percent. But the question is: how many people sold out their positions or are still invested in the hope – justified or not – that Yahoo! will go ever higher?

Human nature being what it is, the crowd will move again. The attraction of easy wealth exerts a seduction that few speculators can resist. There will be more investment bubbles; we just cannot predict where or when.

Manipulating the bubble

Responsible investment means becoming aware of when someone is taking advantage of you. Your mindset can be changed so that others can't influence you against your will. Later in this chapter, we will consider the deeper psychological reasons for investors being gullible and continuing to be ripped off. For the moment, on the assumption that forearmed is forewarned, take a look at some of the best-known schemes that repeatedly pop up in different forms. These include pyramids, sell and store, and pump and dump.

Pyramids – it's not just ancient Egyptians who build them

Pyramid schemes are some of the most commonly investigated speculative investments. They depend on investors recruiting more investors; often it's someone you know who knocks on your door telling you about this great business they're in. And once the news is out that there's profit to be made, the herd begins to move. There may or may not be a product, but in the long run this doesn't matter because the aim of the company behind the scheme is to gain new investors in a never-ending cycle. The promise alone of future high investment returns is usually sufficient to prompt you to join.

There are two forms of pyramid scheme: one is a scam, the other is likely to lose you money but is not illegal. With the scam, the company is completely aware that its product or service cannot produce the advertised returns. Sometimes known as a Ponzi scheme, it is illegal, but continues to entice investors to sign up with the same unfounded promises. Each time a new investor joins, new money is brought in that goes to pay off previous investors and generate a commission for the directors. When the pool of new investors dries up, the pyramid becomes unstable. Hence, someone is not going to get paid. At this point, the directors collect their cuts and take a plane trip to the Bahamas.

The more legitimate form is where the company appoints agents to sell a product and introduce more agents. Each time, a commission is generated and passes to the top of the pyramid. In reality, the product is not what the company is selling; it's selling agencies. Anything an agent sells, from water filters to pet insurance, is extra commission for the directors.

Take the case of Dan Furnley, who decided to invest in ostrich farming. 'For £12,000 you too can be the proud owner of an ostrich,' said the advertising literature the company sent. It went on to state how, after the breeding season a few months later: 'Your ostrich could produce up to forty chicks, which at current market prices can each be sold for £500.' The company behind the scheme, the Ostrich Farming Corporation, also guaranteed an annual 50 percent return, and even promised to buy back the chicks if other buyers couldn't be found. 'Don't forget,' said OFC, 'the demand for ostriches is about to soar as consumers discover ostrich meat.'

Sounds too good to be true? The British Department of Trade and Industry thought so too after receiving complaints from a number of disgruntled British investors. After investigating, the DTI concluded: 'Pigs or ostriches might fly!' It wasn't so much that it was unhappy about ostrich farming, but based on its knowledge of the market in legitimate ostrich farming, the DTI believed that the only way OFC could honor its claims was by selling more ostriches to more investors rather than through the returns generated from the ostriches themselves.

Eventually, OFC was shut down, but not before Dan Furnley and a great many investors eager to make a fast profit had ploughed hundreds of thousands of pounds into the scheme.

As Dan later explained when he spoke to his accountant about the loss he'd made, 'The problem is, it's so easy to believe you're going to make money from these types of investment. All you have to do is make a one-off payment and sit back as your ostrich starts to produce valuable chicks.'

But it wasn't just the prospect of tiny ostrich feet that was the attraction. As an added incentive, when the opportunity to present new investors to the company comes along, you get to take a commission to sweeten the pot. And as each of your recruits brings in more investors, you even get commission on their commission and onwards down the line. It's like a chain letter with a little gift to you each time the letter is forwarded.

These are the classic methods by which pyramids operate. A little psychological reinforcement to reward good performance, while an increasing commitment spurs you on to work even harder. The work you're doing may actually be out of proportion to your profit from the scheme, but once you're hooked into that cycle of behavior, it's incredibly difficult to break free. Investors will even justify their actions to themselves and others. For example: 'I'm not yet working hard enough to gain the full profit as others higher up the pyramid' or 'I just need better sales leads,' and so on.

Eventually, the number of new investors increases dramatically, with each level passing money back up to the top of the pyramid. Those sitting there have to do very little work and have their own personal goldmine, while those further down have to work harder to gain any return whatsoever.

Ponzi schemes – alive and doing very well!

Paying off earlier investors with funds received from later investors is not illegal in all parts of the world, and traps for the unwary investor abound. No more so is this true than in the fledgling capitalist economy of Russia, where the financial services industry is still in its infancy and there's a ready pool of financially uneducated individuals.

The MMM Fund was started by Sergei Mavrodi, a former mathematician. Its stock was not traded on any exchange, instead it made a market in its own stock with the price set by Mavrodi. MMM promoted itself to ordinary Russians with slick TV advertising and guaranteed an annual return of 3000 percent! Speculative investors were positively drooling with greed at the prospect of that level of profit. Within six months, MMM had over five million shareholders and its stock price had risen from $1 to $60.

Without any real assets – or an infinite supply of gullible speculators – MMM was eventually no longer able to draw sufficient numbers of individuals to fund the continued buy-back of stock. It was this procedure that kept bolstering the stock price. The pyramid became unstable and MMM's price smashed to the ground, leveling at 46 cents.

Mavrodi eluded prosecution on charges of tax evasion for the second time, not just because Russia has no law against Ponzi schemes but because he gained a parliamentary seat, which gave him immunity from prosecution. As an interesting aside, the seat had become available because the previous member had been shot.

No one can deny that Mavrodi is a colorful character and perhaps it's a sneaking admiration that lies at the root of people's perception of him. Without doubt, those investors who got burned gave some extraordinary justifications for maintaining their acceptance of his actions. Few seemed to blame him outright. 'It was government officials who'd brought him down,' was one prevailing view. In the new capitalist climate, Mavrodi had become something of a folk hero. Even more puzzling was that the episode didn't dissuade new investors from buying MMM stock after it had crashed. In terrible weather, one young woman stood in line to invest her money and explained her reason for being there: 'I know it's a pyramid scheme but the stock is cheap now and might go up again.'

Hope, foolhardiness, self-delusion, or simply the belief that they were just unlucky compared to those who got out before fear and panic sent the stock price plummeting – whatever the reason these investors believed they had for placing their money in the scheme, they were all manipulated and became part of the bubble. And those who start such bubbles are always looking for better ways to capitalize on investors' propensity for greed.

Sell and store – schemers who possess may leave you in a mess

One way to make schemes work better is when investors have less contact with the product or asset. There is far less responsibility involved. Furthermore, investments such as ostriches require a certain amount of care, which most investors can't provide. What speculative investors want is for the money to come without expending any effort at all. So where there's a demand for a particular kind of product, someone will supply the solution.

With amazing regularity, investors get caught in sell and store schemes. These schemes often use the storage of metals as their investment. Metals don't require feeding or cleaning, just a place to stay!

One such scheme was brought to my attention by a client of mine, Lyndsay Marc. Seated in my office, obviously annoyed and upset, Lyndsay related how she'd found out that morning that the company with which she'd invested in titanium bars had disappeared from the face of the earth leaving a trail of debts behind.

'And titanium is so good,' she was saying, 'it's used in surgical hip replacements and even in golf clubs too. Did you know that?'

I did, as it happened. There had been a mini run on titanium recently and the only reason anyone could find was that golf club makers were using more of the stuff. Titanium has particular qualities that make it useful, such as being light and not being prone to rust. 'How many bars did you buy?' I asked.

'Fifty. And I've got the certificates to prove it.' She added quickly: 'Not as many as some of the people who introduced me to this investment.'

'So it's a few hundred dollars you've lost then?' I asked gently, hoping that things weren't so bad after all and I'd be able to smooth things over for her a bit.

'More like $10,000, you mean!'

I suspected what had happened but didn't want say anything without checking my facts. 'Let me make a call,' I said.

Three minutes later my fears were borne out. Lyndsay had put $10,000 into a metal that, although useful, is not as rare as Regency Titanium's marketing had suggested. It also transpired that the directors had skipped the country but left a warehouse full of titanium. That's one of the drawbacks for the conmen; to start their con again elsewhere, they have to buy fresh as it's too difficult to transport the metal.

Nevertheless, the titanium was worth nowhere near what Lyndsay had paid. Each bar was worth approximately $7.50. Her $10,000 was in an investment worth a total of $375. And that's all she ever saw of it again.

Pump and dump – it isn't just weightlifters who pump any old iron

Small-scale manipulations of bubble markets happen in every conceivable asset. The profits are high for very little work and unscrupulous brokers often lie behind the scam. By working together in a ring and cold-calling potential and former clients, the price of an obscure stock is bid up. But these investors end up with a lemon. When the selling stops, there is nothing supporting the price and down it falls. Hence the stock is said to be pumped to a new price level and then dumped with the investor.

This procedure has been around for a long time in various forms, even before the salesperson's 'art' was honed for the telephone. For example, during the 1920s the scam was carried out with *pools*. A ring buys a large number of shares but before selling to the public, the stock is traded between the members. With an ally on the trading floor, precise information was fed back to the pool members on tickertape price levels. Commonly known as *wash sales* because the illusion of activity was produced, when the price reached the level the pool wanted, the stock was sold to the public. Quietly at first and then more rapidly, in increasing block trades, the effect was to inflate the speculative bubble. By the time the bubble collapsed and unhappy investors were left with all the worthless stock, the pool had taken its profit.

More recently, inflating the speculative bubble has been taken to a new level with the promotion of *chop stocks*. The name refers to the spread between the price that a brokerage house pays for the stock –

usually a micro capitalization, secondary market stock – and the price at which it is sold to the unwary investor. The fraud occurs when these prices bear no relationship to each other. Electronic quotes are a simple fabrication. These stocks are often obtained by the *chop shops* from corporate insiders or through offshore accounts for pennies. Although they may not be allowed to be legally traded, for example the stock is meant to be held for a specific length of time, the restriction is broken. Investors are duped into buying stocks at highly inflated prices and remain in darkness about what's happened until they try to sell. At this point, the broker tries to dissuade you or may even offer you another hot stock to make up your loss – assuming that they haven't gone out of business and the directors haven't been arrested.

According to recent findings, the scale of this fraud in the US is vast. It is estimated that these over-the-counter trades are a $10 billion a year enterprise. A range of middlemen and promoters are involved driving corporate networks with thousands of cold-calling salespeople inflating the stock bubble. Although many are unwitting participants, oiling the wheels all the way to the top are kickbacks and bribes, where corporate officials, consultants, brokers and underworld figures, all take a slice of the pie.

Why do investors get caught?

Let's now have a closer look at some of the reasons that lie behind a tendency to be gullible, and why it's so easy to get sucked in and hand your money over to a poor investment – or someone – when there's little chance of ever seeing it again, let alone making a profit. Some of these reasons are internal and some are prompted from an outside source. Nevertheless, it's *you* who acts. So think of each of these reasons as a step in your mind; the more steps you climb, the greater your gullibility (Figure 17).

It's tempting

Speculation answers a need within you. You want money and to be successful and this appears to be the way to get it. And so easy too. Just put

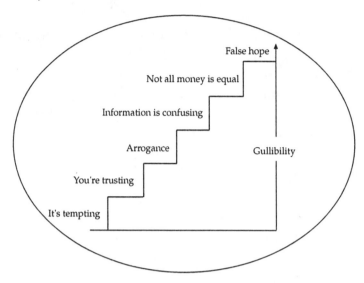

Figure 17 *The psychonomic components of gullibility*

your money into this investment for a while and the profit will be yours. No downside. You can be up there with the big players, you tell yourself.

But you don't see the pitfalls. Your desire and greed are clouding your good judgment. If you stopped for a moment and thought about it rationally, you'd realize that there are many reasons for your chances of success being minimal; most importantly, there is always a downside, however slight.

You trust professionals

Enter the salesperson from a reputable insurance company who tells you that you should relinquish your occupational pension in favor of the one he recommends. Would you trust him? A great many people in the UK found themselves in this situation. They trusted the advice they received and inadvertently found themselves being sold unacceptable products, often by poorly trained agents. The result was one of the biggest fiascos in pensions misselling in recent years, with several of the biggest financial institutions, such as Sun Life of Canada, being reprimanded and fined.

It is OK to follow professional advice, but that doesn't mean that you relinquish all responsibility to check things out before you sign on the dotted line.

☞ Carelessness

It would be carelessness if you failed to assess fundamentals rationally before investing, believing solely in your adviser's trustworthiness. Apart from the few hiccups that hit the headlines when a financial adviser skips the country taking with them their former clients' money, the vast majority of advisers are highly professional individuals and are not out to make you a loss. But what they rely on are proven approaches. For example, you've seen in Chapter 2 how a passive strategy to buying the index can produce a good return over a long-term period. The danger is that by virtue of the strength of the approach, the fund manager is inadvertently gullible, because all they have to do is buy the index spread – they themselves are following the herd. As a result, they may fail to look at the fundamentals of individual stocks and whether they make sound financial sense in the overall portfolio strategy.

At this point, investors can easily believe that the price of one stock in the fund is as good as any other – they are simply constituents. This leads to the false belief that the market is never overvalued. But when stock prices need to be revalued the potential for mistiming trades increases, as it is easier to enter the market at the wrong point in its cycle.

Under these circumstances, a decision to trade is based solely on the adviser's instructions or, as frequently happens when the market nears its top, the sheer abundance of ads for funds that appear in the press. In the short term, this type of gullibility can lead to poor investment returns and, on a wider scale, to the emergence of bubbles.

☞ You fail to be critical

Suppose that you're presented with three numbers, such as 2, 4 and 6, and asked to find the rule they conform to by generating three-number sequences. You can do as many trials as you need and at each stage the experimenter provides feedback by classifying your trials as either conforming or not conforming to the solution. What types of number sequence would you generate?

In this case, the pattern is simple enough and a rule would relate to ascending even numbers, which is precisely what the researchers who conducted this experiment expected. However, what they were also looking for was the ability of subjects to falsify the mental hypothesis underlying the rule they formed. Information must be subject to test without an attitude of conviction before you start. So to test the rule, it's also necessary to attempt to disconfirm it; which, in this instance, is done by generating odd numbers – such as 3, 5 and 7 – to see if the rule holds. Few of the subjects who took part in the experiment showed evidence of having gone this far, and therefore they could only confirm the rule they generated but never falsify it.

Similarly, many investors are unlikely to seek to disconfirm their own beliefs by implementing a more rational rule or tactic. It's another example of the illusion of validity that you saw in Chapter 4, where, once investors already accept an intuitive belief as correct, they have great difficulty in altering their mindset.

Investors may also fail to be critical because they actively seek out information that substantiates their financial attitudes, biases or strategies. As a result, they trust information they receive from both bona fide and dubious sources simply because it appears to be valid, but they haven't actually tested it by attempting to disconfirm it and see under what conditions it doesn't hold true. This leads to many investors' tendency to plough into gold or other commodities where false intuition tells them that there's an opportunity and a salesperson confirms their belief.

Of course, if investors have a vested interest in maintaining their viewpoint because they've already taken a market position, then it's unlikely that they'll try to disconfirm new information. As far as they're concerned, if the market's rising, it will continue to rise – or if the market's falling, it will continue to fall. A failure to be critical and a tendency to overreact to information are once again the result of trusting those experts or marketing procedures that add support to firmly held intuitive beliefs. Everything else is ignored. Rarely, under these circumstances, do investors consider that there are trustworthy sources of disconfirming information. After all, that's like pouring cold water on their confidence and abilities – even though it would lead them to reevaluate their position and be more critical of the advice they're getting.

☞ *You forget that everyone else has their own priorities*

Even when you're dealing with reputable financial companies or individuals, you can still be too trusting. Figure 18 shows how what is most important for you may be least important for others who hold their own particular interests paramount, and vice versa. Each level is a statement that might reflect your priority, but that is the opposite to the priority of the financial company.

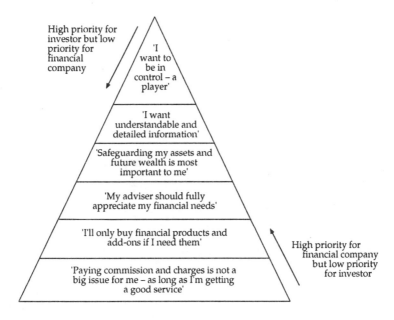

Figure 18 *Everyone has their own priorities*

Arrogance

There are some investors who know full well that they have limited ability to pick good stocks but, strangely, these same investors can believe that they're very good at picking people who are good at picking stocks. If you've ever been to a very boring party where you've been buttonholed by someone who wants to tell you about this great adviser they've got who's making them a packet, then you'll know what I mean.

This arrogance is a result of people believing that they're good judges of character. Although some are, in reality most people look primarily at superficial characteristics such as appearance.

Imagine that you're taking part in an experiment where you're asked to look at pictures of several young men and women and rate them according to whether you think the person is 'nice' or 'not nice'. How do you think you'd react? What psychologists have found is that most people associate the pictures of the better-looking people with not only being nicer, but with a range of other positive characteristics such as being a good student, being kind, trustworthy, reliable and so on.

On this basis, many investors choose an adviser or listen to expert opinion for all the wrong reasons. As a consequence, you can be more easily led into particular deals, parting with your money or following a fashion.

☞ You can handle it

Like someone who says that they can give up smoking any time they want to and are in control, you believe you'll get out when the right moment presents itself. You're not going to follow the herd – you're far too clever for that – you're just going to use it. Sometimes known as the *greater fool theory*, the belief is that everyone else, except you, is acting irrationally. Because of that, there will continue to be support for the bubble as other speculators will keep pushing the price ever higher. And when the tide turns, because you're rational, you'll be able to see the warning signs. The question is, could you really move that quickly? Or is it more likely that you won't notice the signs when they appear and you'll continue to believe that you can squeeze another drop of profit out of the investment?

☞ It appears authentic

The guy in the bar asks whether you want to buy this amazing offer. You may swallow his sales patter and consider his wares, but the chances are – if your head is screwed on your shoulders correctly – you have a pretty good idea that it's not what it seems and that what he's selling probably won't work.

However, many speculative investments are far more enticing than an offer that fell off the back of a truck and there is often a highly efficient business enterprise behind the scheme. Good marketing and advertising are used to influence you, usually in quality financial newspapers and magazines.

A few years ago a friend of mine, Len, showed me an ad offering 18.5 percent return a year. It was a colorful and evocative ad depicting a seventeenth-century galleon sailing the high seas against a gently fading orange sunset. Details of how to invest and where to send the check were printed below. The idea was to invest in transport containers, the type that can be transferred from cargo ship to articulated rig. There were containers of several sizes to suit a variety of pockets. And when the containers were not being used they were stored in warehouses.

I explained to Len that I thought it strange that they were offering a rate of return about 11 points higher than that available in local banks and that alone would make me wary. Certainly, if they were capable of making this type of return on containers, why didn't the company use them themselves?

Len wasn't convinced and said he was putting $6000 into it the following day, the price of the smallest container size. I tried one more argument to dissuade him and asked, 'What exactly do you know about the container industry?'

'As much as anybody else,' said Len with indignation, 'and look at that interest rate they're offering.'

I thought that the conversation had covered this area already and I didn't seem to be making any headway getting my message across. So, I let it alone.

Four months later, I met Len at a party. He looked somewhat disheveled with his hair untidy and two large brown stains on the middle of his tie. 'You were right,' he said, downing a large whisky in one swallow. 'That container company went under. Lost everything. I should have listened when you tried to tell me.'

If it sounds too good to be true, it probably is. The unfortunate fact is that unless the advertiser is known to be involved in criminal activity, there is little legal reason to stop them from attracting you with their slick copy. As a result, you're on your own.

Information can be purposely confusing

Why make information confusing? Because if it were simple, investors would be able to work out whether it made good financial sense. Call me a cynic, but there are examples in many product brochures and ads that appear to deny the existence of understandable, plain language. The result is that potential investors assume that because they cannot understand the information, it must be due to their lack of intelligence.

At this point it becomes far easier to believe that the experts know more than you. So your tendency to believe the product literature, or what you're told, increases. Figure 19 is an example based on ads that have appeared in the *Financial Times*. On the face of it, it seems to be an acceptable ad. But consider how much useful information you're really getting, what is confusing, and what you still need to find out before investing any money.

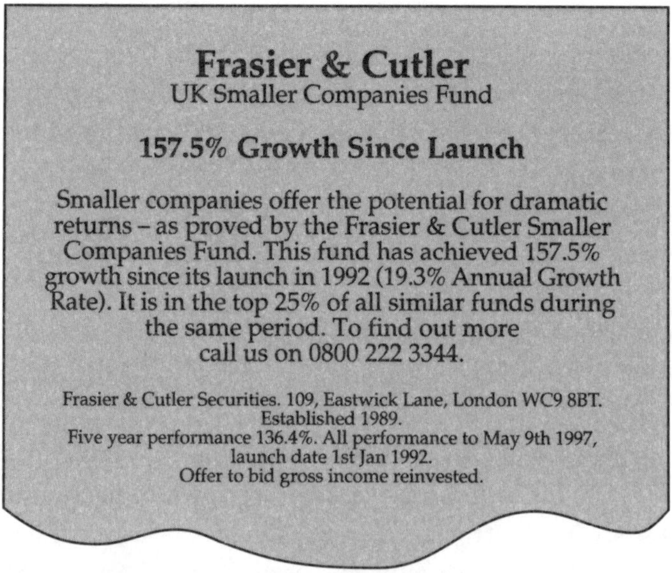

Frasier & Cutler
UK Smaller Companies Fund

157.5% Growth Since Launch

Smaller companies offer the potential for dramatic returns – as proved by the Frasier & Cutler Smaller Companies Fund. This fund has achieved 157.5% growth since its launch in 1992 (19.3% Annual Growth Rate). It is in the top 25% of all similar funds during the same period. To find out more call us on 0800 222 3344.

Frasier & Cutler Securities. 109, Eastwick Lane, London WC9 8BT. Established 1989.
Five year performance 136.4%. All performance to May 9th 1997, launch date 1st Jan 1992.
Offer to bid gross income reinvested.

Figure 19 *Is this a straightforward advertisement?*

What you are seeing here is the common ploy of aggregating the growth over several years so that it looks higher than it is and then inflating it further by showing the final figure based on income reinvested. The trouble is that you end up with several growth figures in the same ad, and you never quite know what the real figure is.

Furthermore, unless you check it out, you don't know what the performance has been for a particular year where the manager may have done quite poorly or how they have performed relative to the market index.

☞ *Lack of confidence*

In the case of bubbles, there can be so many conflicting news reports and media pundits predicting prospects that you don't know who's correct any more. Like you saw in Chapter 6, you believe other investors, who form the majority, must know more than you, so they must be right if they're trading in or out of the market. At times like these, when market information is highly confusing, carefully formulated strategies can easily get forgotten. As a result, not having confidence in your decision-making ability, you subdue your rational thinking processes and follow an 'expert' or the actions of everyone else.

The way to overcome this is to realize that your investment success is largely dependent on you – not on experts, pundits or dramatic stories – and the decisions you make as well as the approach you stick to.

You value some of your money less than other money

Money that you've previously made on an investment or inherited is not thought of as highly as money that you've worked for. This is another example of *found money*, where it has less of an emotional connection to you and is more easily used to fund speculative investments. So the more of this money you have, the more of it you're likely to use. For this reason, large sums of money can be placed in the most outlandish speculations, and often this is done without the intense fear of how you'd manage if it were all lost.

☞ *You confuse amounts of money with buying power*

Because money has a physical or electronic reality – you can touch cash or a check or see its presence as numbers on a computer screen

– it is easier to focus on. The true reality, however, is that the money is only worth what you can do with it and its value can shrink over time.

Locking yourself into a five-year investment paying 6.5 percent, for example, may only be good initially. As the years go by, with inflation at, say, 3 percent, its real value is whittled away so that at the end of the term your buying power has been reduced. This is also known as *money illusion,* because investors imagine that they are wealthier – or will be wealthier – than they are. For many people the concept of real value is hard to grasp.

This effect displays itself when buying any type of asset such as property, bonds, equities or CDs, where investors imagine that they're in a safe investment that will continue to provide a good return.

Take the case of Bert and Jennifer Hampton, who decided to invest $10,000 of their savings. They didn't like the volatility of stocks and wanted something safe. 'Government bonds are what you need,' said the financial adviser at their local bank. Bonds seemed a good prospect, paying 7 percent a year till maturity in 20 years.

But then Bert and Jennifer did some research and looked more closely at what they were proposing to do. The bonds could produce a maximum return of $40,000. Stocks, it seemed, were likely to provide a higher return, in the region of 12 percent a year, and produce a total return of $109,000. Then there was inflation. Bert and Jennifer did a bit more research and decided that the economic outlook was reasonably good and that 4 percent a year seemed like an average ballpark figure for the foreseeable future. They worked out that by 2017, they would have the equivalent in today's buying power of $18,000 if they bought bonds. But with stocks they would have the equivalent of $49,000, a much more substantial amount. After a lengthy discussion, Bert and Jennifer decided to find out more about the prospects for stocks and how safe they really were.

What they found was that, taking a long-term view over several years, stocks were likely to perform better than bonds. In the end, Bert and Jennifer decided that as the $10,000 was 'spare' cash – they already had pensions and insurance – and they wouldn't need to touch it for the foreseeable future, they could afford to live with some risk and go for a portfolio of quality blue-chip stocks.

Money illusion also applies when investors fail to take into account transaction costs, which can actually wipe out any gains. Commission charges, where there is front loading, are often ignored. In these instances, the charges are levied at the beginning of the investment period and can sometimes reduce the fund size to below the amount invested.

False hope

Many investors treat the markets as one big casino. To them, trades are just like a gamble. And like the gambler who is drawn back to the tables time after time, there is the thrill of winning and the hint of danger.

For anyone who has a gambling mentality, there is often some deeper underlying reason for behaving as they do – they could be trying to prove something to themselves or they may gain a warped sense of pleasure when they know that their money can be lost in an instant if the deal turns sour.

Such investors will state that they're looking for that one special deal that's really going to put them on top. That is their hope and their dream. But they get caught up in one speculation after another and lose ever-larger amounts of their personal funds. Furthermore, trading may be undertaken too frequently and at the wrong times. These individuals don't see themselves as gullible, but they can be influenced by any investment, speculation or gamble that answers their psychological need.

Table 19 gives a few examples of how you might react if you're in this position.

Table 19 *When you behave with false hope*

❐ You concentrate on the profit you'll make rather than the likelihood of achieving it.

❐ You fail to realize how, over time, losses mount up.

❐ Each speculation is considered a small loss at worst and potentially highly profitable at best.

❐ Whenever you speculate and lose, but know that others have gained, you justify it as nearly getting it right, rather than accepting you got it wrong.

❏ You're frustrated that you only nearly got it right, which reinforces your belief in your ability and that you'll get it right next time.

❏ Your few subsequent successes, a result of luck more than anything else, are an extra strong reinforcer for further speculation.

Buying on margin or borrowing money to fund the speculation is far more likely under these circumstances. At the extreme, when there are losses, money is taken from one source to cover yourself. But your memory is short and you're soon involved again in the same type of risky speculation.

The result is that bubbles, slick-tongued salespeople or a false belief in your investment prowess exert a strong influence. Hence, it's easy to end up in the most risky types of trades, such as derivatives and commodities, without a full understanding of how these financial instruments work. Even demonstrating that the amount of loss you've taken far exceeds any rational form of investment falls on deaf ears. You are single-minded in your approach and your investment is driven by false hope alone.

What type of trade are you making?

Assuming that you're a rational person, what makes you potentially gullible is a lack of knowledge. Moreover, when you're confronted with a range of possible investment opportunities, human nature being what it is, it's difficult to decide which is best. In Chapter 6, you saw in some detail how choice conflict works. But that's when all the alternatives may have something of value to offer. The choice is made harder when you can't distinguish between good opportunities for profit and bad opportunities that are certain to lose money. In essence, you can't tell the difference between an investment, a speculation and a gamble.

Investments, speculations and gambles

At the heart of this dilemma is being able to determine whether what you're attracted to really is an investment with a fundamentally sound base, where you have control over what happens to your money. Or is there someone else pulling the strings and you are simply dancing to their tune, your personal biases being played while you jump on the bandwagon as the market soars to a new height? It's vital that you understand what type of investment you're taking on and from what standpoint you're approaching it. If you have a good financial approach and your money is going into a good investment, there is a high chance that you'll succeed. But if you're a speculator or a gambler, you're more likely to lose your money.

Another way to think about your approach is to imagine you're a child in a candy store, confronted with a multitude of jars of colored candies and brightly wrapped chocolates. They all glitter in front of your eyes in never-ending rows stacked high to the ceiling. But which ones are going to taste the best?

Out of the hundreds of ordinary candies to choose from, there are reputed to be three that taste 'out of this world'. Those are the ones you want. And just to complicate matters, the other children in the neighborhood are all lined up to enter the store as well. You only have five minutes to decide what you're going to take before the next 'taster' comes in after you.

How would you proceed? Let's look at it from various angles.

The gambler tries tasting all the candies in no particular order. She crams her mouth full of candies until she's fit to burst. After a couple of minutes, she can't even differentiate the tastes, let alone decide if she likes them. It's a matter of pure luck whether she ends up with the prized candies.

The speculator's approach is to attempt to get into the store just as the previous child is leaving so that he can see what's being taken out. He makes a mental note and then rushes into the store and heads straight for the same types of candies and chocolates, dismissing all the rest. When he comes out, he even tells his friends that he got the good candies – but did he? Only the storekeeper knows for sure.

The investor listens to what all the other children are saying. The weight of opinion, when she asks her friends what they think, suggests that candies with gold and red striped bands are the prized ones. There's certainly a lot of them being carried out. But this child wants to make sure because one thing puzzles her: if these candies are so good, why haven't the children who've brought them out eaten them all up? She enters the store and asks the storekeeper if all the candies are on display. 'They are now,' says the storekeeper, lifting out a large jar from behind the counter.

Dipping her hand into the jar, the investor takes a candy, unwraps it and puts it into her mouth – she has never tasted a candy so delicious.

While there is always some risk associated with any investment, it doesn't mean that you're gambling. There is a big difference between putting your money into a sound and fully researched investment where you make less profit than you'd hoped for – or some of its value is lost as the price drops – and placing your money on the 4.30 at the local horse races. That is a gamble.

When 'investments' go wrong

You're irrational and get sucked in

Look at the following list and consider whether you're thinking or acting in any of these ways. The more you are, the more you're speculating; at the extreme, you're gambling.

- ❏ You put money into a scheme but don't really understand how it works.
- ❏ You're dazzled by the fantastic returns shown in a scheme's brochure and rush to send off a check.
- ❏ You believe the salesperson when they say you'll never have to work again.
- ❏ You pick your investments by throwing darts at investment listings or by astrological forecasting.
- ❏ You give your money to an individual or company without checking out their performance or reputation.
- ❏ You know you can lose everything if the deal goes wrong but go ahead anyway.
- ❏ You just need one hot tip to make you rich – and this is the one.
- ❏ You've repeatedly lost money in the past but keep getting drawn back to the same types of scheme.

❑ Win or lose, you never listen to useful advice that would make you stop and think.

❑ You put money into schemes when that money should have been used for your or your family's future.

You're rational but the 'investment' is a gamble

Speculation, gambling and investment don't just apply to the mentality of the individual, but to the scheme or investment itself – the candy. What is the likelihood of the candy going sour? As you've previously seen, risk can be evaluated and with equities you would look at such things as:

❑ the company's ability to pay a dividend – the dividend cover

❑ the amount of debt the company has

❑ whether the company's trading is in safe markets or its trading outlook is uncertain.

Apply these measures carefully and consistently and you'll be on far safer ground. Remember, if the risk is too speculative or it's a gamble, walk away.

When you're assessing a financial opportunity that's offered to you and aren't sure exactly what form it is, Table 20 lists several pointers you can consider.

Table 20 *Investment, speculation or gamble?*

❑ When a gamble goes wrong, you lose all your money. When an investment or speculation goes wrong, you can often recover some of your money.

❑ The greater the risk, the greater the speculation. Ask yourself whether the investment makes financial sense.

❑ Always check out the details. If someone's trying to sell you an 'investment', it's likely to be speculative.

❑ Know what your level of profit is likely to be.

❑ There's no such thing as a speculation – and definitely not a gamble – that gives a 'guaranteed' return; there is with a proper investment.

☐ Make sure that your money is being handled by a reputable and reliable financial institution with a good track record.

☐ Risk is maximum with a gamble and, like on the turn of a card, money can be lost in one go. With good investments – and some speculations – any loss can be staggered, taking months or years to materialize.

☐ Remember that investment requires patience.

☐ Consider if you're buying because everyone else is buying or for your own reasons.

☐ Use benchmark rates. If you find an 'investment' with a much higher rate than is generally available, ask yourself if it's feasible.

Gullibility leads to strange bedfellows

If you have a reduced sense of financial realism, it's more likely that you will cast about looking for some method that will give you control over your actions. It's a perception where you fail to take responsibility for the development of your own investment skills. Someone has the secret, you believe, and it's a question of getting it – that will give you the edge you seek. Your past failures weren't your fault because there was some overpowering phenomenon that you couldn't possibly understand. As far as you're concerned, it just wasn't on the cards. Your losses were out of your hands. Investors, therefore, often turn to fringe approaches such as astrology or seek advice from gurus.

Astrology

As the stars and planets travel at different speeds through their orbits, they form different angles with each other and the Earth and a cycle is produced. It is the relative positions of these bodies at important moments, such as birth, that is the basis of astrological prediction.

Leaving aside individual horoscopes, birth can also apply to the starting of a company and on a wider scale to the birth of nations, such as at the time of the Declaration of Independence when the United States came into existence. On this basis, the fate of the US could be forecasted. Most serious astrologers, however, are more concerned with predicting trends than forecasting specific events; hence, the application of astrology to market movements and, though many financial companies will rarely admit to it, the use of astrological prediction in addition to scientifically based statistical models.

Is there any validity in it? Astrology is certainly one of the oldest 'sciences', dating back to ancient times. But the problem is that although there is often some part of an astrological forecast that appears to account for real occurrences when they happen in the future, statistical studies suggest that there is no real effect. Chance alone accounts for what happens.

Moreover, at the heart of astrology is the assumption that certain events are predetermined. The thinking is that it's 'written in the stars'. This negates human beings' ability to use free will and choose their actions on the basis of rational thought and analysis. Yet human actions do affect this earthly realm according to personal desires, needs and attitudes. The world may not be as destiny intended.

It is this intrinsic variation in human behavior that underlies the workings of financial markets; some of the financial and psychological rules we understand and some we are still learning about – which is a reason for this book. And although the behavior is explainable, it is not preordained. Furthermore, if you get ripped off in a bad deal, the desires of the fraudster and any tendency you have to be gullible are far more likely to be the cause than is any heavenly formation.

Another important point to keep in mind is that the more people there are who believe in this type of forecasting and make investment decisions as a result – however irrational their decisions may be – the more it becomes a self-fulfilling prophesy. Consequently, prices can be pushed up and the approach draws further adherents. But it isn't astrology at work here, simply normal market operation, which is buying or selling pressures and supply and demand.

This isn't to say that planetary configurations don't exert some physical force on the natural world; after all, gravity is caused by stellar bodies. But to extrapolate the effect to account for company performance and the swings of financial markets is an enormous leap and would be folly in the extreme.

Gurus

Confronted with the confusing and seemingly inexplicable nature of financial market events, many investors seek out individuals who are believed to have some extra insight. Seminars costing anything between hundreds and thousands of dollars cater to this desire and are readily attended by novice investors. Yet in their rush to find answers from the gurus, investors often forget that making a lot of money takes work and personal commitment.

Many seminar gurus stress how easy it is to be a financial whizz in the markets by making you believe that all you need is the desire to be rich. They access your greed and minimize the risks involved in speculative investment by placing you in an audience of other people who are all similarly inclined. But think rationally. Who's really going to get rich? You, or the company to whom you've paid thousands of dollars for the seminar?

Perhaps it's the tensions in the way we live that make us search out ready solutions from the archetypal guru who sits on the top of the mountain contemplating the universe. Whatever the reason, it answers a psychological need and there are an awful lot of people out there who want to be acolytes.

There are some very good experts giving advice and seminars on a variety of investment topics. In order to sift out the best ones, here are a few things to consider before you put your hand in your pocket to speculate.

Assessing the gurus

- ❒ Be realistic – you don't become a millionaire overnight or even in a few months (unless you're really lucky and win the lottery!).
- ❒ Consider whether you're being fed the idea that speculation (or gambling) is the way to wealth. How much risk is associated with what you're doing?
- ❒ Does the guru's talk have real content or is it just a barrage of stimulating buzzwords to increase your greed?
- ❒ If you're at a seminar, stop and ask yourself if the vibes from other

people are fueling a belief within you that this really is a simple way to make money.

❑ Don't be coerced into financing trades by borrowing.

❑ Do the advertised projected returns make rational sense? How many stock market miracles offering 300 percent are there likely to be?

❑ Ask yourself whether what you're advised to buy has intrinsic worth or whether it's intrinsically pretty worthless.

❑ Remember, it takes work to learn the techniques of good-quality investment, but you have to do it (or you can seek out the expertise of reputable advisers).

❑ Look at the guru's track record.

❑ How much is it costing you to learn from the guru?

❑ Has there any previous legal action against the guru?

❑ Who is Rick from Ripoffsville? Are the endorsements genuine or a marketing ploy?

Following homespun gurus

What about taking the advice of investors who are just like you?

Over the last few years, the Beardstown Ladies Investment Club has become something of a media sensation, with loads of investors avidly following their advice. There's also something rather quaint about imagining several little old ladies sitting around a backroom table in a bar down in Beardstown, Illinois, discussing high finance and hatching their latest dawn raid on Wall Street. And, according to their bestselling book, they've done exceedingly well, with an annualized return between 1984 and 1993 of 23.4 percent.

Figures recently released by Price Waterhouse auditors put a rather different slant on things, however. It seems that the Beardstown Ladies had overstated their performance slightly and only made an annualized 9.4 percent. During the same period, the S&P 500 had risen over 14 percent per year. The ladies have got an explanation, in fact they have two: they use a different method of calculation; and more recently, there was a computer error of which they weren't aware when the figures were inputted! Of course. That makes sense! It's all a pity really, because I was rooting for them. It would have been strangely satisfying to find that a group of daring, elderly ladies can take on seasoned professionals at their own game and win.

Clubbing, the investment way

Notwithstanding the Beardstown Ladies' performance, should you join an investment club? That's safer, surely, than following gurus. You'll make a few bucks and you'll get to make a lot of friends along the way.

In fact, investment clubs are an excellent way of learning about investment in the stock market. But, just as you need your wits about you when you assess any approach or scheme – or hear homespun recommendations from club members who've been heavily hyped by a media looking for a ratings boost – so, too, do you need to maintain your financial realism when you invest in a club alongside other people.

You cannot afford to be excessively trusting of other people's motives – or their choices of investment. They all have personal reasons for becoming members of the club, whether it's friendship, a wish to show off their knowledge, a desire for great wealth, an eagerness to dominate others with their opinions, or even a repressed need to be a guru. These, arguably, are the greatest temptations, because an emotional tie to the group is formed over and above a straightforward common interest in investment. The investment club becomes the key reference group that informs your attitudes and behavior. Hence, while the whole process may be completely legitimate, once the factor of relationships enters the picture, very soon it's the dominant group opinion that matters more than an individual one. Eventually, this translates into how investment decisions are made.

In the long run, as the Beardstown Ladies have no doubt realized, they would have made more money investing in index funds together or even individually. But, of course, they wouldn't have had so much fun.

Becoming investment conscious

It's a sad fact that investors are continually falling into avoidable traps. They take bad advice, buy the wrong products, get caught up in schemes and follow the crowd as bubbles develop.

Even if it's not your fault that you lost money, reading the small print, watching out for charges and understanding sales tactics are practical steps that will protect you from the sharks out there. And, if you don't know or understand something when dealing with reputable companies, don't feel guilty about asking. If you can't get an understandable answer, then go somewhere else where you will. More importantly, before you hand over money to any type of speculation or investment, consider who's really going to benefit. 'Let the buyer beware' is the old storekeepers' saying, and it is just as true today with investment and financial services.

For whatever reason you may be gullible, successful investment requires that you take a good, long, hard look at the reasons behind your investment actions. You need to rely on yourself, not on any line that might be fed to you by good marketing, smooth-talking salespeople, or the latest media darling. In other words, don't be a sucker and don't let the fraudster's favorite motto – there's one born every minute – become a reality, with you as a stuffed and mounted trophy!

11

Think Money, Think Relationships

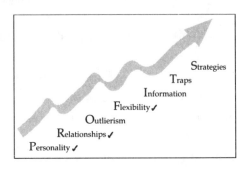

Strategies
Traps
Information
Flexibility ✓
Outlierism
Relationships ✓
Personality ✓

I T'S HUMAN NATURE TO MENTALLY COUNT YOUR FUTURE WEALTH EVEN before the ink is dry on the check you paid for your investment – after all, if you didn't think you were going to make a decent return, why bother investing in the first place? But to make investments by focusing on how much money you're going to make is only seeing part of the picture. In the same way, it's easy to come away from books like this and believe that by understanding your personality you'll gain all the insights into financial success that you're seeking.

What is vital is the ability to take a wider perspective and not center on one particular investment component while excluding others, because then you would miss the core idea. The common element running through many of the things I've talked about is that *relationships* are formed, altered or broken depending on how the investment proceeds.

And what an amazing range of relationships there are. You might deal with another solitary investor who you're matched up with through a broker or you may deal with millions of investors as the market pace hots up. At the same time, you may be influenced by your partner and any other key reference group that you're attached to. Underlying these relationships is the relationship between the varied parts of your own personality. All these external and internal relationships are a source of joy, greed, fear, panic and conflict. And all must be integrated or harmonized for the maximum possible gains.

Therein lies the crux of a psychonomic approach to profitable investing. Understand the relationships that promote investor behavior and market swings begin to make some sort of sense. It's about more than mere money, because investors don't just buy stocks, they buy a concept, an idea or a story – and they buy it from another investor or the company issuing the stock, who have their own stories, emotional needs and personal biases. These are complex interactions, constantly undergoing change.

From individual relationships to psychonomic prosperity

Any investor with an iota of sense will realize that to form a winning investment strategy in the face of this emotional and market onslaught is going to require some work. Yet the implications of psychonomics are far more wide ranging than accelerated personal success. Misguided motives may indeed cause investors to act purely for the money, but all things have value beyond an immediate financial return; not just the simple, weightless factors of an investment or a business, but value on which individuals, communities and societies depend. These are the ties that, through an interest in what other people are doing, don't merely bind individuals together but make life worth living in terms of future potential. Art, science and literature, as well as the maverick inventor or nonconformist thinker, make a society culturally rich.

Of course, it's important to make a decent investment return, but this should never destroy the creative spirit and the quality of our interactions with one another. Our relationships create true value. Consequently, underlying successful investment – as well as the truly contrarian perspective – is always the question: how is society going to benefit from this? And you only have to look at how fascinated people are by new technology to realize that many investors are thinking ahead. Those investors who are only considering how much short-term profit they're gong to make are usually the ones leading the speculative bubbles.

What is interesting is that if we center on money alone as the primary goal, then paradoxically we don't make as much as we'd hoped for. In *Making Democracy*, Robert Putnam looked at the relationships underlying economic performance from the point of view of social capital, focusing on communal identification and affiliations. What he found was that relatively high levels of social capital in northern Italy between the 1970s and 1980s were associated with strong economic growth, while relatively low levels of social capital in southern Italy were associated with poor economic growth. Besides the breadth of social connections and shared goals, trust is the other major component viewed as responsible for economic prosperity, and there has been a considerable amount of work in this field in recent years.

A number of international polling groups have joined forces to produce the World Values Index, a systematic measure of the extent to which people trust each other. These results are used to compare trust and economic wellbeing. As Stephen Knack of the American University and Phillip Keefer of the World Bank showed, there are various countries around the world that demonstrate how strong relationships create wealth. Although the cultural climate and pressures are vastly different – and may not be appropriate for all people in terms of international cross-fertilization of social and business practices – in these places individuals feel a greater connection to the system, have more incentive to invest and businesses feel greater security about their future. Norway and Switzerland, for example, foster high trust and have a high level of investment as a share of gross domestic product.

While we can't say for certain that high levels of social interaction don't come about as a result of economic prosperity, instead of the other way around, we can say that the web of relationships that form a healthy society are vital. In psychonomic terms, social, psychological and economic factors are connected. What we see, therefore, is that socially and culturally it is undoubtedly the case that non-financial wealth increases with the quality and extent of relationships. But if the economic assumption is also true – and, of course, it has a ring of obviousness about it – then the more interaction there is between people, the greater the likelihood there is of business, trade and investment opportunities developing; and, as a result, more chance of investment markets rising as economic prosperity increases.

Conversely, once these relationships break down, fail to be formed in the first place, or become skewed in some way, then it's likely to be because personal biases, self-delusions and susceptibility to a warped set of values are exerting their influence. For both corporate employees and investors, there is no longer any trust or feeling of obligation to the common good, which stops the exchange of information, ideas, creative involvement, financial incentives and investment opportunity. Under these circumstances, markets can only fall.

Towards investment success

Subjective evaluation, biases, personal desires, and relationships are fundamentally intertwined with rationality. How people and things are valued is affected, either directly or indirectly, by thinking and behavior. Ultimately, this affects business, companies and stock prices. Get the balance wrong and an assortment of emotional traps are produced, with effective forward planning becoming forgotten as the prime financial goal of easy riches or economic prosperity expands within individuals' mental horizons. At this point, all that's left is greed, fear and self-delusion at its most primitive level, where an investor or corporate leader thinks: 'I want what I want and I want it now! And I'll be damned if I'm going to let anything or anyone stand in my way!'

On the world stage, therefore, economies, markets and fashions all continue to interact and change. In parallel with this, within individuals' internal markets, attitudes and biases cause people to be enticed by personal desires and fantasies. All these forces are battling for supremacy in your outlook too. As a result, because many investors fail to appreciate their internal psychological relationships – in addition to external relationships governing market and economic behavior – high investment profits remain an elusive dream.

The key to success is to rise above what is happening. Panic is not an option. In each chapter of this book, some of the problems you might be faced with have been demonstrated to help you make a more balanced evaluation of investment opportunities and inform your decision making. Bearing in mind what I've said about successful investment being a mixture of objective and subjective assessment, and the need to harmonize the external market with your internal market, here are a few summarizing guidelines to keep you on the straight and narrow and help you achieve your financial goal.

Psychonomic guidelines for success

What you will have learned from Part One

☐ P.R.O.F.I.T.S. underlies psychonomics and means using your internal market in harmony with the external market. It incorporates Personality, Relationships, Outlierism, Flexibility, Information, Traps and Strategies.

☐ There's your personal rationality and there's the rationality of the markets. If the market's behaving crazily, you don't have to follow it.

☐ Active short-term trading is associated with higher volatility, risk and speculation.

☐ Short-term trading is not the same as long-term dealing and requires a different approach.

☐ Listen to experts but make your own mind up.

☐ Only go against the crowd for a good reason; don't be a contrarian for the sake of it.

☐ Only go with the crowd if you're going that way anyway.

☐ The market is cyclical – however long a bull or bear market lasts, it will change. If you have a fundamentally good investment, sit on it and wait.

☐ Don't be afraid to cut your losses – you'll be safeguarding your funds and will have gained experience.

☐ Remember that short-term investments are inherently more unstable than long-term ones. So if you're going to be a short-term investor, can you keep your head when you bounce on the bumps?

☐ Know your information sources and what they can provide for you – interpret and use the information wisely.

☐ Understand that short- and long-term investment horizons require different strategies.

☐ Don't fall in love with an investment.

☐ Don't let unfounded media stories dictate your investment choices.

☐ Remember that the ingredients of contrarianism are sound evaluation with only a dash of gut instinct – not the other way around.

☐ Stick to your strategy and don't be pushed, pulled or panicked into dealing.

☐ Assess overreaction objectively by fundamental valuation.

- ☐ Have confidence, be pragmatic, invest appropriately to your sleep factor and believe in your abilities.
- ☐ Ask yourself, from all possible angles, whether the investment is worthwhile for your needs.
- ☐ Keep your approach simple, straightforward and consistent.
- ☐ Don't overstay your welcome – know when you can't make any more profit from an investment and move on, before it begins to go into reverse.
- ☐ When the stock market is near or at its all-time high, and the media pundits are full of euphoria about how wonderful the markets are, that's the time to get out.
- ☐ Beware of hot tips – never plough into an investment without checking things out.

What you will have learned from Part Two

- ☐ Be ruled by your head, not your heart.
- ☐ Make time to assess your previous financial performance.
- ☐ Set clear investment goals.
- ☐ Remember that many aspects of your life situation are connected and that investment is only one of them.
- ☐ Start making changes in your financial situation with small investment steps, before you make bigger ones.
- ☐ Don't let conflicting emotions, unrealistic expectations or unresolved feelings dictate how you invest.
- ☐ Learn from experience – the bad as well as the good – so that the next time around, you'll do better than before.
- ☐ Rationality in investment is about keeping desires, biases and other personal characteristics balanced – not suppressed.
- ☐ Be flexible in your thinking and in your approach, so that you're receptive to opportunities when the market turns, if it's an appropriate course of action.
- ☐ Watch how successful investors apply rationality in their approach, but develop your own style.
- ☐ Be realistic about your perception of risk as well as the real risk of an investment.
- ☐ Patience in investing often pays dividends.

❑ Know your investment profile so that you can use a strategy that suits you best.

❑ Don't act on a whim – buy investments that you know something about.

❑ Never use borrowed funds for speculative investment and never, ever buy on margin if you can't cover it.

❑ Know what level of speculative risk you're taking on and decide whether you're comfortable with it.

❑ Don't let unscrupulous people manipulate your propensity for greed by dazzling you with glitz, or by making you believe that it's easy to become wealthy and that you can have it all if you follow their (expensive) advice.

❑ Remember that everyone has their own priorities that are not the same as yours.

❑ Don't let a trusting nature, arrogance or false hope make you gullible.

❑ Believe in your own abilities and not in fringe approaches.

❑ Don't follow the speculative bubble like a lemming – this only leads to the cliff edge.

❑ Remember, the stock market – and other bargains – will be there tomorrow. So don't buy just because everyone else is buying and you think there will be no more 'candy' for you! The barn door may close, but another one will open somewhere else.

❑ Don't leave everything to professionals – it's your money, so take an interest in it.

❑ True wealth – that also leads to economic prosperity – is dependent on relationships.

❑ Invest, don't gamble.

The language of investment psychology

I have covered many different psychological concepts in the book that explain how investment pitfalls occur. Below, therefore, is a selection of terms to keep in mind.

Anchoring: a falling or rising price, where each subsequent price is compared to its immediate previous one in the minds of later investors; a reluctance to revise long-held beliefs.

Barn door closing effect: a perception that there is a limited window of opportunity to act.

Choice conflict: the inability to choose between investment alternatives.

Confirmation bias: the selective use of information that supports previous personal beliefs.

Decision bias: an encompassing term for such effects as choice conflict, framing and a range of biases; deciding on a course of action based on perceived benefit.

Disposition effect: the inability to sell a stock if it falls below the level at which it was bought.

Endowment effect: investments owned are imbued with higher value than may be realistic.

Found money: money easily come by, other than by working.

Framing: the way a decision is considered (don't ask: should I sell this stock, but rather: would I still be a buyer?).

Habituation effect: becoming locked into an investment behavior pattern.

Herd instinct: the tendency to act in accordance with the crowd.

Hindsight bias: the tendency to remember and magnify past successes and minimize or forget past failures.

Illusion of validity: seeing confirmatory evidence of personal beliefs in graphs or patterns of investment data.

Key reference group (KRG): the family, social or cultural group with which you identify most strongly.

Loss aversion: losing is felt far more keenly than gaining.

Money illusion: a perception that there's more money than there really is – i.e. tax or inflation is forgotten.

Negative emulation: the desire to copy or be like another individual, based on superficial characteristics such as the trappings of wealth.

Order bias: also known as nontransitivity, how the order in which investors examine alternatives affects what they choose.

Over- and underreaction: in terms of crowd effects, the tendency of markets to move with excessive momentum.

Overconfidence: market highs or investment successes lead to a belief that things will only keep on improving.

Preferential bias: the tendency to make a choice that is in accordance with personal preference.

Prospect theory: a theory about how investors weigh up the chance of gain or loss in relation to perceived risk.

Psychonomics: an approach that seeks to assess value by taking account of weightless, financial and psychological factors.

Recallability bias: the recall of information that then interferes with how a present investment decision is made.

Reflexivity: a term popularized by George Soros, suggesting how investment behavior is modified in the market by changed behavior and changed perception, all reinforcing each other.

Representativeness fallacy: the tendency to predict investment outcomes from highly limited amounts of data.

Risk aversion: the tendency to avoid risk for a variety of reasons, where risk may be real or perceived.

Snowball effect: also known as cascade effect, an information transmission-based momentum effect, whereby an investment price can move for no obvious financial reason.

Social capital: the financial outcome resulting from a particular web of relationships.

Stability misperception: an assumption that lack of market or price movement represents stability and that volatility represents instability.

Status quo bias: also known as investment inertia, the tendency to want to keep things as they are.

Sunk cost bias: investments are imbued with extra value depending on how much time, money or effort went into obtaining them.

Uncertainty: in a market sense, a factor responsible for volatility.

Weightless value: the non-financial component of a company's overall value.

Psychonomics: it's more than about money

Profits Without Panic has been a journey through the remarkable array of human experiences that can cause you to sidestep rational decision making or fall into psychological traps. My view throughout the book has been that everyone who has a true desire to develop their investment outlook can achieve it. Essentially, it all boils down to the relationship between your internal world and the outside world. When these two worlds work in psychonomic harmony, you safeguard yourself against investment pitfalls and place yourself in the most profitable position to benefit when financial opportunity strikes.

By now, you should have a fairly good idea what this all entails and what feeds into your personal approach and your unique decision-making skills. Rationality, biases, attitudes, beliefs and style are all part of this process. Forget their importance to investment, and at best you will only be mediocre.

Is it a recipe for success? I don't say that psychonomics, with its stress on psychological components, has all the answers to making high profits, but it can go a long way. The alternative, dismissing psychology entirely, is certainly not an option. It was the economist John Maurice Clark, writing in 1918, who suggested that those who ignore the psychological principles governing people's behavior cannot ignore human nature – that of the crowd or their own – and are apt to apply wild theories to explain events. We have come full circle. If you understand the real drives that produce your investment behavior, and don't let your biases and emotions get the better of you, then your decisions will be rational ones.

If all you have learned from this book is to appreciate the reality of what's happening around you over and above what you think is happening, then you truly are on the road to investment success.

Psychonomic Value Inventory

THE PSYCHONOMIC VALUE INVENTORY (PVI) IS A METHOD OF systematizing the assessment of a company's underlying health and strength for more accurate and profitable investment.

It can be used to assess a single company, but it is best suited to comparative evaluation, that is, whether one company is healthier than another.

This Level 1 PVI is for personal, non-commercial use, and is a simplified version of a broader and more complex PVI test for professional portfolio construction and management. However, using this PVI requires some knowledge of the basic yardsticks currently employed in conventional investment evaluation, as well as basic arithmetic skills.

The test is divided into two parts, according to a psychonomic model of investment, and looks at weightless assets and financial assets as constituents of the intrinsic value of a stock. Part 1, Weightless Assets Strength, centers on subjectively determined company factors, and the test items examine customer targeting, competitive advantage and changes in market information. Part 2, Financial Assets Strength, centers on the company's reported numerical data and the test items examine past and future financial and market performance, and basic ratios. Consequently, general research about the company will often be required before a definitive response can be given, but all the latest information is readily available from published sources.[1] This Level 1 test, however, confines itself to externally observable factors that affect corporate performance and does not require too detailed a knowledge of the internal operational workings of the company.

Note that because the PVI focuses on companies themselves and their real worth, momentum effects caused by investors buying and selling can cause discrepancies between the results of the test and market value. For example, the test may suggest staying clear of a stock but its market price has been rising sharply; or indeed, the test suggests that a stock you hold is strong and healthy but its market price has been dropping, leading you to consider selling. This is an intentional effect and, hence, you should always be wary of entering the market simply because other investors are pushing stock prices up or down. In addition, users are reminded that the PVI is for guidance only and the constructors of the test take no liability for any ultimate choice of trade you might make or any decision about market timing.

For each of the statements or questions, circle the appropriate number that most reflects your chosen company's current status. As the test is sensitive, you are advised not to guess but to find out the information to the best of your ability.

	Exceptional or high amount of evidence	Considerable amount of evidence	Moderate amount of evidence	Small amount of evidence	No evidence

Part 1 Weightless Assets Strength

Customer targeting

	Exceptional or high amount of evidence	Considerable amount of evidence	Moderate amount of evidence	Small amount of evidence	No evidence
A range of quality products or services that are well liked or used (e.g. Coca-Cola, AOL, Colgate-Palmolive)[2]	4	3	2	1	0
A clearly defined brand image, name or logo with good customer recognition	4	3	2	1	0
Meets shift in consumer demands as market environment changes	4	3	2	1	0
Has diversified – or adapted – into different national or international markets[3]	4	3	2	1	0
Good long-term prospects with respect to future market share and penetration, or products or services with a rising demand	4	3	2	1	0
A good track record of listening to the feedback of customers and clients	4	3	2	1	0
A significant proportion of repeat business – goodwill built up from previous customers or clients, brand loyalty etc.	4	3	2	1	0

Name of company: Date of assessment:

Competitive advantage

The following statements seek to determine the position of the company compared to similar companies and competitors in the same sector, and how it attempts to gain an advantage in the market it operates.

	Exceptionally	Considerably	Good but room for improvement	Slightly	Not at all
A market leader, known and respected in its corporate sector	4	3	2	1	0
Margins above industry levels – evidence that the company knows what it's doing in its sector[4]	4	3	2	1	0
Evidence of ability to take advantage of, or meet, changes in industry or government standards[5]	4	3	2	1	0
Management demonstrate the ability to think for themselves, rather than following the business crowd because it seems the best thing to do	4	3	2	1	0
Effective implementation or use of new technology and procedures	4	3	2	1	0
Is not purely industry – or customer – driven but demonstrates some vision in innovating or developing its own revolutionary ideas	4	3	2	1	0

Changes in market information

The next set of statements points to how a change in market perception of a company is related to the release of news and information. In turn, this modifies the weightless value of a company as trading pressure alters.

	Exceptional or significant evidence	Considerable amount of evidence	Moderate amount of evidence	Small amount of evidence	No evidence
An important deal, acquisition or R&D breakthrough that will enhance earnings, market penetration or prospects	4	3	2	1	0
Other major or quality companies involved jointly or as partners in agreements, new contracts or deals	4	3	2	1	0
Stock repurchasing or directors' dealings (are they buying back their company's stock rather than dumping it?)	4	3	2	1	0
Presence of institutional holdings, e.g. pensions or life assurance companies	4	3	2	1	0
Plans appropriately (e.g. real estate construction company buys land when it's cheap)[6]	4	3	2	1	0
Chairman's statements, AGMs and company reports show full and open disclosure of performance of divisions, management remuneration packages, objectives, successes and failures[7]	4	3	2	1	0
Is company information, released or reported, upbeat? Acceptable to you? Understandable?	4	3	2	1	0

Part 2 Financial Assets Strength

Past and future financial and market performance

The following items refer to performance over the last several years. Experienced investors often favor a three- to six-year period in their analysis. So, for example, a sustained increase in earnings per share (EPS) during the previous five years, and with other indicators suggesting corporate strength, is likely to be a good predictor of future performance.

As previously, for each item, circle the number that most closely fits the present situation of the company that you are assessing. Note that 'Unchanged or erratic' might include two or more small directional changes during the selected period.

Chosen period is __ years

	Major increase over period	Slight or steady and consistent increase over period	Unchanged or erratic over period	Slight or sustained decrease over period	Major decrease over period
EPS	4	3	2	1	0
Dividend yield	4	3	2	1	0
Cashflow	4	3	2	1	0
Debt exposure/borrowings[8]	0	1	2	3	4
Relative strength (year-on-year change)	4	3	2	1	0

Ratio analysis

The ratios set out below in Basic ratios (1) indicate what the market thinks of a company. A high ratio – that is, high against the historical or sector average – indicates a stock that is sought after by investors, while a low ratio indicates that the market doesn't feel inclined to buy it.[9] However, good companies that have low ratios have been repeatedly shown to do well in the long term, as they suggest strength and a company that is well run. Hence, the market eventually realizes its value.

E, B and S in the headings refer to earnings, book value/net assets, and sales respectively. You may compare each of the ratios with the previous year's figure, a longer historical average based on your chosen period, or the sector average, as you prefer. You may also use a forecasted value from analysts' figures to project a future estimate of performance and strength. Overall, whatever method you choose, remember to be consistent.

While Basic ratios (1) examines performance from a market viewpoint, Basic ratios (2) is more company-centered and assesses whether or not a company's financial strength is increasing for the benefit of its stockholders.

Basic ratios (1)

	Considerable decrease/ very low relative to sector average	Some decrease/ low relative to sector average	Very slight change (within 10%)/ unchanged	Some increase/ high relative to sector average	Considerable increase/ very high relative to sector average
PE ratio	4	3	2	1	0
PB ratio	4	3	2	1	0
PS ratio	4	3	2	1	0

Basic ratios (2)

	Large or considerable decrease/ very low	Some decrease/ low	Very slight change (within 10%)/ unchanged	Some increase/ high	Large or considerable increase/ very high
PEG ratio[10]	4	3	2	1	0
ROE[11]	0	1	2	3	4
Dividend/payout ratio[12]	4	3	2	1	0

Scoring

Add up all the numbers you've circled in Part 1, Weightless Assets Strength, and divide by 20 to get the average subtotal. Similarly, add the numbers circled in Part 2, Financial Assets Strength, and divide by 11. Then add both subtotals together to obtain the psychonomic intrinsic value, P_i, score for your chosen stock.

$$\text{Part 1 subtotal (score/20)} =$$
$$\text{Part 2 subtotal (score/11)} =$$
$$P_i \text{ (total of 1 and 2)} =$$

A P_i score below 4.5 indicates a stock with obstacles to overcome, and that should possibly be avoided unless there's a very good reason for believing in its imminent superior performance or recovery. A score between 4.5 and 6 indicates a healthy stock with significant potential, although caution is still required. A stock with a P_i score above 6 is a stock that has an increased probability of an above-average return in the future.

These P_i scores are best used as a type of sieve to compare and separate out the strongest of several stocks.

Notes

1 Information sources to use include: in the US, Value Line, Standard & Poors Stock Reports, *Wall Street Journal*, annual company reports, business magazine articles on particular companies, *Barron's*; in the UK, Extel, Macarthy, *Financial Times*, *Investors' Chronicle*.

2 A range of useful products – not simply a short shelf-life item catering to a fad.

3 Take into account problems of particular markets – such as sales weakness for many companies operating in Asia between 1997 and 1998 – which hinders geographic diversification.

4 Profit and sales margins should ideally be higher than similar companies, or companies working in the same markets.

5 Some evidence that the company is well placed to benefit readily from new, industry-wide quality standards by, for example, a new product or service that satisfies the changed requirement. The same logic is applicable to an imposed regulation, such as emission or environmental controls, which new products might exploit.

6 Does the company have foresight?

7 There should be no feeling that the company's management is playing a game for its own ends or that something is being hidden from present and potential stockholders.

8 Little or no debt – or the company is significantly reducing debt – is the ideal. However, sometimes debt is warranted if funds are being raised for long-term planning (this relates to note 6 above).

9 With a rapidly declining stock price – however E, B and S are moving – the ratio will decrease. This may be because the market has taken a dislike to the stock for no obvious reason, in which case it may have underlying strength and there is a buying opportunity. Or the stock is, in reality, poor quality, in which case the assessment is anomalous and you should stay well clear of buying. Analysis of Weightless Asset Strength and background research will provide the answer.

10 The price–earnings ratio divided by the growth rate for the following year. This item can be looked at either by considering how the PEG has moved relative to its previous level or by considering its performance within its generally accepted range. A stock with a PEG below 0.7 is considered very low and is taken to be indicative of increased potential. A PEG between 0.7 and around 1.0 is low and suggests a company to watch. A PEG between 1.0 and 1.5 is high, while over 1.5 is very high and suggests a stock fully discounting future performance (a PEG with a negative growth value, mark as '0'). However, these figures also depend on the type of market that exists – i.e. bull or bear – and how the market rates stocks and particular sectors at any given time.

11 Return on equity is the net earnings divided by stockholders' funds, expressed as a percentage. This ratio provides a measure of performance and how well a company is doing for its stockholders. Increases or decreases over a given time period are indicative of a company's ability to transform itself. Companies that produce a very low return of, say, less than 12 percent are generally thought to be working insufficiently hard for their stockholders, while a very high return would be in excess of 40 percent.

12 The dividend divided by the earnings. The lower the ratio, the more a company believes in plowing profits back into its business. This ratio can be compared to a previous one or assessed from the point of view of its generally accepted range. A very low DP ratio, between 0.1 and 0.3, indicates a stock with increased growth potential (often a fast-expanding company). A low DP ratio, between 0.3 and 0.5, indicates a company that is a little less concerned with developing its business and a little more concerned with producing income for stockholders (often an older-established company). A DP ratio below 0.1, mark as '1', as this suggests a company that can't – or won't – pass on anything to stockholders. A very high ratio would be in excess of 0.8.

Further Reading

Buffett, Mary and Clark, David (1997) *Buffettology*, Rawson Associates.

Carswell, John (1960) *The South Sea Bubble*, Cresset Press.

Dreman, David (1982) *The New Contrarian Investment Strategies*, Random House.

Fisher, Phillip A (1996) *Common Stocks and Uncommon Profits*, John Wiley.

Fridson, Martin S (1993) *Investment Illusions*, John Wiley.

Graham, Benjamin (1986) *The Intelligent Investor*, Harper & Row.

Gurney, Kathleen (1988) *Your Money Personality*, Doubleday.

Hagstrom, Robert G (1994) *The Warren Buffett Way*, John Wiley.

Kindleburger, Charles P (1996) *Manias, Panics, and Crashes*, John Wiley.

LeBon, Gustave (1982) *The Crowd: a Study of the Popular Mind*, Cherokee.

Lefevre, Edwin (1995) *Reminiscences of a Stock Operator*, John Wiley.

Lo, Andrew, MacKinlay, Craig and Campbell, John (1997) *The Econometrics of Financial Markets*, Princeton University Press.

Lynch, Peter (1990) *One Up On Wall Street*, Penguin.

Mackay, Charles (1932; 1852 edition reprint) *Extraordinary Popular Delusions and the Madness of Crowds*, L. C. Page.

Malkiel, Burton G (1973) *A Random Walk Down Wall Street*, W.W. Norton.

O'Shaughnessy, James P (1996) *What Works on Wall Street*, McGraw Hill.

Pring, Martin J (1993) *Investment Psychology Explained*, John Wiley.

Sadtler, David, Campbell, Andrew and Koch, Richard (1998) *Breakup!* Capstone.

Schwed, Fred Jr (1940) *Where Are the Customers' Yachts?* Simon & Schuster.

Shiller, Robert (1989) *Market Volatility*, MIT Press.

Siegel, Jeremy (1994) *Stocks for the Long Run*, Irwin.

Smith, Adam (1968) *The Money Game*, Random House.

Slater, Jim (1992) *The Zulu Principle*, Orion.

Soros, George (1994) *The Alchemy of Finance*, John Wiley.

Thaler, Richard H (1992) *The Winner's Curse: Paradoxes and Anomalies of Economic Life*, Free Press.

Thaler, Richard H (ed.) (1993) *Advances in Behavioral Finance*, Russell Sage Foundation.

Train, John (1980) *The Money Masters*, Harper & Row.

Von Neuman, John and Morgenstern, Oskar (1944) *Theory of Games and Economic Behavior*, Princeton University Press.

Sources of information

Most of the following information can be readily found at the reference sections of major libraries or through a friendly broker.

USA

Morningstar Guide to Mutual Funds
Value Line Investment Survey

UK

Company Refs, Hemmington Scott
Extel Information and Data Services
Macarthy Information and Press Cutting Services (also known as Macarthy Cards)

For information about the commercial version of the Investor
Profile, non-financial corporate auditing and assessments,
weightless portfolio construction, or to arrange lectures and
seminars, please write to the author
c/o the publishers at the address at the front of the book,
or e-mail to ajmyers@msn.com

Index